THE GODDESS LAKṢMĪ

American Academy of Religion Academy Series

edited by
Barbara A. Holdredge

Number 95

THE GODDESS LAKṢMĪ
The Divine Consort in South Indian
Vaiṣṇava Tradition
by
P. Pratap Kumar

P. Pratap Kumar

THE GODDESS LAKṢMĪ
The Divine Consort in South Indian Vaiṣṇava Tradition

Scholars Press
Atlanta, Georgia

THE GODDESS LAKṢMĪ
The Divine Consort in South Indian Vaiṣṇava Tradition

by
P. Pratap Kumar

Library of Congress Cataloging in Publication Data
Kumar, P. Pratap, 1952–
The goddess Lakṣmī : the divine consort in South Indian Vaiṣṇava tradition / P. Pratap Kumar.
p. cm. — (American Academy of Religion academy series ; no. 95)
Includes bibliographical references and index.
ISBN 0-7885-0198-4 (cloth : alk. paper). — ISBN 0-7885-0199-2 (paper : alk. paper)
1. Lakshmi (Hindu deity) I. Title. II. Series.
BL1225.L3K86 1997
294.5'2114—dc21 97-21914
CIP

Printed in the United States of America
on acid-free paper

In loving memory of my mother

TABLE OF CONTENTS

Acknowledgements.....ix

Abbreviations.....xi

Chapter 1 Introduction..... 1

Chapter 2 Śrī-Lakṣmī in Historical Perspective.....11

Chapter 3 Śrī-Lakṣmī in the Pāñcarātra Āgamas.....21

Chapter 4 Śrī-Lakṣmī in the Writings of Yāmuna and Rāmānuja.....51

Chapter 5 Śrī-Lakṣmī in the Writings of Parāśara Bhaṭṭar.....77

Chapter 6 Śrī-Lakṣmī in the Writings of Piḷḷai Lokācārya.....95

Chapter 7 Śrī-Lakṣmī in the Writings of Veṅkaṭanātha.....111

Chapter 8 Tradition: Continuity and Change (clarifying issues in understanding Śrī-Lakṣmī).....133

Chapter 9 Afterword.....149

Appendix 1 Text of *Catuśślokī* of Yāmuna.....161

Appendix 2 Text of *Stotraratna* of Yāmuna.....163

Bibliography.....165

Index.....177

ACKNOWLEDGEMENTS

This work was originally written as part of my doctoral studies during the years 1987-90. During the last three years I have revised it in light of comments from various scholars in Europe, especially those of Prof. Bronkhorst and Prof. R. Mesquita, who gave me off-prints of several of his articles on the Śrīvaiṣṇava tradition. In the course of my research, many people have assisted me in many different ways, and it is only appropriate to acknowledge with gratitude their contribution to this task. I am greatly indebted to Prof. Lakṣmī Tātācārya, who clarified many issues and also made it possible for me to use the resources and materials available at the Academy of Sanskrit Research, Melkote. I am also grateful to the Librarian, Mr. Narasarāja Bhaṭṭar, for his valuable insights and assistance in the library. This study would not have reached completion but for the kind cooperation and guidance provided by Prof. John B. Carman, who was then the Director of the Center for the Study of World Religions, Harvard University. He made it possible for me to spend the year 1988-89 at the Center, and also gave me free access to his personal library. From the beginning of my research, Prof. Carman spent a lot of his time discussing with me various issues related to the goddess and read all the chapters with patience and scholarly care, and offered his valuable comments. I sincerely thank him for all his help.

I wish to record my sincere gratitude to the members of my doctoral committee at the University of California, Santa Barbara: Prof. Gerald J. Larson (Chair), Prof. Ninian Smart, and Prof. Barbara Holdrege, all of whom gave me their valuable comments, and also a great deal of freedom to go to various places to use necessary resources. Specifically, I wish to thank Prof. Larson for strengthening my skills in Sanskrit and broadening my understanding of many philosophical problems peculiar to Indian Philosophy. He also laid the foundation for my background in the History of Religions, since this work is attempted from that standpoint.

I am also grateful to a number of scholars both in India and in the United States, who gave their valuable time in discussing with me some of the issues related to the topic of my research. Among them, I should mention Prof. Vasudha Narayanan, Prof. Dennis Hudson, Prof. Francis X. Clooney, Prof. George Hart, and Kausalya Hart (both of them taught me Tamil when I was at Harvard), and many other scholars whom I met at various stages of my work. I would specially like to thank my first teacher of Vedānta, Prof. Eric J. Lott, who provided me with the initial background and laid the foundation for my doctoral work.

Many of my friends and colleagues in the department at the University of California, Santa Barbara assisted me in dealing with problems that arose in the course of my use of the computers. Prof. George Hart, University of California, Berkeley provided me with his program for the diacritics, which saved me a great deal of time writing the diacritics by hand. A special word of thanks to my friends and colleagues, Brian Wilson and Cybell Shattuck, who went through every single page carefully and suggested changes. I thank all my friends and my wife, who gave moral support during the writing of the book. The major part of the funding for this study was given by the Lutheran World Federation, Geneva, during the years of my doctoral study. I wish to sincerely thank them for their generous support. Last but not the least, I wish to thank Ed Levy for copy editing this text.

ABBREVIATIONS

Ah. S	Ahirbudhnya Saṃhitā
BG	Bhagavad Gītā
LT	Lakṣmī Tantra
Mbh	Mahābhārata
MRL	Medieval Religious Literature (J. Gonda)
RV	Ṛg Veda
Rām	Rāmāyaṇa
SB	Śatapatha Brāhmaṇa
SBE	Sacred Books of the East
Vaj. S	Vājasaneya Saṃhitā
JS	Jayākhya Saṃhitā
SS	Sāttvata Saṃhitā

CHAPTER ONE

INTRODUCTION

Significance of Śrī-Lakṣmī in the Interpretation of the Śrīvaiṣṇava Tradition

In the present study I attempt, first, to explore an understanding of the Goddess as articulated in the writings of the teachers of the Śrīvaiṣṇavas. Second, I also try to explore the interpretive process of the tradition in order to see how the various streams of thought are integrated into a coherent tradition. Thus, I use the notion of Śrī-Lakṣmī as a key to explore the workings of the interpretive process within the Śrīvaiṣṇava tradition. That is, through an exploration of the understanding of Śrī-Lakṣmī, I shall simultaneously lay out the interpretive process of this tradition. The understanding of Śrī-Lakṣmī is closely tied to the ongoing interpretive process of the Śrīvaiṣṇava tradition. Other concepts may also be useful to study the interpretive process of the tradition, but it seems to me that the notion of the Goddess demonstrates the various transitions in the interpretive process more clearly than the other concepts, and thus provides us with an overall picture of the Śrīvaiṣṇava history during its formative stages. Exploring the notion of the Goddess clearly spells out not only the various elements that became significant for the tradition, but also shows how they are sustained. This study also shows that the sustaining factor is the ritual tradition, namely, the Pāñcarātra Āgama tradition. In a broader sense then, exploring the notion of the Goddess unveils the interpretive process of the tradition and further establishes the significance of ritual as a sustaining factor in Śrīvaiṣṇava history.

As the interpretive process continues, what becomes clear is that while the teachers of the tradition tried to be loyal to preceding teachers, they nevertheless brought in new aspects and dimensions to the understanding of the tradition. Each generation had to deal with questions that were emerging as relevant to them, and thus made attempts to clarify their positions so that the tradition might survive through the coming generations.

Significance of the Question of Śrī-Lakṣmī for the Community

The Śrīvaiṣṇavas unequivocally affirm the presence of the divine consort in the context of ritual, especially her mediatorial role. This applies to all the teachers from the beginning of the Śrīvaiṣṇava tradition. The Śrīvaiṣṇava ritual remains incomplete without her presence. By the same token, she is not seen apart from the ritual. In other words, while Śrī-Lakṣmī is vividly present in the ritual, she remains hidden in the philosophical writings. This is illustrated from the fact that, no matter how they understood and what status they accorded to her in relation to Viṣṇu, all the teachers gave her prominence both in their hymns and particularly in the context of ritual. Although the question of the divine consort was not the major issue on which the community of Śrīvaiṣṇavas divided themselves into two sects, namely, the Northern (*Vaṭakaḷai*) and the Southern (*Teṅkaḷai*) during the eighteenth century C.E., it certainly became a sensitive and crucial issue in the course of the subsequent interpretive process. The significance of the issue may be seen in light of the subsequent debate between the thirteenth century theologians Piḷḷai Lokācārya and Veṅkaṭanātha.

The question of the divine consort also has a wider significance in view of the fact that the Śrīvaiṣṇava tradition is predominantly a *bhakti* oriented theistic tradition. One of the crucial questions common to all the theistic traditions, whether Hinduism, Christianity, or even certain sects of the Buddhist tradition such as Mahāyāna Buddhism, is how grace is mediated to human beings. While different traditions made attempts to respond to that question in their own ways from within their own frames of reference, the Śrīvaiṣṇavas responded by positing the reality of the divine consort as the mediator between the Lord and the devotees. Nonetheless, whether all the teachers of the tradition saw the divine consort as the mediator is a moot point. In view of the fact that Rāmānuja was relatively reticent about the divine consort in his philosophical writings and remains vague even in his devotional writings, scholars in the field, such as J. B. Carman, justifiably think that it is unnecessary to posit the divine consort as the mediator since the Lord himself combines in him the two natures, the transcendent (*paratva*) and the accessible (*saulabhya*). The issue, however, cannot be decided so simply, because not only do we find references to the divine consort in the most significant passages in the works of Rāmānuja, such as the *maṅgalaśloka*-s, but also the subsequent teachers tend to draw their support for their views on the divine consort from both Yāmuna and Rāmānuja. Certainly, after Piḷḷān[1] and Bhaṭṭar, the notion that the divine consort is the mediator becomes clearly established no matter what status is accorded to her in relation to the Lord. Carman writes:

> This theoretical difference does not seem to have affected the practical significance of the goddesses for all Śrīvaiṣṇavas. They are almost always iconically represented along with Viṣṇu, and their favor (especially that of

1. The significance of the divine consorts in the theology of Piḷḷān is attested to in the work done by J. B. Carman and Vasudha Narayanan. See J. B. Carman & Vasudha Narayanan. *The Tamil Veda: Piḷḷān's Interpretation of the Tiruvāymoḷi* (Chicago: University of Chicago Press, 1989), pp. 74-77.

> Śrī) is prayed for by the devotee before he or she approaches Viṣṇu himself.[2]

Thus, the question of grace is intrinsically related to the question of the divine consort in the Śrīvaiṣṇava tradition. In trying to understand the Śrīvaiṣṇava tradition, historians of religion have the burden of clarifying the issues as clearly as possible from within the interpretive process of the tradition. My attempt in this study, therefore, is not only to bring to the attention of scholars, both within and without, the significance of the question of the divine consort, but also to clarify the issue through the commentarial sources and the devotional hymns of the teachers, as well as through the Pāñcarātra tradition that had been vigorously defended and assimilated into the tradition by the early teachers.

Some Methodological Considerations

The present work is a historical and interpretive study of the understanding of the Goddess Śrī-Lakṣmī in the writings of the early teachers of the Śrīvaiṣṇava tradition between the tenth and the thirteenth century C.E. It is historical in the sense that an attempt is made to study the understanding of Śrī-Lakṣmī in the writings of the early teachers in a chronological order. The study is based primarily on the texts and commentaries of the teachers. Although I depended largely on the actual writings of the teachers themselves, during my field trip to India I made attempts to discuss various issues related to Śrī-Lakṣmī with scholars both within and outside the tradition. Those discussions, indeed, helped me to understand better the issues and their implications for the Śrīvaiṣṇava community.

Thus, the study reflects how the early teachers of the tradition perceived the Goddess in their specific times. In each period, the community of Śrīvaiṣṇavas appropriated the understanding of those teachers and passed it on to the succeeding generations. In passing on their tradition to the succeeding generation, however, each generation made its own authentic contribution to the ongoing interpretive process on the basis of its own individual experience of the Goddess. Although broadly speaking it is supposed to be the community's overall understanding, the teachers of the tradition became the spokesmen of the community. In other words, the teachers of the tradition were virtually the custodians of the understanding of the community. They interpreted the role and the significance of the Goddess in ways that made sense to the community at that specific time. In that sense, the present study is an attempt to identify those various developments in the community's understanding of Śrī-Lakṣmī during the formative period.

Even though the study is concerned primarily with expounding the understanding of Śrī-Lakṣmī within the Śrīvaiṣṇava tradition, in

2. Ibid., p. 75.

order to place their understanding in the wider context of the Hindu tradition, an attempt is made to provide the antecedent background related to Śrī-Lakṣmī in the Vedic and epic materials. The present study, however, does not primarily concern itself with the question of the survival of those early notions in the Śrīvaiṣṇava tradition, although that in itself could form an interesting and significant study that other scholars might pursue.

This study also does not cover the Āḷvār tradition, which is identified as one of the most significant streams culminating in the Śrīvaiṣṇava tradition. In view of the fact that I limited my research to the Sanskritic tradition beginning with Yāmuna and ending with the thirteenth century teachers, I am hesitant to undertake and include a study of the Āḷvār hymns at this point in my research.

The Śrīvaiṣṇava tradition proper begins with Nāthamuni, to whom the Śrīvaiṣṇavas attribute the compilation of *Nāḷāyira Divya-prabandham*, a work that contains all the hymns of the Āḷvārs as remembered during the time of Nāthamuni. Apart from this collection of hymns in Tamil, Nāthamuni's other Sanskrit works, such as *Yogarahasya* have not survived. The Śrīvaiṣṇavas believe that Nāthamuni's teachings were appropriated and assimilated by Yāmuna, whose writings really form the basis for the subsequent interpretive process. Yāmuna was followed by Rāmānuja, whose writings became canonical for the subsequent tradition. The present work also includes an exposition of the writings of Bhaṭṭar, Piḷḷai Lokācārya, and Veṅkaṭanātha. As explained in the chapter on Bhaṭṭar, I have omitted an exposition of Piḷḷān's work. In spite of the above limitations I hope that this work presents the early developments of the understanding of Śrī-Lakṣmī in the Śrīvaiṣṇava tradition.

Since this study is intended to be a descriptive analysis of the writings of the early teachers, no attempt is made to assess the validity of the positions of these teachers. All that is attempted here is an exposition of the writings of the early teachers and an explanation of their positions as faithfully as possible and as adequately as I was able to understand them. As an outsider to the tradition, I am aware of my limitations in fully grasping all the various dimensions related to the understanding of Śrī-Lakṣmī.

Some Comments on the Pāñcarātra Tradition

Upon studying the writings of the early teachers and in the course of my discussions with the traditional pundits, it became clear to me that a fuller understanding of Śrī-Lakṣmī cannot be gained without seriously studying the relevant Pāñcarātra Āgama texts. Of the Pāñcarātra texts that I surveyed, five (*Sāttvata-*, *Pauṣkara-*, *Jayākhya-*, *Pādma-*, and *Parama Saṃhitā*-s) do not deal with Śrī-Lakṣmī at any significant length, although some of them do contain some *mantra*-s related to the worship of Śrī-Lakṣmī (e.g., *Jayākhya Saṃhitā*). The only two Pāñcarātra texts that deal with Śrī-Lakṣmī rather substantially are the

Lakṣmī Tantra and the *Ahirbudhnya Saṃhitā*. I focus primarily on the *Lakṣmī Tantra*, since it deals with Śrī-Lakṣmī more directly than the *Ahirbudhnya Saṃhitā*, and make use of the latter as a reference point. However, I refer to the older Pāñcarātra texts where necessary in order to make some general comments regarding the Goddess in the Pāñcarātra tradition. The second chapter deals with the various images of Śrī-Lakṣmī presented in the Pāñcarātra tradition.

Since I shall be using the *Lakṣmī Tantra* more extensively than any other Pāñcarātra text, some explanation about the place of that text in the Śrīvaiṣṇava tradition may be in order. The *Lakṣmī Tantra* obviously incorporated many Tantric notions related to Śakti, and one might tend to look at it as a Tantric text.[3] It originated in South India, specifically in the context of the Pāñcarātra tradition that had already been assimilated into the Śrīvaiṣṇava tradition. Unlike many other Pāñcarātra texts, the *Lakṣmī Tantra* can be dated with reasonable accuracy. Since we do not find any reference to it in the writings of Yāmuna, Rāmānuja, and Bhaṭṭar, it probably was not in existence until after the eleventh century C.E. The first reference that we find is in the *Prapannapārijāta* of Nāthādūr Ammāḷ, Veṅkaṭanātha's teacher, who lived around the twelfth century C.E. Later we find ample references to it in the writings of Piḷḷai Lokācārya and Veṅkaṭanātha who lived between the twelfth and the thirteenth centuries C.E. It is therefore clear that the text of the *Lakṣmī Tantra* was available to the Śrīvaiṣṇava teachers by this time, and was used by them in their interpretation of the tradition.

The context of the text is clearly the Śrīvaiṣṇava tradition. By the twelfth century C.E. we have a highly developed and clearly articulated Śrīvaiṣṇava tradition, which drew its ritual tradition quite openly from the Pāñcarātra tradition. The connection between the Pāñcarātra tradition and the Śrīvaiṣṇava tradition is established without any doubt by the early teachers of the Śrīvaiṣṇavas. The fact that the twelfth and thirteenth century teachers clearly identified the *Lakṣmī Tantra* as a Pāñcarātra text and as part of the Śrīvaiṣṇava tradition and used it in their interpretive process makes the text more relevant to the Śrīvaiṣṇava ritual tradition, especially in dealing with Śrī-Lakṣmī. We certainly do not have any direct reference in the *Lakṣmī Tantra* to the Śrīvaiṣṇava tradition as such. Although it is a Pāñcarātra text, the people who accepted and used it as an authoritative text for the interpretation of their tradition were the Śrīvaiṣṇavas. There is no doubt that there is a great deal of material in the *Lakṣmī Tantra* that fits within the Tantric tradition, but of course, the same could be said about almost all the Pāñcarātra texts. There are many notions in the Pāñcarātra tradition that resonate with the Tantric tradition in general.

---

3. See Sajukta Gupta, in her introduction to the translation of the *Lakṣmī Tantra*, identifies the text as a Tantric text. See Sanjukta Gupta, trans., *Lakṣmī Tantra: A Pāñcarātra Text* (Leiden: E. J. Brill, 1972).

As a matter of fact the Pāñcarātra is also known as Tantra Śāstra.[4] The presence of many Tantric notions in the Pāñcarātra texts may be attributed to the influence that the Tantric tradition (both the Buddhist and the Hindu) exerted on many Hindu rituals over a long period of time. Therefore, it is no surprise that the Pāñcarātra ritual tradition had appropriated many Tantric notions and practices. The *Lakṣmī Tantra*, in dealing with Śrī-Lakṣmī, a theme that is also integral to the Tantric tradition, might have appropriated Tantric notions more systematically than many other Pāñcarātra texts. Nevertheless, the text, in so far as it clearly reveals the author's knowledge of Upaniṣadic notions (e.g., Brahman as Pure Consciousness) and attributes those notions to Śrī-Lakṣmī, shows that the author is clearly concerned with integrating the text into the Vedāntic scheme as interpreted in the Śrīvaiṣṇava tradition. Furthermore, there is clear internal evidence in the text that distinguishes between the Pāñcarātra system and the Tantra system. It clearly speaks of the *mantra*-s of the Tantra texts as inferior.[5] In that sense, the text seems not only to distance itself from the Tantra system but also to present enough evidence suggesting that it belongs to the Śrīvaiṣṇava tradition and it was authenticated as such by the Śrīvaiṣṇava teachers who came after Bhaṭṭar.

The use of Tantric notions and categories does not necessarily qualify the text as part of the Tantric tradition. The text of the *Lakṣmī Tantra* clearly speaks of Lakṣmī and Nārāyaṇa as the divine couple, much the same way as they are addressed in the hymns of the Āḻvārs and also in the Sanskritic hymns of the Śrīvaiṣṇava teachers.

The fact that the text belongs to a later period when Śrīvaiṣṇava theology has already been developed becomes crucial because what the *Lakṣmī Tantra* attempts is to integrate the aspect of the divine consort into the total scheme of Śrīvaiṣṇava theology. To that extent, the text provides an Āgamic basis for integrating the Lord and his consort into the Viśiṣṭādvaitic scheme. In other words, the *Lakṣmī Tantra* fulfils and complements what the earlier Pāñcarātra texts (e.g., *Sāttvata-*, *Pauṣkara-*, and *Jayākhya Saṃhitā*-s) did not cover. That is to say, the early Pāñcarātra texts discussed mainly, *inter alia*, the divine nature of Viṣṇu through the formula of six auspicious qualities. And what the *Lakṣmī Tantra* does is to apply the formula of six auspicious qualities to Śrī-Lakṣmī and place her on a par with the Lord Viṣṇu. In the absence of the *Lakṣmī Tantra* both Yāmuna and Rāmānuja did not have a proper Āgamic basis on which to discuss the question of the divine consort in their theological treatises. This is perhaps one reason why both Yāmuna and Rāmānuja were relatively

4. As per the question of the Tantra and the Āgama, Gonda identifies the two as the same—the former being in vogue in the North and the latter in the South of India. See J. Gonda, *Die Religionen Indiens* (Stuttgart: W. Kohlhammer Verlag, 1963), 58, f.n. 37. Nevertheless, insofar as Gonda does not provide any explanation as to how the two, namely, the Tantra and the Āgama, are one and the same, this question must be left open for future scholarship to clarify.

5. *LT*. 22:32-36

reticent about the divine consort, although they did give her prominence in the context of ritual. Although the early Āgamas (*Sāttvata-*, *Pauṣkara-*, and *Jayākhya Saṃhitā*-s) did not define clearly the status of the divine consort in relation to Viṣṇu, they did, however, include *mantra*-s used in the ritual in relation to Śrī-Lakṣmī. By the time of Piḷḷai Lokācārya and Veṅkaṭanātha, the *Lakṣmī Tantra* as a text was available, and both of them used it to discuss the question of the divine consort. Both Piḷḷai Lokācārya and Veṅkaṭanātha found Āgamic basis in the *Lakṣmī Tantra* for their divergent views on the divine consort, and they refer to passages in the *Lakṣmī Tantra* to support their points of view. In that sense, the *Lakṣmī Tantra* provided them an Āgamic basis for integrating the divine consort into their theological scheme.

Although scholars in the field, such as J. B. Carman and Vasudha Narayanan, identify the Pāñcarātra tradition as a significant influence on the Śrīvaiṣṇava tradition, no study has been done to show specifically how much the Pāñcarātra tradition influenced and shaped some very important aspects of the Śrīvaiṣṇava tradition. To that extent my study of the understanding of Śrī-Lakṣmī is a specific attempt to explore the Pāñcarātra connections in the Śrīvaiṣṇava tradition. I do not, of course, pretend to have explored all possible aspects related to the understanding of Śrī-Lakṣmī and the Pāñcarātra influence.

An Overview of the Present Study

In the following chapters, I will discuss how various teachers of the Śrīvaiṣṇava tradition tried to integrate the notion of the divine consort into the total scheme of Viśiṣṭādvaita/Śrīvaiṣṇava tradition. The first chapter serves as an outline of the background of some important notions related to Śrī-Lakṣmī. The second chapter provides the Pāñcarātra Āgamic background for integrating the divine consort in the interpretive process of the tradition. The reason for introducing a discussion on the Pāñcarātra Āgamas, especially the *Lakṣmī Tantra*, in the second chapter is to see the correspondece of ideas between the early teachers and the Pāñcarātra Āgamas on the one hand, and on the other, to see how much the teachers who came after Bhaṭṭar were influenced by the ideas of the Pāñcarātra tradition generally and the *Lakṣmī Tantra* particularly. Chronologically speaking, an analysis of the *Lakṣmī Tantra* should have come after Yāmuna and Rāmānuja. Since the second chapter also in a general way analyses the older Pāñcarātra texts, I chose to place it before the third chapter, in which I deal with Yāmuna and Rāmānuja. Thus, I do not intend to create the impression that Yāmuna and Rāmānuja were influenced by the *Lakṣmī Tantra*, but rather to merely indicate the correspondence of ideas between the *Lakṣmī Tantra* and the two early teachers. Nonetheless, in so far as the older Pāñcarātra texts clearly include Śrī-Lakṣmī within the ritual context, it is conceivable that both Yāmuna and Rāmānuja were aware of it and incorporated her in their respective theologies. In that sense, they seem to clearly follow the Pāñcarātra tradition. Chapter three discusses the initial developments in the Śrīvaiṣṇava theology dealing with Śrī-Lakṣmī. The writings of both Yāmuna and Rāmānuja are discussed in the same chapter, as both have argued in favor of the Pāñcarātra Āgamic basis for the Śrīvaiṣṇava ritual tradition. It is precisely that very Āgamic basis that also provided them scope for integrating the divine consort in their interpretive process. Both of them, however, limited themselves to the Vedāntic materials and did not go very far. On the other hand, Bhaṭṭar takes the discussion far beyond the Vedāntic materials and uses the epic and the Purāṇic materials rather extensively. In chapter four, I attempt to show Bhaṭṭar's distinctive contribution to the discussion on Śrī-Lakṣmī. Unlike Yāmuna and Rāmānuja, Bhaṭṭar deals with the question of the divine consort more directly, which perhaps can be attributed to the fact that by his time the Śrīvaiṣṇava theology has already begun to grapple with theological issues that remained unclarified. Since both Yāmuna and Rāmānuja had already established the Śrīvaiṣṇava theology on firm Vedāntic grounds, the interpretive process after them moves on to take into account rather thorny and delicate theological issues, such as the question of the divine consort. The works of Piḷḷān and Kureśa already show their concern to clarify some difficult areas of interpretation. Bhaṭṭar's contribution is certainly a step forward in the direction of integrating the divine consort into the Vedāntic system that Yāmuna and Rāmānuja had developed.

By the twelfth and the thirteenth centuries C.E., with the appearance of the text of the *Lakṣmī Tantra*, which provided an Āgamic basis for integrating the divine consort, the interpretive process of the tradition reaches a significant point, one where the teachers of the tradition are faced with serious theological debates from within. Among other theological differences, the question of the divine consort became a key issue over which the teachers of the period became divided. During this time the debate was between two important theologians, namely, Piḷḷai Lokācārya and Veṅkaṭanātha. In chapter five, I discuss the theological framework of Piḷḷai Lokācārya and attempt to show the way in which he tried to integrate Śrī-Lakṣmī into his theological scheme. In chapter six, I present the theological framework of Veṅkaṭanātha and attempt to elucidate his position on Śrī-Lakṣmī. On the one hand, Piḷḷai Lokācārya sees the role of the divine consort as essentially one with the Lord and functionally inferior to him. She is crucial in the mediation between the Lord and his devotees. On the other hand, for Veṅkaṭanātha she is on a par with the Lord both essentially and functionally. Both philosophers attempt to draw support from their predecessors. In chapter seven, I attempt to clarify the positions of each teacher and try to identify the factors that influenced their understanding of Śrī-Lakṣmī. I further attempt to show how the understanding of each of them is consistent from within his own framework. In chapter eight I try to layout the overall interpretive process in the Śrīvaiṣṇava tradition. In the same chapter I will also outline some unresolved and unexplored issues for further research.

In the appendix section, I include the texts and the translations of the Sanskrit hymns of Yāmuna—*Catuśślokī* and selected verses from *Stotraratna.* The translations of *Catuśślokī* and *Stotraratna* appear as part of the main text in chapter 3 and the texts appear in the appendix. While I make use of *Catuśślokī*, *Stotraratna,* *Śrīvacanabhūṣaṇa*, and *Śrīstuti* in the course of my discussions, I do not provide any additional comment on *Śrīstava* of Kureśa. A complete and substantial analysis devoted solely to the hymns of all the teachers could form an interesting and significant study which I might pursue at a later stage of my research.

While it is obvious that I bring my limitations to the study, I submit that my clarifications and interpretations of the issue of the divine consort are potentially significant in the ongoing process of our understanding of the Śrīvaiṣṇava tradition. My attempt here is only to begin a discussion that will open up further avenues of clarification of the larger issues involved. Hopefully, scholars both inside and outside the tradition find this study useful.

CHAPTER TWO

ŚRĪ-LAKṢMĪ IN HISTORICAL PERSPECTIVE

The Śrīvaiṣṇava community in its understanding of Śrī-Lakṣmī relies largely upon the past traditions of the vast and diverse Hindu tradition. In order to maintain its orthodoxy the tradition also relies upon the Vedic and epic materials. In other words, the goddess Śrī-Lakṣmī that is worshipped in this tradition as the divine consort of Viṣṇu is the same goddess that also appears in the Vedic tradition. Although much of the later understanding of the goddess, in large measure, comes from the Pāñcarātra and the subsequent Purāṇic traditions, one must first look at the Vedic and epic materials in order to develop a historical perspective of the continuity and change that occur in the conceptions of Śrī-Lakṣmī in these ancient materials. In so far as the community itself looks to the Vedic and epic materials, a historian of religions cannot overlook those important sources if one wants to be faithful to the task of describing how the community itself wants to remember its tradition, both past and present.

In the present chapter, I explore the understanding of Śrī-Lakṣmī in the Vedic and epic materials. Since several scholars before me have already done this work, in order to avoid duplication in the present study I will only briefly highlight the various issues involved in understanding Śrī-Lakṣmī. Although I occasionally make reference to other scholars who have dealt with those issues relating to Śrī-Lakṣmī, in my analysis I have drawn primarily on Gonda's study of relevant Vedic materials and Hiltebeitel's study of the *Mahābhārata*.

Two important issues have been discussed by scholars such as Gonda,[1] Jaiswal,[2] Geldner,[3] Oldenberg,[4] and Hiltebeitel[5] with regard to Śrī: 1) the etymological and conceptual imports of "*śrī*" as common noun; and 2) the depiction of Śrī as a goddess associated with Viṣṇu. While others have commented on Śrī in significant ways, the studies of Gonda and Hiltebeitel provide systematic accounts of Śrī.

---

1. J. Gonda, *Aspects of Early Viṣṇuism (*Utrecht: NVA Oosthoek's Uitgevers Mij, 1954), pp. 176-231.

2. S. Jaiswal, *Origin and Development of Vaiṣṇavism (*Delhi: Munshiram Manoharlal, 1981), pp. 89-109.

3. K. F. Geldner, *Der Rigveda in Auswahl,* 2 (Stuttgart, 1909).

4. H. Oldenberg, "Die Vedischen Worte fur "Schön" und "Schönheit" und das Vedische Schönheitsgefühl", in *Nachr. Königl. Ges. d. Wiss.* (Göttingen, ph-h. Kl. 1918), p. 35ff.

5. Alf Hiltebeitel, *The Ritual of Battle: Kṛṣṇa in the Mahābhārata (*Ithaca & London: Cornell University Press, 1976), pp. 143-91.

The Etymological and Conceptual Significance of "Śrī"

Gonda has shown that in early Vedic Saṃhitā literature (e.g., Ṛg, et al.) the term "*śrī*" is used only as a substantive and not as a goddess. Gonda disagrees with the German rendering of the noun "*śrī*" by terms such as *Schönheit* used by Geldner and Grassman, who seem to have favored a more æsthetic definition of the term as luster, radiance, splendor, beauty, grace, etc. At the same time Gonda also disagrees with Oldenberg's æsthetic point of view, saying:

> Nor can I subscribe to Oldenberg's view that the frequency of the passage in which *śrī* is connected with derivatives of *dṛś* proves the former's primary sense of "erfreulicher Anblick." Such texts as 7:15:5; 2:1:12; 1:122:2 only show that *śrī* its manifestations, consequences, and attendant circumstances can be, and often are, visible, that the possession of *śrī* can be displayed. Passages like 5:3:4 *tava śriyā sudṛśo deva devāḥ purū dadhānāmṛtam sapanta* "durch deine, des Schönen, Herrlichkeit (*samṛdhyā*/s) O Gott, mehren und wahren die Götter die Unsterblichkeit;" 4:23:6; 5:44:2 etc., do not necessarily imply that *śrī* was employed by the poet from the æsthetic point of view.[6]

Bartholomae and his disciples have translated *śrī* and *śrāy* as found in the *Avesta* as *Schönheit*—beauty. Lommel also translates these words by *schön* etc., which Oldenberg has adopted. But Gonda finds himself restless with such æsthetic categories, as he feels that the primary sense of *śrī* has to do with material prosperity. He says such æsthetic meanings are only vague:

> There is no denying that this vague meaning can do duty in most cases, but the question arises whether at least part of the relevant passages will not gain in depth and importance if we replace the above translations, which, though adopted by Oldenberg are only seldom a necessity, by renderings resulting from the assumption that the primary sense of the IIr (term) *śrī* —was some thing like "prosperity," "well-being," and not "beauty."[7]

Gonda gives credit to Oldenberg for correctly relating *śrī* to *śriṇāti* rather than to *śrāy—śrāpayati* (to cook). He, however, disagrees with Oldenberg's hypothesis that the base meaning for the root *śrī* in the Vedic period meant *Schönheit*. For him the idea of prosperity constitutes the primary meaning. As far as Oldenberg's hypothesis is concerned, he does not stand alone on this. As indicated above, other scholars, such as Bartholomae and Lommel, have considered beauty as an important meaning of *śrī*. Monier-Williams includes a wide range of æsthetic categories as part of the meaning of the term *śrī*.[8] As the

---

6. Ibid., 180.

7. Ibid., p. 204.

8. Monier Monier-Williams, *A Sanskrit-English Dictionary (*Delhi, Patna, Varaṇasi: Motilal Banarasidass, 1974), p.1098. Monier-Williams includes terms such as light, luster, radiance, splendor, or beauty, beauteously, gloriously. Cf. *śrīyase*, du. *śriyau*, beauty and prosperity; *śriya-ātmajāḥ*—sons of beauty; R.V.—

epic materials show, the meanings related to the æsthetic categories and the meanings related to material prosperity are not totally unrelated. It is also difficult to assign a particular meaning as the primary meaning of the term because it is the context in which it is used that necessarily clarifies the meaning, and therefore, there need not be a primary meaning that is permanently assigned to the term. In the context of the texts that he cites in his article, Oldenberg perhaps rightly sees the meaning of the term *śrī* corresponding with æsthetic categories.[9]

Gonda favors the rendering indicated by Sāyaṇa's explanation of the term *śrī* by words such as *saṃpad, saṃṛddhi*, and *vibhūti*—all of which indicate material prosperity more than anything else.[10] Although Gonda disagrees with the rendering of the term *śrī* by *Schönheit*, he admits that it is difficult to distinguish between well-being or prosperity and the outward appearance. Gonda further shows that the term *śrī* is found in association with *bhūti*—(growth, thriving, prosperity)[11]—in the Atharvaveda (12:1:63); and that *śrī* and *prajā* (offspring) are sometimes found in the same context (e.g., *Śatapatha Brāhmaṇa*, 2:3:1, 13; 4:4:2,4; *Aitareya Āraṇyaka*, 5:3:2).[12] He also shows the association of *śrī* with *yaśas* (glory);[13] and with *kṣatra* (ruling power).[14] He further deals with related words such as *śrīmat* (possessed of fortune), *śreman* (superiority), *śreyas* (more splendid/excellent) and *śreṣṭha* (most excellent) in order to elucidate the idea of economic, social, and political pre-eminence. To emphasize his point Gonda also shows the opposition between *śrī* and *pāpmān*: those who perform the sacrificial acts properly prosper while those who perform them in the wrong way suffer evil. In other words, because of one's evil deeds, one is alienated from *śrī* which results in material poverty. Gonda further lists the combinations of *śreṣṭha-śiras* (idea of head of a community); *śreṣṭha-jyeṣṭha* (best, most excellent—pre-eminent); *śreṣṭha-baliṣṭha* (most powerful); *śreṣṭha-varṣiṣṭha* (eminent); *śreṣṭha-vaśiṣṭha* (wrong reading for *vasiṣṭha*, meaning most excellent)—all pertaining to the idea of eminence, leadership, prominence, and so forth which is also linked with the notion of rulership or kingship. As we shall see, Hiltebeitel also emphasizes the connection of *śrī* with the idea of sovereignty in his study of the *Mahābhārata*.

While Gonda, drawing upon the material from the Vedic texts, tries to show that the primary meaning of the term *śrī* is material prosperity, Hiltebeitel, drawing his material from the epic sources and

prosperity, welfare, good fortune, success, auspiciousness, wealth, treasure, riches.

9. Oldenberg, op.cit. (referred to in Gonda, p. 204.).

10. Gonda, op.cit., p. 176.

11. Ibid., p. 181.

12. Ibid., p. 183-84.

13. Ibid., p. 185.

14. Ibid., p. 188.

specially from the *Mahābhārata,* tries to show that *śrī* is basically associated with sovereignty. In the treatment of Hiltebeitel, Śrī is already a goddess in her own right whereas Gonda's treatment centers around the term *śrī* as common noun.

Hiltebeitel makes four points: 1) Śrī is connected with royalty; 2) she is concerned with royal virtues; 3) she confers or transfers these virtues through the sacrificial horse to the king; 4) Śrī herself comes to the king with the royal virtues.[15] The basic texts to which he refers are the *Śatapatha Brāhmaṇa* and the *Mārkaṇḍeya Purāṇa*. The other important reference that he makes is to the "Śāntiparvan" of the *Mahābhārata*, which contains the story of Indra snatching Śrī away from Prahlāda by deceit.[16] With the departure of Śrī from Prahlāda his *aiśvaryam* (sovereignty) is gone. Hiltebeitel says:

> This final blow to Prahlāda's *aiśvaryam* is reminiscent of the hopelessness which overcomes the Pāṇḍavas at the loss of Draupadī, Yudhiṣṭhira's last stake in the dice game.[17]

Although Gonda and Hiltebeitel emphasize different notions as fundamental to the understanding of Śrī there is no disjunction between the notion of prosperity (Gonda) and the notion of sovereignty (Hiltebeitel). Both conceptions depend on each other and are complementary. Sovereignty presupposes prosperity while prosperity is certainly a part of sovereignty. Nor, as mentioned earlier, is there any disjunction between the notion of prosperity and that of beauty. In fact in the *Viṣṇusmṛti* (ca. third century C.E.) there is a description of Śrī by Bhūdevī, the goddess of the earth. After having addressed Viṣṇu regarding her concern for her maintenance and having subsequently received a whole set of laws that human beings would have to follow to maintain the earth, Bhūdevī turns to Lakṣmī (Śrī) and praises her in the following way:

> Thou art repose (final liberation), the highest among the four objects of human pursuit; thou art Lakṣmī; thou art a support (in danger); thou art Śrī; thou art indifference (the freedom from all worldly pursuits and appetites which is the consequence of final emancipation); thou art victory; thou art beauty (*saundaryam*); thou art splendor (of the Sun and the moon personified); thou art renown; thou art prosperity; thou art wisdom; thou art power of expression; thou art purifier (XCIX.4).[18]

The above passage includes a wide range of attributes that aptly depict Śrī as a goddess in her own right. These categories include both æsthetic categories as well as categories related to sovereignty ("thou art victory") and prosperity. The passage does not provide any

15. Hiltebeitel, op.cit., p. 149.
16. *Mahābhārata.* 12:124:54-60.
17. Hiltebeitel, op.cit., p. 159.
18. *The Institutes of Viṣṇu (Viṣṇusmṛti//Viṣṇu Sūtras*), trans. Julius Jolly, SBE (Oxford: Clarendon Press, 1880), p. 297.

indication as to which one of these attributes is primary, although the way Bhūdevī uses "thou art" as a refrain at the beginning of every attribute seems to imply that all these categories have equal significance in the context of her request to Viṣṇu.

Thus, in understanding Śrī, both in this context and elsewhere, there seems to be no radical separation between æsthetic categories and the material categories. Such a distinction not only seems to be artificial but also does not provide a complete and coherent picture of who Śrī is both in the Vedic and the epic materials as well as in other texts. By making a distinction between *śrī* as a common noun and Śrī as a goddess one might be able to provide subtle arguments in favor of one or the other. But such a radical distinction between *śrī* as a common noun and Śrī as a goddess is unhelpful in gaining an insight into the overall understanding of Śrī. Obviously the Vedic notion of *śrī* becomes part of the later conceptions of Śrī as a goddess. In any case, the later traditions claim that their understanding of Śrī is basically derived from the Vedic notion of *śrī*. The Śrīvaiṣṇava tradition certainly makes this claim and refers to the *Śrīsūkta* portion of the Ṛg Veda Saṃhitā.

The significance of these categories in understanding Śrī must be seen in the context of Śrī's role in sustaining the world order along with her inseparable consort Viṣṇu, as we will discuss in the following chapter.

The Association of Śrī-Lakṣmī with Viṣṇu

Both Viṣṇu and Śrī appear in Vedic literature. While Viṣṇu appears as a minor god, the term *śrī*, as we have seen, is not yet used to refer to a goddess. In the Ṛg Veda Viṣṇu is usually recognized as an aspect of the Sun, while later Vedic texts associate him with sacrifice (SB 1:1:2:13).[19]

According to the formula developed in the *Taittirīya Āraṇyaka* which is still recited during the worship of Viṣṇu in Śrīvaiṣṇava temples, Nārāyaṇa, Vāsudeva, and Viṣṇu are identified as one.[20] The *Śatapatha Brāhmaṇa* mentions Nārāyaṇa who, at the request of Prajāpati offered sacrifice thrice (SB 12:3:4:1). Nārāyaṇa is also mentioned in connection with Puruṣamedha sacrifice, which is performed by the Puruṣa Nārāyaṇa litany (SB 13:6:2:12). In the same text, Nārāyaṇa is said to have performed the Pāñcarātra sacrifice and gained superiority over the other deities (SB 13.6.1.1). In other words, the Puruṣamedha sacrifice and the Pāñcarātra sacrifice are identified as the same (*etaṃ puruṣamedhaṃ pañcarātraṃ yajñakratum*). Although the *Śatapatha Brāhmaṇa* does not identify Nārāyaṇa and Viṣṇu as one, there seems

19. For a detailed account of Viṣṇu's origins see Gonda, op.cit., chap. 1

20. "*nārāyaṇāya vidmaha Vāsudevāya dhīmahi, tan-no Viṣṇuḥ pracoḍayāt,*" *Taittirīya Āraṇyaka*, 10th prapāṭhaka.

to be some indirect connection made between the two. For instance, in SB 13.1.8.8 and SB 13.2.2.9 Viṣṇu and the sacrifice are identified; in SB 13.6.1.2 Puruṣa and the sacrifice are identified. Taking these references together, then, it seems to imply that Puruṣa Nārāyaṇa and Viṣṇu might have been understood, in the *Śatapatha Brāhmaṇa*, as representing the same deity.

According to the editors of *The History and Culture of Indian People*,[21] Vāsudeva, referred to in Pāṇini's *Aṣṭādhyāyi* (fifth century B.C.E.), was deified as Bhagavat by the second century B.C.E. Furthermore, according to the accounts of Megasthenes, the Vāsudeva cult can be traced back to the fourth century B.C.E. By the time of the *Bhagavad Gītā*, Vāsudeva-Kṛṣṇa was identified with the Vedic deity Viṣṇu.[22] The identification of Nārāyaṇa with Viṣṇu can be traced in the *Baudhāyana Dharma Sūtra*.[23] In the *Mahābhārata*, however, Nārāyaṇa is identified with Vāsudeva-Kṛṣṇa. According to archeological evidence, iconic representations of Viṣṇu-Vāsudeva can be traced to earlier than the beginning of the Common Era. The four-armed figure of the deity is found on the coin of the Pāñcāla King Viṣṇumitra. Again, a Kuṣāṇa seal-matrix attributed by Cunningham to Haviṣka contains a representation of a four-armed Viṣṇu with *śaṅka* (conch), *cakra* (wheel), *gada* (mace) and a ring-like object.[24]

The earliest representations of Śrī-Lakṣmī in historical records have been found in the Bhārhut Stūpas. There are four representations, one seated and three standing: Śrī (Beauty), Āśa (Hope), Śraddhā (Faith), and Hṛī (Modesty). In addition, there is another representation in Bhārhut Stūpa—of Śirimā, who may be the same as Śrīmati. From these and other figures historians have drawn the conclusions that the cult of these goddesses was widespread by the beginning of the Common Era, between third century B.C.E. and the first century C.E.[25]

Gonda, quoting from Hartmann, points out that Śrī as a distinct goddess did not appear before the *Vājasaneya Saṃhitā* and further identifies her with a pre-Āryan fertility goddess. Although the Ṛg Veda Saṃhitā presents only the substantive *śrī* (whether it meant prosperity or beauty) the *Śrīsūkta* provides some valuable information about Śrī. She is "moist" (*ārdra*); she is perceptible through her "odor" (*gandhadvāra*); "well-supplied" (*nityapuṣṭa*); "abounding in dung" (*karīṣin*), and that she delights in the sound of elephants. Her appearance is compared to that of gold or of the Sun. She is described

---

21. R. C. Majumdar, ed., *The History and Culture of the Indian People*, vol. 2. (Bombay: Bharatiya Vidya Bhavan, first published in 1951, third impression, 1960), p. 433.

22. Ibid., p. 435.

23. Ibid., p. 435.

24. Ibid., p. 438.

25. Ibid., p. 470.

as "shining brightly" (*jvālantī*), "having the hue of light" (*candra*) and as "splendid" (*prabhāśa*).[26]

As mentioned earlier, the first mention of Śrī as a distinct deity comes from the *Vājasaneya Saṃhitā*. In the same text Śrī and Lakṣmī appear as two different goddesses. They are presented as co-wives of Āditya. According to Gonda, this tradition continued even up until the epic period. Thus in the *Mahābhārata* (Critical Edition III. p. 127, 151) and the *Rāmāyaṇa* (3:46:17) Śrī and Lakṣmī are invoked together. Majumdar et al., however, contend that these passages may be later interpolations.[27]

Gonda also agrees with Hartmann that Śrī and Lakṣmī were different figures at the beginning and later became merged in the Upaniṣads. He, however, does not quite agree with her contention that the "original dual personality of the goddess survives in the well-known representation of Viṣṇu with two wives"[28] (i.e., Lakṣmī and Bhūdevī/Bhūmi). Gonda rightly thinks that Bhūdevī is another divine character.[29] Furthermore, in the dialogue that I noted earlier from the *Viṣṇusmṛti* it is clear that Lakṣmī and Bhūdevī/Bhūmi are distinct divinities.

Gonda also disagrees with Hartmann's contention that Lakṣmī originally meant *alakṣmī* and was the goddess of poverty,[30] and asserts rather that Lakṣmī "may originally have been the divinity representing the signs, evidence, or prognostications (of luck and prosperity)."[31]

Returning to the question of the figures Śrī and Lakṣmī and their subsequent merging, we have noted that Gonda agrees with Hartmann's opinion that the merging might have taken place in the Upaniṣads. There is also another suggestion that their merging might have occurred around the epic period.[32] While there is no satisfactory evidence for either point of view, the merging of Śrī and Lakṣmī seems plausible, in view of their seemingly overlapping attributes and characteristics, certainly over a period of time between the Vedic texts and the epic texts. Most certainly by the epic period, we have clear indication of Śrī and Lakṣmī being one and the same, as for

---

26. Gonda, op.cit., p .213.

27. R. C. Majumdar, op.cit., p. 470.

28. Gonda, op.cit., p. 214.

29. Loc. cit., p. 214. Gonda refers to usages like Viṣṇu-Śrī—*mahīyukta* (joined by the earth), and *devyau śrībhūmyau* (goddesses Śrī and Bhūmi) (*Atri Saṃhitā*, 4:22); *devasya dakṣiṇe pārśve śriyaṃ vāme mahiṃ tathā|* *Śrībhūmidevyoḥ* (Śrī on the right side of God, and the (goddess) Earth on his left and so on; Śrī and Bhūmi of God) (*Atri Saṃhitā*, 16:18), etc.

30. Ibid., p. 217, f.n. 33.

31. Ibid., p. 217 and also see pp. 215-17 (for distinction between Lakṣmī-Lakṣman).

32. I refer to the implied suggestion in R. C. Majumdar, op.cit., p. 470.

example, in the *Mahābhārata* (12:225:1ff). Śrī calls herself Lakṣmī, Bhūti, and so on.[33]

This takes us to the next question as to when Śrī-Lakṣmī became associated with Viṣṇu. From the evidence of the Purāṇic narratives it may be hypothesized that Śrī-Lakṣmī was bestowed upon Viṣṇu after the churning of the ocean. Gonda has pointed out that before being permanently associated with Viṣṇu, Śrī-Lakṣmī was connected with various other gods. In the *Śrīsūkta* Lakṣmī is associated with Agni and Jātavedas (stanza 1ff; 13ff). In the Vedic period Śrī and Lakṣmī were considered to be consorts of Puruṣa (Vaj. S. 31:22) who is identified as Prajāpati. In the *Śatapatha Brāhmaṇa*, Agni was considered as possessing Śrī (SB 8:6:2:4; 5:4:3:15). In the *Mahābhārata*, Śrī is depicted as the wife of Kubera (Mbh. 2:10:19). She is also depicted as the wife of Dharma in both the *Mahābhārata* and the *Viṣṇupurāṇa* (1:7:2).[34] Again, in the *Mahābhārata*, Śrī is said to have left Bali for Indra, and subsequently Indra also loses her (Mbh. 12:225:1ff). This story is also referred to in the *Rāmāyaṇa* (6:50:25). The lost goddess was finally recovered by the gods by churning the ocean, and after the churning of the ocean she is bestowed upon Viṣṇu. Due to her association with many divinities before finally settling with Viṣṇu, she is characterized as "inconstant" (*cañcalā*). Coomaraswamy remarks that if she clings to Nārāyaṇa it is only to enjoy his constant changes of form.[35]

In the "Śāntiparvan" of the *Mahābhārata*, Bali, after having lost Śrī to Indra, reminds Indra by saying:

> This Royal Prosperity (*rājaśrī*) which you have obtained and which you consider to be incomparable formerly dwelt in me. Contrary to that, she does not remain in one place (*naiṣā hyekatra tiṣṭhati*). Indeed, she has dwelt in thousands of Indras who were superior to you. Fickle (*lolā*), having abandoned me, she has come to you . . . . Do not brag O Śakra. If you go on this way, having abandoned you she will quickly go to another. (12:217:57-59).
>
> From delusion (*mohāt)*, you long for this Royal Prosperity (*rājaśrī*). Imagined to be stable (*sthira*), she is not for you, nor for us (*na ca asmākam*), nor for others. Passing over many others she now dwells in you. Having remained in you for a certain time, O Vāsava, (she will prove to be) inconstant (*cañcalā*). Like a cow abandoning one drinking hole, she will go again to another (12:220:44-46).[36]

As mentioned above, Śrī-Lakṣmī subsequently leaves Indra to finally stay with Viṣṇu. When Śrī-Lakṣmī leaves Bali and comes to Indra, she

---

33. Cf. Mbh. 3:37:33; Rām. 3:46:17. Certainly by the Āgamic period Lakṣmī and Śrī are seen as one and the same. Cf. *Srīprasna Saṃhitā*, 26:1ff—the name Lakṣmī and Śrī are used interchangeably in the whole of the chapter. *See* especially 26:33.

34. Cf. Mbh. 1:66:13.

35. A. K. Coomaraswamy, "Early Indian Iconography: 2, Śrī-Lakṣmī" in *Eastern Art,* vol. 1 (1928-29), p. 178. (Referred to by Hiltebeitel. op.cit., p. 163).

36. Quoted from Hiltebeitel, op,cit., p.163.

points to two interesting elements that seem to regulate her goings about: 1) that "time alone causes (her) goings about" (Mbh. 12:218:10); and 2) that "I have come to you of my own accord" (*māṃ svayam anuprāptam*) (Mbh. 12:221:80) which means that she chooses to come to anyone on her own initiative and not being controlled by any other god. The first principle, time (*kāla*), is identified in the *Bhagavad Gītā* with Viṣṇu (BG 11:32), which means that after she comes to Viṣṇu, he becomes her regulating principle, although he does not curtail her freedom.

Earlier we noted that in the Ṛg Veda Saṃhitā, Viṣṇu is depicted as an aspect of the Sun. Association of Śrī's appearance with that of the Sun in the "Śrīsūkta" may be the earliest allusion to the subsequent association of Śrī-Lakṣmī with Viṣṇu in post-Vedic literature. The earliest historical record of the association of Śrī-Lakṣmī with Viṣṇu comes from the Gupta period. The Junāgarh inscription of Skandagupta mentions Viṣṇu as the "perpetual resort of Lakṣmī." Again, in the Sārnāth inscription of Parakālāditya, Lakṣmī is mentioned as the wife of Vāsudeva. Furthermore, in one Kadaṃba record, dated ca. 500 C.E. the narrative begins with the adoration of Bhagavat with Śrī on his breast. Some inscriptions carry the names of both wives "Śrī-Pṛthvī Vallabha."[37] Gonda is in agreement with the idea that the association of Śrī-Lakṣmī with Viṣṇu can be traced to the Gupta period. He notes:

> The pantheon of the Gupta period is, further, relatively simple: Viṣṇu accompanied by Lakṣmī seated on the Garuḍa, or sleeping on the cosmic serpent, Rāma and Kṛṣṇa.[38]

He further says:

> But Śrī-Lakṣmī who appears on the coins of the Guptas and after them, and who appears as the wife of Viṣṇu on the inscriptions, especially during the time of Skandagupta (ca. 460), and whose role has been attributed neither to the Indo-European nor to the line of Sāṅkhya teaching on the Puruṣa and Prakṛti, has found her definitive place in the middle of the first millenium.[39]

In summary, the conception of Śrī-Lakṣmī in the Vedic materials is seen in relation to prosperity, well-being, and beauty, and in the epic

---

37. R. C. Majumdar, op.cit., vol. 3, p. 424f.

38. J. Gonda, *Die Religionen Indiens*, vol. 2 (Stuttgart: W. Kohlhammer Verlag, 1963), p. 115. (Das Pantheon der Gupta-Zeit war noch verhältnismässig einfach: Viṣṇu auf dem Garuḍa sitzend, von Lakṣmī begleitet oder auf der Weltschlange schlafend, Rāma und Kṛṣṇa). Translation is mine.

39. J. Gonda, *Die Religionen Indiens*, vol. 2 (Stuttgart: W. Kohlhammer Verlag, 1963), p. 116. (Śrī-Lakṣmī aber, die auf den Münzen der Guptas und ihrer Nachfolger erscheint und inschriftlich zuerst zur Zeit des Skandagupta (um 460) als Viṣṇu Gattin auftritt und deren Rolle weder indo-griechischem Einfluss noch in erster Linie der Sāṅkhya-Lehre von Puruṣa und Prakṛti zugeschrieben werden darf, hat in der Mitte des ersten Jahrtausends ebenfalls ihren definitiren Platz gefunden). Translation is mine.

materials, Śrī appears as a minor goddess. She is characterized as "inconstant." She represents auspiciousness, prosperity, royalty, and beauty. She becomes associated with Viṣṇu only much later, during the Gupta period. Although Viṣṇu becomes her regulating principle her freedom is not curtailed or diminished. The Vedic and the epic materials do not make reference to her involvement in the process of creation, maintenance, and dissolution. Although she becomes associated with Viṣṇu, the idea of their inseparability and one-ness does not appear in the Vedic and the epic materials. It is the Pāñcarātra and the later Purāṇic materials that provide us with that understanding of Śrī-Lakṣmī. It may be noted that perhaps the transition of Śrī-Lakṣmī from the inconstant one to the inseparable one can only be understood in light of the *avatāra* concept that becomes associated with Viṣṇu and is developed subtantially in the Pāñcarātra and the Purāṇas. Although it might be too much to claim that the later Hindu poets have developed the notion of incarnation to deal with the problem of the inconstant nature of Śrī-Lakṣmī, the fact remains that with the emergence of the idea of incarnation associated with Viṣṇu, the goddess Śrī certainly remains inseparable from him. As we shall see, it is this inseparable nature of the goddess that is characteristic of the Śrīvaiṣṇava materials and forms the basis for the discussion of the status of the goddess.

CHAPTER THREE

ŚRĪ-LAKṢMĪ IN THE PĀÑCARĀTRA ĀGAMAS

In establishing the ritual tradition of the Śrīvaiṣṇavas, Yāmuna, Rāmānuja, Veṅkaṭanātha (Vedānta Deśika) and the subsequent teachers defended the Pāñcarātra tradition quite vigorously as being orthodox, and very much in line with the Vedic tradition. In the later chapters, I shall be dealing with this defense by the early teachers and explore the extent to which they appropriated the Pāñcarātra notions in their overall understanding of Śrī-Lakṣmī. For the purposes of this chapter, however, I shall limit myself to laying out the understanding of Śrī-Lakṣmī in the Pāñcarātra tradition. Before I do that, it would be useful to discuss some of the presuppositions in understanding the Pāñcarātra tradition. Since my primary task is to expound the understanding of Śrī-Lakṣmī, I have focused primarily on the *Lakṣmī Tantra* which deals with Śrī-Lakṣmī more extensively than the other texts. Nevertheless, in discussing the presuppositions of the Pāñcarātra tradition I shall also refer to other older Āgama texts to supplement and to substantiate what is provided in the *Lakṣmī Tantra.* This is by no means to suggest that the early Śrīvaiṣṇava teachers (such as Yāmuna and Rāmānuja) were influenced by the *Lakṣmī Tantra*, for the text in my view, is certainly a later text. Since several scholars such as F. O. Schrader, J. Gonda, J. A. B. van Buitenen, H. Daniel Smith, and Sanjukta Gupta[1] (among other Indian scholars) have provided useful and substantial introductions to the Pāñcarātra literature that include discussions of issues such as the meaning of *pāñcarātra,* etc., I shall briefly lay out the main tenets of the Pāñcarātra tradition.

---

1. For a detailed introduction to the Pāñcarātra literature see F. O. Schrader, *Introduction to the Pāñcarātra and the Ahirbudhnya Saṃhitā* (Madras: Adyar Library, 1916). Also see H. D. Smith, *A Bibliography of the Pāñcarātra Āgamas* (Baroda: Gaekwad's Oriental Series, 1975). This is found to be very useful as it includes chapter-wise the contents of printed Pāñcarātra texts. See also S. Gupta, *Lakṣmī Tantra* (Leiden: E. J. Brill, 1972), pp. xv-xxxvi. Also see J. Gonda, *Medieval Religious Literature in Sanskrit* (Weisbaden: Otto Harrassowitz, 1977); also see J. A. B. van Buitenen, "The name 'Pāñcarātra,'" in *History of Religions* (Chicago, 1962). Besides, all critical editions of the Pāñcarātra texts that are published in Sanskrit have valuable introductions in Sanskrit; in some texts there are also introductions in English (e.g., *Śrī Praśna Saṃhitā,* trans. Seetha Padmanabhan).

General Background and Philosophy of the Pāñcarātra

The name "Pāñcarātra" presents a problem to scholars as it is not clear what exactly is referred to by it. Nevertheless, several different theories are proposed within the various texts themselves, and also by some modern scholars. It is, perhaps, useful to list some of the ones that I have been able to survey:

1) The *Pādma Tantra* (1.1.68) calls this literature the "department of knowledge, a great esoteric doctrine."
2) The Mahābhārata (12.326.99 ff) says, "this *mahopaniṣad* connected with the four Vedas and relating to the Sāṅkhya and Yoga and therefore named Pāñcarātra."
3) The *Parama Saṃhitā* (1.1.68) calls it "*Yogatantra*"—which deals with five qualities (*guṇa*-s) of the gross elements (*mahābhūta*-s) that are called *rātri*-s of the embodied soul; and speaks of the union of five primary elements (*pañcamahābhūta*-s), five subtle elements (*tanmātra*-s), the principle of individuation (*ahaṃkāra*), intelligence (*buddhi*), and the principle (*avyakta*) from which the material world arises. These five are called *rātri*-s of the the Puruṣa. Therefore the doctrine is called "Pāñcarātra."
4) *Nāradīya Pāñcarātra*, a late text, emphasizes five kinds of knowledge—that which leads to the ultimate reality; to final emancipation; that which produces *bhakti*; that which leads to mastery of Yoga, and that which relates to mundane knowledge.
5) *Śrīpraśna Saṃhitā* (2.40) explains *rātri* as nescience (*ajñāna*) and *pañca* as "to destroy."[2] Therefore, this system is called that which destroys ignorance.
6) Some traditional scholars point out that the Pāñcarātra deals with five duties of the Vaiṣṇavas—*tapas, puṇḍra, nāma, mantra,* and *yoga.*
7) Some other traditional scholars point out that it deals with the five parts into which a day is divided for ritual purposes, namely, *abhigamana* (approaching the Lord—morning prayers), *upādāna* (fetching flowers), *ijyā* (worship), *svādhyāya* (study of the Vedas), and *yoga* (meditation).
8) Others say that it deals with the fivefold manifestation of the Lord—*para, vyūha, vibhava, arcā*, and *antaryāmin.*
9) van Buitenen tries to locate the meaning in the context of rituals and not so much in the philosophy. He relates it to an ascetic practice of staying "five nights"—one night in a village for every five nights in a town.[3]

2. It is not clear how the meaning "to destroy" is arrived at; the root *pac* means to cook, ripen, to develop, mature, heal, etc. See Monier-Willimas, p. 575, cols. 1 and 2.

3. J. A. B. van Buitenen, *Yāmuna's Āgamaprāmāṇya* (Madras: Rāmānuja Research Society, 1971), pp. 1-38.

10) Gonda tends to support van Buitenen's interpretation but also points to the influence from the "five-day sacrifice" (*pañcarātraṃ yajñakratum*) mentioned in the Śatapatha Brāhmaṇa (13.6.1.1) where Nārāyaṇa was identified with Puruṣa of the Vedas. There, Nārāyaṇa is described as the "originator of the Pāñcarātra rite."[4]

While all these above are possible explanations of the name *Pāñcarātra* there, nevertheless, seems to be no consensus on the meaning of the words *pañca* and *rātri*.

The authorship of the Pāñcarātra texts is anonymous, although most of the texts seem to have come from south Indian origin. The dating of the texts is also not easy. All we can provide, on the basis of the available information, is a rough estimation of the dates when they were first available. Thus, from the writings of Yāmuna, we know that he was familiar with *Īśvara Saṃhitā*, *Parama Saṃhitā, Śāṇḍilya Saṃhitā, Sanatkumāra Saṃhitā, Indrarātra Saṃhitā* and *Padmodbhava Saṃhitā*. Rāmānuja refers to *Sāttvata-, Pauṣkara-* and *Parama Saṃhitā*-s. Schrader places the *Ahirbudhnya Saṃhitā* in the eighth century C.E. on the basis that it belongs to the "original *Saṃhitā*-s."[5] Sanjukta Gupta places the *Lakṣmī Tantra* between the ninth and the thirteenth centuries.[6] Thus, the *Jayākhya-*, *Parama-*, *Pauṣkara-*, *Sāttvata-*, and the *Ahirbudhnya Saṃhitā*s, among a few others, may have been in existence by the eighth century C.E. Among all the *Saṃhitā*-s, the *Sāttvata-*, *Pauṣkara-*, and the *Jayākhya Saṃhitā* are considered the three gems and also are considered the oldest and therefore more authoritative.

The subject matter of the Pāñcarātra texts is normally divided into four parts—*jñāna* (knowledge), *yoga* (meditation), *kriyā* (dealing with temple construction), and *caryā* (rules prescribed for daily worship). Not all the texts are divided so clearly, nor do they all deal with all four parts. So far, to my knowledge, only *Pādma Saṃhitā* deals with all four parts.

The philosophy of the Pāñcarātra is based on the belief of one ultimate end (*ekāntika* which literally means "one as the end"). It affirms Viṣṇu as the supreme reality, with all his divine aspects. He is pre-existent, beginningless, and infinite. He is characterized as Pure Bliss, Omniscient, Omnipresent. He is further characterized by six auspicious *guṇa*-s (qualities)—*jñāna* (knowledge), *aiśvarya* (sovereignty), *vīrya* (virility), *śakti* (power/potency), *bala* (force), and *tejas* (energy). He is associated with his consort, Śrī-Lakṣmī, who is identical and yet distinct from him. She is described as his Śakti. Śrī-Lakṣmī as Viṣṇu's Śakti has two aspects—Kriyā Śakti (Active Force), who is identical with Viṣṇu's resolve to become active; and Bhūti Śakti, who forms the material reality. While the *Ahirbudhnya Saṃhitā*

---

4. J. Gonda, *Medieval Religious Literature in Sanskrit* (Wiesbaden: Harrassowitz, 1977), pp. 39-139.
5. Schrader, op.cit., p. 20-22.
6. Gupta, op.cit., pp. xix-xx.

attributes five functions to Viṣṇu, the *Lakṣmī Tantra* attributes the same to Śrī-Lakṣmī.[7] Those functions are known as Viṣṇu's *śakti*-s. They are: *tirodhāna* (obscuration),[8] *sṛṣṭi* (creation), *sthiti* (maintenance), *saṃhṛti* (dissolution) and *anugraha* (favoring). In the cosmological theory of the Pāñcarātra there are three phases in the creation—pure creation, intermediary (nonpure) creation, and lower (impure) creation.

In the pure creation, Lakṣmī becomes manifest with the six auspicious qualities described above. These six auspicious qualities form the material for the pure creation. The first beings to emerge are, the *vyūha*-s: Saṃkarṣaṇa, Pradyumna, and Aniruddha. In other words, the six qualities form three groups. In each group two qualities predominate while the other qualities remain dormant. Thus, *jñāna+bala* forms Saṃkarṣaṇa (Individual Soul/*Jīva*); *aiśvarya+vīrya* forms Pradyumna (*Manas*); *śakti+tejas* forms Aniruddha (*Ahaṃkāra*).[9] The *vibhava*-s (*avatāra*-s which are thirty-nine), the *arcā* and the *antaryāmin*, the creation of the Highest Heaven (*Parama Vyoma/Vaikuṇṭha*), the exalted ones (*nityasūri*-s), and the eternally liberated ones (*nityamukta*-s) all belong to this pure creation. The older texts seem to project the idea that at the time of dissolution the Highest Heaven with its beings is dissolved. The later texts, however, seem to favor the idea of the continuation of the Highest Heaven.[10]

While the pure creation emanates from the *kriyā śakti*, the intermediary creation, which is called nonpure creation (*śuddhetara*, because it is a mixture of both pure and impure), emanates from the *bhūti śakti*. During the intermediary creation there are two manifestations from the *bhūti śakti*—*kūṭastha puruṣa* (aggregate of souls) and *māyā śakti* (non-spiritual energy). Both of these actually emanate from the *vyūha* called Pradyumna. The disembodied souls that are bound by *karma* originate from the *kūṭastha puruṣa* at the time of creation and return to it at the time of dissolution. The material universe belongs to the *māyā śakti*. After the manifestation of the *kūṭastha puruṣa* and the *māyā śakti*, the *vyūha*, called Aniruddha, becomes responsible for the emergence of *śakti* (identified as *mūlaprakṛti*—root-matter), and from *śakti* emerges *niyati* (restriction—subtle cause); from *niyati* emerges *kāla* (time); from

7. Cf. *Ah. S.* ch. 14; *LT*. ch. 12.

8. According to *LT*. 13-14 —*tirobhāva* (to disguise one's nature); in *Ah. S.* 14.1ff.—*tirodhāna* (obscuration) or *nigraha* (obstruction).

9. *LT*. ch. 6. The *Sāttvata Saṃhitā* elaborates on the worship of the four-fold Viṣṇu and pays a great deal of attention to his six auspicious qualities. See *Sāttvata Saṃhitā*, (with commentary by Alasiṅga Bhaṭṭa, ed. V. V. Dwivedi, Varanasi, 1982), chaps. 3-6. The *LT* account of the distribution of the six auspicious qualities among Saṃkarṣṇa and others agrees with that of the *Sāttvata Saṃhitā*. See *SS*, chaps. 3. vv 6-7.

10. It is interesting to note that one of the points of difference between the two sects of the Śrīvaiṣṇavas has to do with the question whether the *nitya muktas* (eternally liberated ones) participate in the creative process.

kāla emerges the *sattva guṇa*; from the *sattva guṇa*, the *rajo guṇa-s*; from the *rajo guṇa*-s, the *tamo guṇa*-s. *Niyati* is the subtle regulator, while *kāla* is the mysterious power different from the usual sense of time. The three *guṇa*-s, then, form the uniform mass called the *avyakta* (unmanifest) or *mūlaprakṛti* (root-matter) for the purpose of the material creation.

The lower creation begins with the evolution of the *tattva*-s. Unlike the classical Sāṅkhya system, there are three principles involved in the process of the lower creation. In the classical Sāṅkhya system, the mutual relation between the *puruṣa* and *prakṛti* is not clear. In the Pāñcarātra system, however, the mutual relation between *puruṣa* and *prakṛti* is regulated by *kāla*. Analogous to the Sāṅkhya system, the *tattva*-s emerge from the *mūlaprakṛti* in the following way: From the *avyakta prakṛti* (unmanifest root-matter) emerges *mahat*; *buddhi* is an aspect of *mahat* and not identical with *mahat* as in the Sāṅkhya system. From *mahat* emerges the *ahaṃkāra* (ego), and from *ahaṃkāra* the *manas*. From *ahaṃkāra* emerge the five *mahābhūta*-s (space, wind, fire, water, and earth), five *tanmātra*-s (sound, touch, form, taste, and smell), five *buddhīndriya*-s (hearing, feeling, seeing, tasting, and smelling), and five *karmendriya*-s (speaking, grasping, walking, excreting, and generating).

With the appearance of the *tattva*-s, the cosmic night ends, and the cosmic day begins. First, there appears the cosmic egg from the navel of Viṣṇu (*padmanābha*), which contains all the *tattva*-s. As the egg grows bigger, a shining lotus appears wherein Aniruddha creates Brahmā with four faces. Brahmā then creates 1) four youths (Śanaka, etc.) who refuse to have offspring, 2) the androgynous Rudra (Śiva), and 3) six Prajāpati-s (Marīcī, etc.). From the Prajāpati-s emerge the sentient and the nonsentient beings.[11]

The cosmic day ends with the dissolution. At the time of dissolution everything dissolves into Viṣṇu and all souls (*jīva*-s) asleep in his womb. There are three kinds of *jīva*-s at the time of dissolution. The first are the liberated *jīva*-s who occupy the upper part of the Lord's womb, the *jīva*-s that are fit for liberation occupy the middle part, and the *jīva*-s bound by the *karma*-s are relegated to the lower part. Total emancipation is not identity with the Lord as in the Advaita system, but rather the *jīva*-s remain latent in the womb of Viṣṇu. In other words, as Schrader puts it, the *jīva*-s are in the "perfect embrace of the divine couple."[12]

According to the *Ahirbudhnya Saṃhitā*,[13] the liberated *jīva* is omniscient, omnipotent, and omnipresent. Even though it is atomic in nature, its consciousness is omnipresent (*sadā vibhu*). The *Lakṣmī Tantra*, on the other hand, points out that the *jīva* acquires these divine

11. For more details on the three levels of creation see F. O. Schrader, op.cit., pp. 31-98.

12. Schrader, op.cit., p. 100.

13. Cf. *Ah. S.*, chap. 6

attributes at the stage of liberation and only then becomes omniscient and omnipotent. It further says that since all the fetters are removed, *jīva* acquires the nature of Śrī-Lakṣmī and becomes nonatomic.[14]

Some Presuppositions in the Pāñcarātra Āgamas

1) The Pāñcarātra literature presupposes and makes extensive use of such Sāṅkhya philosophical categories as *puruṣa, prakṛti, mahat, buddhi,* etc., though not in the same way as the Sāṅkhya understands them (*LT.* 4:43; 5:35; 6:20,23; 12:39,40). For instance, the Pāñcarātra use of the category of *guṇas* is not the same as that of Sāṅkhya. The Pāñcarātra texts refer to *guṇa*-s basically as *jñāna* (omniscience), *śakti* (potency), *bala* (force), *aiśvarya* (lordship), *vīrya* (virility) and *tejas* (brilliance) These six *guṇa*-s are said to be both material and instruments for the pure creation; three of them are connected with *bhūti* and three with the *kriyā* aspect of *śakti.* According to the *Lakṣmī Tantra* these six *guṇa*-s, when manifested by Śrī-Lakṣmī in equal proportion, are called collectively Vāsudeva. (But according to the *Sāttvata* and *Ahirbudhnya Saṃhitā* it is Viṣṇu who manifests the six *guṇa*-s).[15] It must also be noted that Pāñcarātra literature does refer to *sattva, rajas*, and *tamas* as *triguṇa.* These are only modifications of *jñāna, aiśvarya*, and *śakti* respectively.[16] These *triguṇa*-s are associated with creation, maintenance, and destruction as follows: *rajas* relates to the creative process, *sattva* relates to the process of maintenance, and *tamas* relates to the process of dissolution.[17]

The other point to be noted here is that the Pāñcarātra interprets *puruṣa* differently from Sāṅkhya. While in Sāṅkhya *puruṣa* is the inert and inactive principle, in Pāñcarātra it is identified with Vāsudeva/Viṣṇu by whose command Śakti (*prakṛti*) opens her eyes (*unmeṣa*).[18] In other words, the *puruṣa* seems to take the initiative in the Pāñcarātra, though *Lakṣmī Tantra* attributes the initiative to Śrī-Lakṣmī. As we shall see later, Śrī-Lakṣmī herself takes the initiative

---

14. Cf. *LT.* 13.32. It is interesting to note that in the question of the *jīva* being atomic or nonatomic and its capacity to participate in the creative process all subsequent debate in the Śrīvaiṣṇava history is already reflected. Both the *Ahirbudhnya Saṃhitā* and the *Lakṣmī Tantra* seem to have occasioned a similar debate, and therefore the subsequent debate on the nature of the *jīva* and its liberation cannot be understood apart from the Pāñcarātra texts.

15. *LT.* 4:43; (when I refer to *LT* it will be S. Gupta's translation of *Lakṣmī Tantra,* and the Sanskrit text —Krishnamacharya, V., ed. *Lakṣmī Tantra—a Pāñcarātra Āgama* (Madras: The Adyar Library and Research Center, Reprint, 1975.). Cf. *Ahirbudhnya Saṃhitā*, 2:28; 5:29; 6:25; 21:9; *Śrī Praśna Saṃhitā*, 26:8. Also see SS. chap.3. vv.4-5.

16. *LT.* 3:6.

17. *LT.* 3:7-8.

18. *Prakāśa Saṃhitā,* 1:1:53.

and wills the creative process.[19] In the *Lakṣmī Tantra* both *puruṣa* and *prakṛti* are aspects of Śrī-Lakṣmī herself, represented by Agni and Soma in the ritual formula.[20]

What is interesting about the Pāñcarātra literature, however, is that it takes Sāṅkhya categories and synthesizes them with its own philosophical categories, which in turn are derived from the Upaniṣads and the Purāṇas, and to some extent from the Vedas.[21] The synthesis of all the various categories achieved in the Pāñcarātra literature appears to be so natural and cohesive that one tends to think that perhaps all the various streams of categories found their culminating point in the Pāñcarātra tradition. The theory of creation as pure, mixed, and nonpure seems to be original to the Pāñcarātra.

2) The most important contribution of Pāñcarātra literature to the post-Vedic Hinduism is its idea of the five forms (*pañcarūpyam*) of existence of Viṣṇu (also known as *prakaras*): *para, vyūha, vibhava, arcā*, and *antaryāmin*.[22] We often do not find all the five being mentioned in the same text of the Pāñcarātra. The *Ahirbudhnya Saṃhitā* mentions only three forms, namely, *para, vyūha*, and *vibhava;*[23] the *Lakṣmī Tantra* mentions only four forms, namely, *para, vyūha, vibhava*, and *arcā*[24] by referring to them as "*rūpa-catuṣṭayam*."[25] It must be made clear that here "*rūpacatuṣṭayam*"

---

19. *LT*. 4:5. Because of this concern for the female principle as the initiator, *Lakṣmī Tantra* is perhaps closer to the Sāṅkhya notion of *prakṛti* than the other Pāñcarātra texts. It must also be pointed out, however, that Sāṅkhya is ambiguous as to whether it is *puruṣa* or *prakṛti* that takes the initiative. But some interpreters of Sāṅkhya attribute the initiative to *prakṛti*.

20. *LT*. 29:2 ff.

21. The notion of *puruṣa* is from the *Ṛg Veda*; the notion of Prajāpati Brahmā is from the Purāṇas; the notion of Brahman is from the Upaniṣads, and so on. Cf. Gupta, op.cit., p. xxiv.

22. Although these terms can be translated into English as "transcendent," "manifestation," "evolution," "image," and "indweller" respectively, I shall not translate them in order to retain their technical meaning and significance.

23. It is possible that originally there were only three forms and that the fourth and the fifth (*arcā* and *antaryāmin*) were later additions. Cf. *LT*. 10:9ff. which mentions only three forms of God : *arcā, vyūha, and vibhava*. However, *LT*. 2:60 mentions *arcā* also. But *Ahirbudhnya Saṃhitā*'s account and the account of *LT*. 10:9 ff. taken together makes it appear that the earlier understanding was of only three forms. Also see *Ah. S.* 11:63a-64b: *tat para vyūha vibhava svabhāvādinirūpaṇaṃ| pāñcarātrahvayaṃ tantraṃ mokṣaikaphalalakṣaṇam||*

24. *LT*. 2:60 : *mantramantreśvara nyāsāt sāpi ṣāḍguṇya vigrhā| parādy-arcāvasāne asmin mama rūpacatuṣṭayam||*

25. In *LT*. 2:60 S. Gupta translates *rūpacatuṣṭayam* as referring to *Para, Vyūha, Vibhava*, and *Arcā* forms of existence. Pandit V. Krishnamacharya takes *rūpacatuṣṭayam* to mean the *prakāras* (*Para*, etc.,) and the latter to refer to four *Vyūhas* (Vāsudeva, etc.). But S. Gupta does not make such distinction. Whenever *cāturūpyam* or *catūrūpyam* (as in *LT*. 2:60; 4:25) occurs, she assumes that it referred to *Vyūhas*. The problem of this nature arises because of *LT*'s inconsistent use of the term *cāturūpyam*. Certainly in *LT*. 2:60, *rūpacatuṣṭayam* clearly referred to *prakāras* (*Para, Vyūha*, etc.). Nonetheless, in 4:25 and 7:19-24, *cāturūpyam* referred to four states of existence, namely, *turya*, etc. (Cf. 11:9) which in turn

does not refer to "*caturvyūha*-s." The five *prakara*-s or *pañcarūpa*-s (*para, vyūha, vibhava, arcā* and *antaryāmin*) include *caturvyūha*-s.

There is, however, an essential difference between *rūpa-catuṣṭayam* (*para, vyūha, vibhava,* and *arcā*) and *cātūrūpyam* referring to *caturvyūha*-s (Vāsudeva, Saṃkarṣaṇa, Pradyumna, Aniruddha) because *cātūrūpyam* specifically refers to the second category, namely, *vyūha*, in the five forms (*pañcarūpas*) of Viṣṇu (*para, vyūha*, etc.). Therefore, for the sake of general understanding of Pāñcarātra categories it is useful not to confuse the two terms, namely, *rūpacatuṣṭayam* and *cātūrūpyam*. When the *Lakṣmī Tantra* uses *rūpacatuṣṭayam* it refers to *para, vyūha, vibhava, arcā* and *antaryāmin*, although only the first four are included. Similarly, when the *Lakṣmī Tantra* uses *cātūrūpyam* it refers to the four *vyūha*-s, namely, Vāsudeva, Saṃkarṣaṇa, Pradyumna, and Aniruddha. There is, however, some inconsistency in the use of the two terms in the *Lakṣmī Tantra*.[26] Generally speaking, all the *Saṃhitā*-s understand *caturvyūha*-s as referring to Vāsudeva, Saṃkarṣaṇa, Pradyumna, and Aniruddha.[27]

3) While the Purāṇas and the Itihāsas advocate the theory of *avatāra*, the Pāñcarātra literature advocates the *Vyūha* theory of creation by drawing upon the categories of Sāṅkhya. In the *Vyūha* theory, Viṣṇu through his Śakti, Śrī-Lakṣmī, manifests his six attributes.[28] And when the six attributes of Viṣṇu are manifested, a millionth particle of him as the will to create (*sisṛkṣā*) initiates creation.[29] This particle then produces the three groups of creation, pure and nonpure creation (*śuddhāśuddhātmako vargastayā kroḍīkṛto 'khilaḥ*).[30] The manifestation of six attributes (*jñāna* etc.), which is the "absolute Lord" (*parameśvaram*) itself,[31] assumes four forms of manifestation, which is usually referred to as "Purāṇas" or "*cāturvyūha*."[32] In other words, *vyūha*-s are the first beings that come into existence. The term *vyūha* is difficult to translate. As Gonda rightly points out, the term indicates "that these figures are regarded

---

refers to the four *Vyūhas*. Again in 18:29, in which Śrī speaks of manifesting four forms as Śāntā, the term *catūrūpyam* is used, which clearly refers to *Vyūhas* (51:29). From these it is obvious that the *LT*'s use of *catūrūpa* is inconsistent.

26. See footnote above.

27. *Saṃhitās* here refer to *Āgamas* which are also called *Saṃhitās* although the term "*tantra*" is also used (e.g., *Lakṣmī Tantra*).

28. The totality of six attributes (*jñāna*, etc., *guṇas*) constitute the body of the Highest Personal Being who is called both Vāsudeva as well as Śrī-Lakṣmī. The *Ahirbudhnya Saṃhitā* speaks in terms of Viṣṇu's attributes and his will to create. But the *Lakṣmī Tantra* speaks in terms of Śrī-Lakṣmī's attributes and her will to create. Cf. *Ah. S.* 2:28; 5:29; 6:25; *LT.* 2:38.

29. *LT.* 2:36; 4:4; 3:3; In the *Ahirbudhnya Saṃhitā* and other texts it is the will of Viṣṇu. *Ah. S.* 14:7-8; 8:36; 3:27-28.

30. *LT.* 2:37.

31. I use "itself" instead of "himself" because the absolute God—*parameśvara*—includes both Vāsudeva and Śrī-Lakṣmī.

32. *LT.* 2:40.

as representing an effective arrangement of the parts of a coherent whole."[33] The *Lakṣmī Tantra* shows that Śrī-lakṣmī, as *bhūti śakti*[34] and *kriyā śakti,*[35] is chiefly responsible for the manifestation of the *vyūha*-s. In the *Lakṣmī Tantra*, Śrī-Lakṣmī refers to these *vyūha*-s as "my fourfold state."[36] In the ultimate analysis, however, each *vyūha* is identified with Viṣṇu himself because Śrī-Lakṣmī is none other than Viṣṇu's *ahaṃtā*[37] and *paravyūharūpa* of Nārāyaṇa.[38] She is considered as the eternal state of existence of Vāsudeva. Later on in this chapter, I shall discuss the point whether Śrī-Lakṣmī and Nārāyaṇa are ultimately one or whether they form two separate entities. The *Lakṣmī Tantra* makes a special effort to show that it is Śrī-Lakṣmī who initiates the *vyūha*-s.[39]

In the process of pure creation the first *vyūha* to emerge is primeval *jñāna*, called Saṃkarṣaṇa; then follows *aiśvarya*, called Pradyumna, who is followed by *śakti* called Aniruddha. Thus, including Viṣṇu, there are altogether four *vyūha*-s.[40] In other words, the first *vyūha* is actually the unmanifest primeval *jñāna* who is Viṣṇu himself. In the manifest state, that primeval *jñāna* is called Saṃkarṣaṇa, and thus the chain follows.

The term *vyūha* has been explicated by Schrader as *vi+uḥ* (*vi*=asunder, *uḥ*= to shove), which means the "shoving asunder of the six *guṇa*-s into three pairs."[41] In the form of Viṣṇu all six *guṇa*-s are equally manifest. But in the other three *vyūha*-s the *guṇa*-s are distributed in the following combination—*jñāna* and *bala* in Saṃkarṣaṇa; *vīrya* and *aiśvarya* in Pradyumna; *śakti* and *tejas* in Aniruddha.[42] This does not mean that in each of the three *vyūha*-s from Saṃkarṣaṇa onward only two *guṇa*-s are present. Schrader rightly points out that since each *vyūha* is Viṣṇu himself, while all the

---

33. Although S. Gupta translates the term with "manifestation" (*LT*.2:40), Gonda thinks that translations such as "expansion," "emanation," "conglomeration," etc., are inadequate . (Cf. Gonda, *Viṣṇuism and Śivaism*, p. 50f, and 165. Also see Gonda, *MRL*. p. 60.

34. *bhūti-śakti* is vast expansion of divine power (*mahāvibhūtirityukto vyāptiḥ sā mahati yataḥ*| *LT*. 2:9).

35. *kriyā-śakti* is the primary form of divine *śakti*—she creates, protects, and destroys the creation; it is said to belong to Agni and in destruction it is said to attain the form of disc (*cakra*)—*āgneyī prathamā mūrtiḥ śaktirdivyā kriyāvayā*| *sahasrāsvarūpeṇa sṛjatyavati hanti ca*|| *LT*. 30:63. Also see *LT*. 31:1 ff.

36. *vivakṣayate yadā sā me śāntayaś cāturātmyatā*. *LT*.2:41.

37. *LT*.2:11-12 (*ahaṃtā brahmanastasya sāhamasmi sanātanī*)., also see *LT*. 2:13-14 (*bhavatastasya devasya sā bhavoḥ ahamiti*), see also 8:10-15; 4:2ff.

38. *LT*. 8:10-15.

39. *LT*. 2:3

40. *LT*. 4:7-10 ff; also cf. *Viśvaksena Saṃhitā* in *Tattvatraya*. pp. 125-27.

41. F. O. Schrader, op.cit., (*Intro. to Pāñcarātra*), p. 40. Cf. Monier-Williams, *Sanskrit-English Dictionary*, p. 1041. col.1

42. *LT*. 4:14-16.

guṇa-s are equally present, only two become manifest in each *vyūha* that begins from Saṃkarṣaṇa.[43]

It is interesting to note that these *vyūha*-s refer to the epic characters in the Mahābhārata i.e., Kṛṣṇa's elder brother, son and grandson respectively in the following way: Saṃkarṣaṇa refers to Balarāma or Baladeva; Pradyumna refers to Kṛṣṇa's son; and Aniruddha refers to Kṛṣṇa's grandson. The oddness of this association, however, is that Balarāma precedes Kṛṣṇa in the Mahābhārata epic while Saṃkarṣaṇa (Balarāma) emanates from Viṣṇu, thus appearing in the subsequent stage. The crucial point of this *vyūha* theory is that there seems to be an effort made here to preserve the *ekāntika* doctrine, namely, that ultimately reality is one (Brahman). Gonda remarks:

> This *vyūha* doctrine may be considered another attempt at maintaining the fundamental monotheistic starting-point whilst incorporating some adorable doubles or manifestations of the Highest Being, and at assigning to these positions and functions a systematic explanation of the universe. At the same time it is an attempt at conceiving God as the unaffected and changeless One who nevertheless is the cause of all change; an attempt also at harmonizing theology with mythology and some elements of evolutionist philosophy.[44]

This idea is further supported by Śrī-Lakṣmī's defense of the *vyūha*-s as being essentially of the same nature. Śrī-Lakṣmī tells Śakra (Indra):

> O Lord of heaven, it is erroneous to think that there is any essential difference between these (manifestations). In order to stress the particular activity associated with each (such differentiations) are envisaged (by scripture).[45]

4) Both the *Lakṣmī Tantra* and the *Ahirbudhnya Saṃhitā* keep Viṣṇu in the background and advocate the primary role of Śrī-Lakṣmī in the context of the process of creation. Other texts, however, clearly attribute the primary role to Viṣṇu—e.g., *Parama Saṃhitā, Jayākhya Saṃhitā*. Gonda generalizes the positions when he says,

> Since Viṣṇu's transcendent aspect (*paraṃ brahma* "the Highest Brahman") remains in the background Pāñcarātra philosophy is mainly concerned with the one force (*Lakṣmī*), which as *bhūti* is *causa materialis* and *kriyā causa instrumentalis* of all existence, vitalizing and governing the world.[46]

5) Finally, the Pāñcarātra texts unequivocally presuppose Śrī-Lakṣmī's permanent association with Viṣṇu both as his beloved consort, who

---

43. Schrader, loc.cit., p. 40. Also see *LT*.4:21-22; 6:15-16.

44. Gonda, op.cit., (*MRL*), p. 60.

45. Translation taken from S. Gupta, *LT*. p. 2. (*LT*.4:23— *naivaiṣāṃ vāstavo bhedaś cintanīyo divaspate| tattatkāryaprasiddhyarthaṃ kṛto'sau kalpanāvaśāt||*). Cf. *Ah. S.* 12:55.

46. J. Gonda, op.cit., (*MRL*), p. 59.

always sits on his lap,[47] as well as his *bhūti śakti* and *kriyā śakti*, who is the substratum of the universe. The aspect of relationship between Viṣṇu and Śrī-Lakṣmī is further developed in this chapter.

The Essential Nature of Śrī-Lakṣmī—Ontological Status of Śrī-Lakṣmī as Creator

In the Pāñcarātra Āgama texts, Śrī-Lakṣmī's status is no longer one of a minor deity associated with only material prosperity, royalty, and beauty as in the earlier traditions from the Vedic through the epic times. Although Śrī-Lakṣmī continues to represent the spheres of material prosperity, sovereignty, and beauty the dominant role attributed to her in the Pāñcarātra tradition is one of creator, participating in the creative process along with her consort Viṣṇu (Nārāyaṇa). The *Lakṣmī Tantra*, the major text that develops a fuller understanding of Śrī-Lakṣmī, projects her as the ultimate source of all existence. Her basic function is to create, maintain, and dissolve the universe. She is characterized by her urge to create (*sisṛkṣā*).[48] She is the *jagannirmāṇaśakti* of the supreme Lord.[49] She pervades the whole universe in the form of I-hood (*ahaṃtā*) of Nārāyaṇa.[50]

The essential nature (*svarūpa)* of Śrī-Lakṣmī that is characteristic of *sisṛkṣā* is to manifest herself in diverse forms:

> I am the prowess (*bala)* of these (created objects); they manifest my forms; I manifest (myself) as one, two, and three. . . . and again as fifty and again as sixty-three. And as goddess *cintāmaṇi* (the wish fulfilling one) I manifest in many forms.[51]

Śrī-Lakṣmī has not only many forms in general, but it is important to note that she has a set of forms in each different context, as indicated in the above passage, though they all are basically related to the creative process.[52] Her manifestations depend not only on the mental

---

47. *LT.* 38:2; 36:121-31—in the context of ritual the adept should visualize Śrī-Lakṣmī as seated on the lap of the supreme self (Viṣṇu). She is also seated on the left side of Viṣṇu—*Paramata Saṃhitā*, 4:80. The *Jayākhya Saṃhitā* speaks of the eternal presence of Lakṣmī and other goddesses in the form of the Lord, and further describes Viṣṇu as Śrīpati. Just as the rays of the Sun reflect in the ocean, Śrī is present in the Lord through his power. See JS. ch. 6, vv. 77-78.

48. *LT.* 5:2; 14:3.

49. *Ah. S.* 3:42 (*yā tasya jagannirmāṇaśaktikā*).

50. *LT.* 2:6 (*ahaṃtayā samākrāntaṃ tasya viśvamidaṃ jagat*—this whole universe is pervaded by his (Nārāyaṇa's) *ahaṃtā* (Śrī-Lakṣmī).

51. *ahaṃ ca balameteṣām madrūpatvaṃ vidanti te| ekadhā ca dvidhā caiva tridhā caivāhamūrjitā||*
pañcāśaddhā punaścaiva punaścāham triṣaṣṭidhā| udemi bahudhā caiva cintāmaṇiriveśvarī|| (*LT.* 52:3-5 translation mine).

52. *LT.* 43:56-65; 44:4; 45:88-100; 45:3-11; 9:6-7; 50:124-26.

capacity of the adept but also on her own inherent nature to manifest herself in different forms in different contexts.

Because of their basic commitment to *ekāntika* doctrine,[53] the Pāñcarātra Āgama texts generally admit Brahman as the basic principle of existence. When that principle of existence is differentiated, the existing principle is called Nārāyaṇa and its state of existence is the supreme Lakṣmī.[54] In other words, during the unmanifest period Śrī-Lakṣmī exists in Brahman while enfolding the universe within herself.[55] She is both the *unmeṣa* (expansion) as well as *nimeṣa* (dissolution—literally contraction).[56] She is also the Śakti of Nārāyaṇa characterized both by her desire to create (*sisṛkṣalakṣaṇa*) as well as her will to sleep (*suṣupsālakṣaṇa*).[57] The import of the terms *sisṛkṣā* and *suṣupsā* here is to indicate that Śrī-Lakṣmī is in charge of both creation and dissolution. She encompasses the whole range from creation to maintenance to destruction by means of her six attributes, namely, *jñāna* and so forth. *Jñāna* is her primary manifestation, in which Lakṣmī and Nārāyaṇa are said to be one ("Indeed, then, the form of mine and that of Nārāyaṇa consist of *jñāna*"—*atastu jñānarūpatvaṃ mama nārāyaṇasya ca*).[58] This point regarding the relationship between Lakṣmī and Nārāyaṇa is elaborated subsequently. *Aiśvarya* is said to be her will (*icchā*) to create. The source of the universe is called her *śakti*. Her capacity to sustain the creation is known as *bala*. As material cause she is known as *vīrya*, which is characterized by changelessness (*vikāraviraho vīryam*). And her capacity to accomplish everything is known as *tejas* (*parābhibhava sāmarthyaṃ tejaḥ*—literally ability to subjugate or dominate).[59]

Śrī-Lakṣmī's first manifestation is called pure creation (*śuddhasṛṣṭi*). Prior to her manifestation in the pure creation, her state

---

53. The Pāñcarātra tradition propounds the doctrine of *ekāntika* which posits three realities, namely, *Īśvara* (Lord), *Cit* (Sentient Beings) and *Acit* (Insentient Beings). The three realities form one single reality. In other words, the *cit* and the *acit* form part of *Īśvara*.

54. *LT*. 2:15.

55. *LT*. 2:21 *kroḍīkṛtyākhilaṃ sarvaṃ brahmaṇi vyavatiṣṭate*|| However, this verse has to be read along with the verse 24 and 25 in order to avoid the implication that Lakṣmī and Brahman as such are two different realities. Ultimately both Brahman and Lakṣmī as *ahamtā* of Nārāyaṇa are identical with *jñāna* (*jñānātmakaṃ paraṃrūpaṃ brahmaṇo mama cobhayoḥ*|| *LT*. 2:25b) and *jñāna* is the essential nature of God. Therefore, the combination of Lakṣmī-Nārāyaṇa is called Brahman. *LT*. 2:16.

56. "*unmeṣa*" literally means opening of eyes and "*nimeṣa*" is closing of the eyes or contraction. *unmeṣa* and *nimeṣa* are the waking and the sleeping states respectively of God. While the former refers to creation and sustenance of the universe, the latter refers to its dissolution. Cf. S. Gupta, *LT*. p. 10, f.n. 1; and also Cf. Schrader, op.cit., pp. 33-34.

57. *LT*. 2:22-23.

58. *LT*. 2:27b. (Translation is mine).

59. *LT*. 2:26-34.

is called inertness, which includes a fourfold form—Vāsudeva, Saṃkarṣaṇa etc. (*caturvyūha* form).[60] At this stage she is also called Śānti. Her state during which the pure creation, namely, Saṃkarṣaṇa, Pradyumna, and Aniruddha, emerges is called her active state.[61] Her intense activity, however, is seen in her stage as Aniruddha.[62] During the *vyūha* state the six attributes are formed in different combinations to issue forth the respective *vyūha*-s. Thus, *jñāna* and *bala* are combined in Saṃkarṣaṇa; *aiśvarya* and *vīrya* are combined in Pradyumna; and *śakti* and *tejas* are combined in Aniruddha.[63] But when Śrī-Lakṣmī is in her Brahman state all six attributes are present in their undifferentiated state.[64]

The next stage of her manifestation is called the nonpure course of creation (*śuddhetara sṛṣṭi/traiguṇya paddhati*). During this stage the essential triad, namely, *vijñāna*, *aiśvarya*, and *śakti* of Śrī-Lakṣmī are operative. Due to her own will (*svasvātantryavaśena eva*)[65] there is a change of form in the essential triad, namely, *jñāna, aiśvarya*, and *śakti* (*rūpam āsīt jñānādike trike*).[66] Thus, from *jñāna* emerges *sattva*, from *aiśvarya* emerges *rajas*, and from *śakti* emerges *tamas*.[67] These three *guṇa*-s are associated with the three functions of Śrī-Lakṣmī in the following way: during the process of creation *rajas* predominates; during maintenance, *sattva*, and during dissolution, *tamas* predominates.[68] Now the point is that in all of these transformations, Śrī-Lakṣmī's essential nature does not change. In other words, while retaining her essential nature, which is identical with Brahman, she first evolves into pure creation (*vyūha*-s), which consists of all six

60. *LT*. 2:42; 7:5-7.

61. *L.T*. 2:49-51; also see Gupta, op.cit., p. 13, f.n. 2 . (These three divinities may have been tutelar deities at an earlier time. Cf. *LT*. 6:12; also cf. Schrader, op.cit., p. 45).

62. According to *LT*. 2:47 ff. Pradyumna is the creator of the manifest world and Aniruddha is the sustainer. (See Gupta, *LT*. p. 12. f.n. 4). Also, *LT*. 4:18 agrees with 2:47 ff. But 4:19 reverses the order and makes Aniruddha the creator, Pradyumna the sustainer and Saṃkarṣaṇa the destroyer. Cf. Schrader, p. 44 ff.

63. *LT*. 2:53-54; 4:14-16; *Ah. S*. 5:17-18; 21-24.

64. *LT*. 2:54.

65. *LT*. 3:3.

66. *LT*. 3:5a.

67. *LT*. 3:5-6; cf. *Ah. S*. 6:52-63—Here the English terms such as emerge, evolve, develop etc., are misleading because of their association with the concept of evolution from a lower stage to a higher stage as in the case of evolution of human beings from lower species. But here in the context of Pāñcarātra Āgama understanding the term "evolution" (if we can use such a term—Gupta uses it in her translation of *LT*.) means evolution of a lower principle from a higher principle, e.g., from *jñāna* (which is identical with Śrī-Lakṣmī in her state of Brahman) evolves *sattvaguṇa*. This idea of evolution from higher stage to lower stage is illustrated by the metaphor of transparent sugarcane juice becoming molasses (*yathaivekṣurasaḥ svaccho guḍatvaṃ pratipadyate*‖ *LT*. 3:5b). This explanation holds good even for the Sāṅkhya understanding because there too the evolution is supposed to be from higher stage (*mahat*) to the lower stages.

68. *LT*. 3:7-8; 4:36, 64.

divine attributes. Then, again without changing her transcendental form, a small part of herself, which is known as Mahālakṣmī, evolves into the *traiguṇya* complex. When dominated by *rajas* she is called Mahāśrī; when dominated by *tamas* she is called Mahāmāyā, and when dominated by *sattva* she is called Mahā-vidyā.[69] All three of these divinities have their ancillary divinities each with specific functions.

These three divinities, namely, Mahāśrī, Mahāmāyā, and Mahā-vidyā, in association with Pradyumna, Saṃkarṣaṇa, and Aniruddha, respectively, give rise to three pairs (male and female).[70] In other words, Mahāśrī-Pradyumna are related to *rajas*; Mahāmāyā-Saṃkarṣaṇa are related to *tamas*; and Mahāvidyā-Aniruddha are related to *sattva*. From here on, that is, after the emergence of the *traiguṇya*-complex, it is interesting to trace the development of *pradhāna* and the further development of the manifest material world therefrom. Viriñci, who is a part of Pradyumna in association with Bhāsā, who is a part of Saṃkarṣaṇa, produces the cosmic egg; Śaṅkara, who is a part of Saṃkarṣaṇa, in association with Gauri, who is a part of Aniruddha, broke the egg open; then Brahmā, who is part of Pradyumna created *pradhāna* in that egg which was then preserved by Keśava, who is a part of Aniruddha, in association with Padmā, who is a part of Pradyumna.[71] This *pradhāna* is characterized by both reality as well as nonreality, and its source is the *traiguṇya* complex; its nature is void (*vyoma*). Further, this *pradhāna* is the source of everything while it in itself is undecaying (*akṣaram*).[72]

Hṛṣīkeśa, who forms part of Aniruddha,[73] then turns the principle of unmanifest *pradhāna* (*avyakta pradhāna*) into water on which he, along with Padmā and Vidyā,[74] lie asleep (meditative sleep). While asleep, out of his navel emerge three aspects—the lotus representing the life principle (*prāṇa*), the male representing Hiraṇyagarbha, and the female representing *buddhi*. These three aspects together constitute the *mahat* (Padmā, male, and female are together called *mahat—Padmapuṃstrī samālaṃbān mahatvaṃ tasya śabdyate||*).[75]

---

69. *LT*. 5:2-5.

70. Cf. *Ah. S*. 6:14, 43-51 where Māyā-Śakti, Niyati, Kāla are identified with Mahālakṣmī (Mahāśrī), Mahāvidyā and Mahāmāyā (Mahākālī); also see Schrader, p. 73-74.

71. *LT*. 5:7-17.

72. *LT*. 5:19.

73. *LT*. 5:12.

74. S. Gupta notes that this idea of Hṛṣīkeśa accompanied by Padmā and Vidyā may be an echo of the mythological concept of Viṣṇu's two consorts —Lakṣmī and Sarasvati, named Śrī and Bhū in Pāñcarātra texts. Cf. S. Gupta, *LT*. p. 28. f.n. 4.

75. *LT*. 5:31-32b; also see 20-21. The category of *mahat* here seems closer to the classical Sāṅkhya understanding in that the *mahat* in *LT* is constitutive of three aspects—*prāṇa, puruṣa*, and *buddhi*. In other words, *buddhi* and *mahat* are identical stages in Sāṅkhya system where as in Pāñcarātra system *buddhi* is seen as one aspect of *mahat*. For that matter it must be noted that *mahat*, as in the

When *mahat* is stimulated by Śrī-Lakṣmī, *ahaṃkāra* emerges and from *ahaṃkāra* follow the subsequent stages called *tanmātra*-s and *buddhīndriya*-s, etc.

Now, in all of these it is Śrī-Lakṣmī's *kriyā śakti* that goes through the successive stages.[76] Further, there is a dialectic involved here. On the one hand Śrī-Lakṣmī maintains her transcendental form, and on the other hand, she forms the basis of objective reality. Thus, she is part of both the pure creation as well as the nonpure creation (*śuddha* and *śuddhetara*).

Śrī-Lakṣmī as Pure Consciousness

Even though Śrī-Lakṣmī, through her own act of will, desires and creates both the pure creation as well as the nonpure creation, she herself evolves into both sentient and insentient objects. Further, these sentient and insentient objects, whether pure or nonpure, are in fact part of her own consciousness (*saṃvid*), while consciousness is her real form.[77] The affirmation of Śrī-Lakṣmī as Pure Consciousness is made in the context of polarities such as pure and nonpure (*śuddha-śuddhetara*), sentient and nonsentient (*cetana-cetya*), blue and yellow (*nīlā-pīta*), happiness and sorrow (*śukha-duḥkha*), light and darkness (*tejas-tamas*), positive and negative (*bhāva-abhāva*), and so on; and also in the context of multiplicity including—time, place, action (*kriyā*), subject (*karta*), dative object (*saṃpradhāna*), enjoyment and the enjoyer (*bhoga-bhoktā*), gods, demons, *nāga*-s, *gandharva*-s, etc., men in their diverse groups according to caste and function, cattle, wild creatures, birds, serpents, plants, insects, the fourteen worlds, rivers, islands, oceans[78]—all of these merge in Śrī-Lakṣmī and are pervaded by her. She pervades both polarities and multiplicity by her consciousness, thereby providing a unitary vision of reality. In other words, in Śrī-Lakṣmī both oneness and multiplicity are affirmed but not denied because she herself is said to be *vikalpa* ("polarized thought is one of my forms—*vikalpo'pi madrūpam*).[79] This affirmation of multiplicity and oneness is important in order to affirm the Pāñcarātra philosophical position of *ekāntika*. However, it must not be confused with the Advaita position in which multiplicity is denied at the ultimate

---

Sāṅkhya system (in the Sāṅkhya system *buddhi* emerges in the proximity of *prakṛti* and *puruṣa*), emerges out of three principles—*pradhāna*, Hṛṣīkeśa (aspect of Aniruddha, who in turn is an aspect of none other than the supreme Viṣṇu or Nārāyaṇa) and the two consorts of Viṣṇu, namely, Padmā and Vidyā, who are seen here together, forming one single aspect. For more details on Sāṅkhya notion of *mahat/buddhi* see G. J. Larson, *Classical Sāṅkhya: An Interpretation of its History and Meaning*, Second Edition (Santa Barbara: Ross/Erikson, 1979), pp. 179 ff.

76. *LT*. 5:55.
77. *LT*. 14:5.
78. *LT*. 14:46-54; 15:4.
79. *LT*. 14:9.

level (*pāramārthika*). It must also not be confused with the Bhedābheda position, or even with the Acintyabhedābheda position, wherein the multiplicity and oneness are simultaneously affirmed. The Pāñcarātra system, which is broadly in line with the Viśiṣṭādvaita system, understands this oneness and multiplicity in terms of the whole and its parts. It is precisely for this reason, the *Lakṣmī Tantra* uses the analogy of "gold and earring" as opposed to the Advaita metaphor of "rope and the snake." Just as the existence of gold (*kanaka*) is not perceived apart from the earrings (*kuṇḍala*), and yet certainly exists as an ornament of gold,[80] so also Śrī-Lakṣmī as Pure Consciousness is experienced in the multiplicity of reality and yet is unaffected by the polarities and the multiplicity of reality. Just as the gold earring is part of gold in the ultimate sense, so also the polarities and multiplicity are part of the reality of Śrī-Lakṣmī who is Pure Consciousness in the ultimate sense. The analogous relationship between "gold-earring" and Śrī-Lakṣmī as "Pure Consciousness and multiple and polarized objective reality" must be seen as contrary to the Advaitin model, namely, the analogous relationship between "rope-snake" and "*pāramārthika-vyāvahārika*" levels. While the "gold-earring" metaphor affirms mutual existence, namely, oneness and multiplicity with all its polarities, as part and whole, the Advaitin analogy of "rope-snake" denies the multiplicity and affirms only the reality of Brahman.

It is precisely to affirm the oneness and multiplicity that Śrī-Lakṣmī is characterized as both Pure Consciousness and Pure Activity (I am both Pure Consciousness and Activity—*śuddhā saṃvid kriyā ca ahaṃ*).[81] The relationship between pure consciousness and pure activity may be seen as subject and attribute relationship. While pure consciousness is the essence of her being, the polarized state, which consists of *jñāna, aiśvarya*, and *śakti* is her attribute. She is absolute knowledge and yet voluntarily becomes sentient.[82] The "ever active blissful consciousness" (*nityoditacidānandā*) is perhaps the more apt way of describing Śrī-Lakṣmī, for it combines succinctly the two aspects, namely, pure consciousness and pure activity. She represents both the inactive (*śāntā*) as well as the active (*unmeṣa*) state.[83]

---

80. *LT*. 14:38-39 *kuṇḍlāderyathā bhinnā na lakṣyā kanakasthitiḥ| na ca śakyā vinirdeṣṭuṃ tathāpyastyeva sā dhṛvam|| evaṃ nityā viśuddhā ca śukhaduḥkhādyabheditā|| svasaṃvedanasaṃvedyā mama saṃvinmayī sthitiḥ|*— (just as the existence of gold is not perceived apart from earrings, etc., and cannot be distinguished even though it (gold) indeed exists (is there), so also my existence which consists of *saṃvid*, and is eternal, pure and not affected by pleasure and pain, is realized (*saṃvedya*) only through self-consciousness (*saṃvedana*). (Translation mine).

81. *LT*. 50:150.

82. *LT*. 3:2; 21:5; 50:46b; 7:29.

83. *LT*. 18:20.

Relationship Between Śrī-Lakṣmī and Viṣṇu

Śrī-Lakṣmī as Pure Consciousness and Pure Activity cannot be seen apart from her complex relationship with Viṣṇu (Vāsudeva-Nārāyaṇa). The complexity of the relationship can be seen in such statements as "I lead Hari and am led by Him in (all) activity"—(*hariṃ nayāmi kāryeṣu nīye ca hariṇā svayam*).[84] In relation to Viṣṇu, Śrī-Lakṣmī is described with many attributes, such as *ahaṃtā* of Viṣṇu; eternal Vāsudeva state of existence (*bhāva*); Viṣṇu's ever-existent omnipotent Śakti (*sthirā śakti*); Viṣṇu's function; Viṣṇu's independent absolute Śrī; His supreme Śakti; His unique Śakti consisting of His Lordhood (*Īśvaratā*). While Nārāyaṇa is perfect, all-pervading absolute Brahman, Śrī-Lakṣmī is His state of being known as tranquillity (*śāntā*). As manifest sound (*mātṛkā*), Śrī-Lakṣmī is a projection of Viṣṇu's Śakti. She is the "consort of the unfathomable householder (Viṣṇu)" (*aprameyasya sā hi śrīrgṛhiṇī gṛhamedhinaḥ*|| *LT* 26:16); beloved of Puṇḍarīkākṣa (Viṣṇu); Hari's unique and supreme Śakti, who performs all functions; the one who sits on the lap of the Supreme Self (Viṣṇu); Viṣṇu's eternal self consciousness; Nārāyaṇī, the Śakti inherent in Nārāyaṇa; as Jayā, Śrī-Lakṣmī is seated in Viṣṇu's chest. She is described as the one who has everlasting love for Hari.[85] Furthermore, the JS mentions that Śrī and other goddesses are present always in the Lord. Śrī is present in the Lord just as the rays of the Sun reflect in the ocean. (JS. 6:77-78)

In all of these relationships, Śrī-Lakṣmī appears to be one aspect of the whole while Viṣṇu is the other aspect. But what this really means, in the ultimate sense, is very complex. The possibility is present to argue in favor of both equality in status as well as a subordinate role for Śrī-Lakṣmī. It depends upon whether one looks at Viṣṇu and Śrī-Lakṣmī as two sides of the same reality or at Śrī-Lakṣmī as a mere attribute of the subject.[86]

Before the creation, Śrī-Lakṣmī is said to be indistinguishable from Viṣṇu. While the *Ahirbudhnya Saṃhitā* describes Śrī-Lakṣmī as being indistinguishable from Viṣṇu, the *Lakṣmī Tantra* prefers reversing the order saying that Brahman (the undifferentiated Lakṣmī-Nārāyaṇa) is not differentiated from Śakti at the stage before creation.[87] That state is like a "waveless ocean of nectar" and not subject to expansion and

---

84. *LT*. 50:46b.

85. *LT*. 2:13-14; 19:1; 3:1,14; 6:3; 7:4; 10:7; 11:7; 12:4,12; 13:20; 14:2; 15:9; 17:18a; 18:24,19; 20:32a; 21:4; 22:7-8; 23:1; 26:16; 27:1,4; 32:17; 32:58; 36:69; 36:124a; 38:2b; 40:67; 38:1; 42:3; 42:46; 44:1-3; 45:1; 46:11; 47:3; 48:3; 49:60; 50:8; 50:22-23,102; 52:1.

86. Even if one were to take Śrī-Lakṣmī as a mere attribute one could still make a subtle distinction between an essential attribute and a secondary attribute. As I show later Veṅkaṭanātha makes such a subtle distinction in order to give Śrī-Lakṣmī status on a par with that of Viṣṇu. Vide my chapter on Veṅkaṭanātha.

87. *LT*. 2:11a.

contraction (*udaya* and *asta*).[88] Again, while the *Ahirbudhnya Saṃhitā* and the *Prakāśa Saṃhitā* see the initiative to create coming from Viṣṇu,[89] the *Lakṣmī Tantra* prefers attributing the initiative to Śrī-Lakṣmī.[90] However, the *Lakṣmī Tantra* also makes reference to "the will of God Nārāyaṇa issued from my (Lakṣmī's) potential state."[91] Further, at another point the *Lakṣmī Tantra* also refers to a joint initiative—"a billionth-billionth particle of ourselves (*trayornau*)."[92]

Since both Śri-Lakṣmī and Nārāyaṇa are indistinguishable in the state of undifferentiated Brahman, it is perhaps more appropriate to think in terms of the will of both. This point of view, nonetheless, raises the fundamental issue of whether, in the ultimate analysis, there is total identity or whether Śrī-Lakṣmī and Viṣṇu have their separate identity. It is worthwhile to explore this aspect with Schrader's comment:

> Here it will be necessary to remark that, in spite of frequent assurances as to the real identity of Lakṣmī and Viṣṇu, the two are actually regarded as distinct: even in the *pralaya* they do not completely coalesce but become only 'as it were' a single principle, the Lakṣmī eventually emerging from the great Night being the old Lakṣmī, not a new one. The mutual relation of the two is declared to be one of inseparable connection or inherence like that of an attribute and its bearer (*dharma-dharmin*), existence and that which exists (*bhāva-bhavat*), I-ness and I (*ahaṃtā-aham*), moonshine (sic) and moon, sunshine and sun. Still the dualism is, strictly speaking, a makeshift for preserving the transcendent character of Viṣṇu: Lakṣmī alone acts, but everything she does is the mere expression of the Lord's wishes.[93]

The above view of Schrader, while supported basically by the *Ahirbudhnya Saṃhitā*, has two components: that there is no real identity of Lakṣmī and Viṣṇu even at the undifferentiated state; and that ultimately it is Viṣṇu who wills everything. To put it differently, while Śrī-Lakṣmī has her separate identity, she plays only a subordinate role by carrying out the wishes of the Lord. The *Lakṣmī Tantra* certainly favors a separate individuality for Śrī-Lakṣmī. The text, however, does not project a subordinate role to Śrī-Lakṣmī even though there are some passages that are ambiguous. Schrader tends to take the attributive as subordinate to the substantive. But it is also possible to argue that the substantive does not exist without the attributive. Thus it becomes a moot point to decide which is more important—the substantive or the attributive. Some commentators (for

88. *LT*. 2:10.
89. *Prakāśa Saṃhitā*, 1:1:53.
90. *LT*. 3:5,25; 4:26; 3:12.
91. *LT*. 2:23. Note that here instead of *icchā* (will) the desiderative of *sṛj* is used to refer to the desire of Nārāyaṇa.
92. *LT*. 4:4.
93. Schrader, op.cit., p. 34.

example, Veṅkaṭanātha) within the Śrīvaiṣṇava tradition argued that both substantive and attributive are of equal status.[94]

With regard to the relationship between Śrī-Lakṣmī and Viṣṇu, there are references in the *Lakṣmī Tantra* to indicate identity of the two—"Because He is not different from *bhūti śakti* (Lakṣmī) He is the undifferentiated Brahman."[95] "The ever active *śakti* known as *ahaṃtā* is not different from it (Brahman)."[96] Although such references can be found here and there, the identity that is depicted here is not the kind of identity that is depicted in the Advaita system of Śaṅkara. The identity has to be understood against the background of the *ekāntika* doctrine of the Pāñcarātra tradition, which admits the individuality of the three aspects of the one reality, namely, Supreme Being, the individual soul and the objective universe.[97] However, the Supreme Being in the differentiated level has two aspects, namely, Lakṣmī and Nārāyaṇa. The question of whether Śrī-Lakṣmī is ultimately one with Viṣṇu to the extent that she loses her own individuality or whether she remains distinctively separate even at the stage of *pralaya* (as Schrader points out), that is, in the state of inertness, is indeed a very complex one. The *Lakṣmī Tantra*, on the one hand, speaks of Śrī-Lakṣmī as *ahaṃtā* and *śakti* of Viṣṇu, and sometimes refers to Viṣṇu as the possessor of Śrī-Lakṣmī.[98] On the other hand, it also speaks of Śrī-Lakṣmī as if she herself is the two aspects, namely, Īśa and Īśitavya.[99]

Furthermore, the relationship between Lakṣmī and Viṣṇu is stated in such complex terms as "I am different and not different from Him, like the moonlight of the moon. This unique existence (reality) of ours, though single, appears to be dual."[100] Again, in the context of external worship, the adept is expected to invoke Śrī-Lakṣmī as "distinguishable from the body of Viṣṇu." It is noted, however, that Śrī-Lakṣmī, without leaving (*avihāya eva*) God's form, remains separate (*pṛthak*) from Him (from His body).[101] There is, on the one hand, a claim for duality; but on the other, a claim for preserving the *ekāntika* position of the oneness of all reality. S. Gupta comments, "This duality in perfect unity is the central postulate of the system."[102] But how this duality exists within the oneness of the divine reality seems to remain inexplicable. This duality in oneness does evoke a sense of mystery in

---

94. I have dealt with Veṅkaṭanātha's point of view more elaborately in a subsequent chapter. Vide chap. 6.

95. *LT.* 16:24 (*apṛthagbhūtaśaktitvādadvaitaṃ brahma niṣkalam*).

96. *LT.* 20:5 (*ahaṃtā nāma sā śaktistadabhinnā sadoditā*).

97. Cf. J. Gonda, op.cit., (*MRL*) p. 4.

98. *LT.* 28:3,8.

99. *LT.* 12:4-6.

100. *LT.* 15:10 (*bhinnā'bhinna ca varte'ham jyotsneva himadīdhiteḥ| tāvāvāṃ tattvamekaṃ tu dvidhā bhūtau vyavasthitau||*). Translation from S. Gupta., also see *LT.* 1:43-45; 2:18.

101. *LT.* 38:22-25.

102. S. Gupta, *LT.* p. 240. f.n. 3.

human consciousness. It is precisely this inexplicability of the existence of duality in unity or oneness that, as S. Gupta suggests, provoked the Caitanya school to think in terms of *Acintya-bhedābhedavāda.*[103]

Another way of looking at the complex relationship between Śrī-Lakṣmī and Viṣṇu is to create two levels of reflection—metaphysical (ontological) and functional. Then it follows that ontologically Śrī-Lakṣmī and Nārāyaṇa are one, that is, at the level of Brahmanhood; and at the functional level they remain separate (the level of ritual seems to represent the functional level). But this way of looking at the relationship between Śrī-Lakṣmī and Viṣṇu does not necessarily imply the two levels of existence in the Advaita model (*pāramārthika* and *vyāvahārika*).

It is true that in the context of ritual the *Lakṣmī Tantra* in some places (for example, the rite of *puraścaraṇa*) proposes that the devotee should worship Śrī-Lakṣmī and Nārāyaṇa as two distinct divinities.[104] Again, in the context of worshipping Śrī-Lakṣmī in the form of the *mantra* of Tārikā,[105] the divine couple must always be visualized in the gross form (*sthūlarūpakam*), subtle form (*sūkṣmam*), transcendent form (*param*) and supratranscendent form (*parātītam*) because the incomprehensible manifestation of Lakṣmī-Nārāyaṇa vibrates everywhere as Śakti and Śaktīśā (the possessor of Śakti). While this duality persists in the divine principle, it is further stated that all the objects of the world are seen in relation to Lakṣmī-Nārāyaṇa as protector-protected.[106] In the context of ritual the *Lakṣmī Tantra* also prescribes that Śrī-Lakṣmī and Nārāyaṇa may be worshipped either together or separately.[107] Then, again, in the context of visualizing, Śrī-Lakṣmī is always visualized as seated on the lap of Viṣṇu.[108]

In all of these above instances the duality is ever present in the ritual context. It must, however, be noted that according to the *Lakṣmī Tantra* the duality is seen even beyond the ritual level. But it is a duality that depicts Lakṣmī-Nārāyaṇa as one single principle rather than as two separate principles coming together. They exist together even at the ontological level. The *Lakṣmī Tantra* says, "At the beginning there is one supreme reality consisting of Lakṣmī-Nārāyaṇa."[109] The Lakṣmī-Nārāyaṇa principle of duality, thus, does

---

103. Ibid., p. 80. f.n. 1.

104. *LT.* 42:31 (*āhūya snāpayitvā tau lakṣmīnārāyaṇātmakau*!) note the use of *dvandva*. For the meaning of *puraścaraṇa*—See S. Gupta, *LT.* p. 130. f.n. 7.

105. The *mantra* of Tārikā is a means by which Śrī-Lakṣmī is visualized in the ritual. She becomes identical with the mantra called Tārikā. She is visualized in the form of lotus, Vāsudeva Śakti, Saṃkarṣaṇa Śakti and so on. For more details see *LT* 43:1 ff.

106. *LT.* 43:54-59.

107. Cf. *LT.* 22:21-24; 40:105-7.

108. *LT.* 50:22.

109. *LT.* 26:3. (*ekamādau paraṃ tattvaṃ lakṣmīnārāyaṇātmakam*) Translation mine. Also cf. *LT.* 23:1; 24:1.

not become reduced into one in the sense of cause without effect. But just as effect exists in unmanifest form in the cause, Lakṣmī-Nārāyaṇa exists in one principle even prior to the manifestation possessing the six auspicious qualities (*jñāna, bala, aiśvarya* and so forth). Just as the whole, even while visualized as whole, still has its two sides present, the aspects of Lakṣmī-Nārāyaṇa are present in one reality. This is precisely the reason why the visualization of Śrī-Lakṣmī seated on the lap of Viṣṇu who perpetually embraces her is significant. Viṣṇu embraces Śrī-Lakṣmī with his left arm, while Śrī-Lakṣmī's lotus-carrying hand (right hand) rests on the shoulder of Viṣṇu.[110] The description is very vivid in portraying the two aspects of the one reality in equal balance, in perfect unity. It is interesting to note that the *ardhanārīśvara* symbolism is not only part of the Śaiva tradition, but it seems to emerge in the *Lakṣmī Tantra* in a seminal form. Śrī-Lakṣmī says,

> But in my incarnation as the enchantress holding nectar, God is manifest both as existent reality and as its state of existence (*bhavat* and *bhāva*) perceived in a single form, of which the gods saw the male form whereas the others (i.e., demons, saw) the female form.[111]

The dual principle, namely, *bhavat-bhāva*, male-female, Nārāyaṇa-Lakṣmī, is ever present in single form. Nonetheless, the duality is profoundly, and inexplicably, present too. This unity is not the elimination of the dual principle, but a profound affirmation of duality in perfect unity. It is because of this perfect balance of the two in unity that affirmation of one automatically affirms the other; the presence of one necessarily presents the other; manifestation of one essentially includes the other. This is why the *Lakṣmī Tantra* states that, after the sacrifice is duly performed, Śrī-Lakṣmī, who is pleased with the devotee, manifests herself as *ahaṃtā*. But the devotee's accurate discriminatory knowledge (*sadviveka*) reveals the harmoniousness (*sāmarasyatā*) of Lakṣmī-Nārāyaṇa.[112] In other words, in the manifestation of Śrī-Lakṣmī there is a simultaneous manifestation of Viṣṇu. The important word here is *sāmarasyatā*, which indicates the profound balance of the duality in one reality. The harmoniousness is further stated in such terms as: "I satisfy Viṣṇu with the libation of my *guṇa*-s and I myself (am saturated) by His attributes."[113] It is again repeated with more punch—"I delight Viṣṇu with my attributes and am delighted by Hari's attributes."[114] It is because of the *sāmarasyatā* between them that whatever is done by one is regarded as having

110. *LT.* 50:22-23.

111. *LT.* 8:48-49.

112. *LT.* 24:40-41.

113. *LT.* 50:104b (*tarpayāmi guṇairviṣṇumātmānaṃ tadguṇairapi*|) translation from S. Gupta; *guṇas* here refer to *jñāna, bala, aiśvarya*, etc., which both Lakṣmī and Viṣṇu share together.

114. *LT.* 50:195a (*toṣayāmi guṇairviṣṇuṃ tuṣyāmi ca harerguṇaiḥ*|).

been done by the other— "Whatever action is done by me is said to be done by Him."[115]

This notion of unity in duality based on *sāmarasyatā* affirms two further important notions, namely, the notion of equality of the two aspects, Lakṣmī and Nārāyaṇa, and the notion of inseparability of the two. The passages referred to in previous paragraphs, as well as the general thrust of the text (*Lakṣmī Tantra*), uphold the idea of equality of the two aspects even at the ontological level, since both Lakṣmī and Nārāyaṇa share the divine attributes (*jñāna, bala, aiśvarya,* etc.,) equally. This is why the highest goal, namely, Brahman, is said to be Lakṣmī-Nārāyaṇa.[116] By admitting the notion of equality between Lakṣmī and Nārāyaṇa, the *Lakṣmī Tantra* invariably admits the notion of inseparability: "Indeed there is no existence of mine without that of the Lord. (Conversely), there is no existence of Viṣṇu without mine."[117]

It is, however, important to note that the position of the *Lakṣmī Tantra* does not necessarily represent the understanding of the rest of the Pāñcarātra Āgamas. For instance, the *Ahirbudhnya Saṃhitā* is clearly committed to the worship of Lord Viṣṇu and seems to portray Viṣṇu as higher than his consort. We have earlier noted that according to the *Ahirbudhnya Saṃhitā* it is Viṣṇu who wills everything, while Śrī-Lakṣmī only carries out the wishes of the Lord. Since each Āgama seems to be written with a particular motif, the *Lakṣmī Tantra* may be justified in projecting its own viewpoint. While the status of Śrī-Lakṣmī in relation to Viṣṇu may be a point of dispute among the different Āgama texts, the general thrust in all of them is to maintain the unity as well as the duality.

Śrī-Lakṣmī's Role in the Rituals

The Pāñcarātra texts ascribe a crucial role to Śrī-Lakṣmī in the process of the liberation of the *jīva*-s. The *Lakṣmī Tantra*, by virtue of its implicit understanding of Śrī-Lakṣmī as equal partner of Viṣṇu, goes a step further by making Śrī-Lakṣmī the central focus in the liberation process. For the same reason she occupies the central role in the ritual also.

In the *Lakṣmī Tantra*, the highest goal of the *jīvas* is said to be to please Śrī-Lakṣmī: "By what means are you, who are seated on the lotus-throne, pleased? By what means can one attain your satisfaction (*prīti*), which is the supreme goal (*paramapuruṣārtha*)?"[118] There are

115. *LT*. 11:7 (*mayā kṛtam hi yat karma tena tat kṛtamuccyate*||). (Translation mine).

116. *LT*. 15:11.

117. *LT*. 11:38. (*na vinā devadevena sthitirmama hi vidyate*| *mayā vinā na devasya sthitirviṣṇorhi vidyate*||), One of the manuscripts omits the second line of the verse. Cf. 11:3; 27:43; 9:2; 8:10.

118. *LT*. 15:5; also see v. 6. (Translation mine).

four methods taught in the *Lakṣmī Tantra* to acquire the satisfaction (*prīti*) of Śrī-Lakṣmī: 1) performance of one's duties according to one's caste (*svajātivihitam karma*); 2) knowledge of the principles of Sāṅkhya; 3) meditative devotion (*yoga*); and 4) complete renunciation (*sarvatyāga*). These methods are designated for the learned (*vidvat*).[119] The underlying presupposition here is that it is only through higher knowledge that one can realize the highest goal, namely, Brahman, who is said to consist of Lakṣmī-Nārāyaṇa.

Although all of the aforementioned methods are valid means to higher knowledge, it is the fourth method that is said to be supreme. This method, which is also known as *śaraṇāgati*, has six components: 1) resolving to perform such acts as conform to God's desires (*anukūlasya saṃkalpaḥ*); 2) abandoning all acts that displease God (*pratikūlasya varjanam*); 3) the firm conviction (trust) that God will protect the devotee (*rakṣasyati iti viśvasaḥ*); 4) consigning oneself to God's protection (*goptṛtvavaraṇam*); 5) self-surrender (*ātmanikṣepa*); and 6) humility (*kārpaṇyam*).[120]

The *Lakṣmī Tantra* proposes the middle course, namely, *śaraṇāgati*, as superior to both *apāya* and *upāya* (*apāya=hiṃsa*—theft etc., and *upāya=karman*—religious duties and so on,). Therefore, the devotee should reject both *apāya* and *upāya*. By the same token the devotee should reject the expiatory (*prāyaścitta*) deeds that annihilate sin. The only deeds that the devotee should perform are those which, when performed, bring no reward and those which, when not performed, bring harm. Moreover, the *Lakṣmī Tantra* believes that this is precisely the attitude taken by the Vedas.[121] The *Lakṣmī Tantra* also cautions that this *śaraṇāgati* method, though simple to follow, is difficult to carry out (*upāyaḥ sukaraḥ so'yaṃ duṣkaraś ca mato mama*).[122]

While the *śaraṇāgati* method is prescribed for those who do not desire any fruit from their worship, both those who desire results as well as those who do not should worship Śrī-Lakṣmī in her *mantra* form,[123] because *mantra*-s are efficacious in procuring both material prosperity and emancipation. The *mantra*-s, which must be regarded as "pure embodiments" of Śrī-Lakṣmī, bestow grace upon the adept (devotee) and lead him beyond the phenomenal world by instilling in him a sense of detachment, and thus the adept finally enters the eternal state of Brahman, which is known as Lakṣmī-Nārāyaṇa.[124]

The *Lakṣmī Tantra* classifies *mantra*-s into three categories—superior *mantra*-s, which deal with *vyūha*-s and envisage complete absorption in the supreme Brahman (Lakṣmī-Nārāyaṇa); the

---

119. *LT*. 15:17.
120. *LT*. 17:60-61. For more details on the six *aṅgas*, see vv. 66 ff.
121. *LT*. 17:82-90.
122. *LT*. 17:105b.
123. *LT*. 17:106-7.
124. *LT*. 18:48-50; 21:26-28; 22:29-31.

intermediary type of *mantra*-s, which deal with *vibhava* manifestations of God along with their *śaktis*; and the inferior type of *mantra*-s, which deal with the limited goals of the phenomenal world. The *Lakṣmī Tantra*, however, claims that the superior *mantra*-s fall under the Pāñcarātra system, while the intermediary and the inferior ones fall under the Vedas and the Tantras respectively.[125]

In the form of *mantra*, Śrī-Lakṣmī is considered as *Śabdabrahman*, and she herself dwells in the earthly preceptor to protect the disciples who approach her. For this reason the disciples must regard the earthly preceptor as identical with herself.[126] In the *mantra* form as *Śabdabrahman*, Śrī-Lakṣmī is represented by the alphabetical letters (*mātṛkā*-s). Each part of her body is associated with a particular sound of the letter (e.g., *a* and *ā* form her eyebrows while *i* and *ī* are her eyes, etc.).[127] The point, however, is that in the *mantra* form Śrī-Lakṣmī's cosmic body is represented by the letters in the context of ritual. The various combinations of sounds, then, are nothing less than constructing the cosmic sound that represents the cosmic body of Śrī-Lakṣmī. For instance, when the adept combines *a+u+m* to construct *Oṃ*, each of the letters represents a *vyūha* : *a*—represents Aniruddha, *u*—represents Pradyumna, and *ṃ*—represents Saṃkarṣaṇa, and *bindu* represents Vāsudeva.[128]

In order to worship the *mantra* form of Śrī-Lakṣmī the adept not only must perform certain rituals related to consecration (*nyāsa*) by appropriate hand gestures (*mudra*-s), *bhūtaśuddhi*, and so on, but also, with his mind, he must meditate on the goddess who contains all *mantra*-s. The adept (*yogin*) who meditates with the knowledge that Śrī-Lakṣmī herself is the Lord Viṣṇu will not be born again.[129]

Then again, since Śrī-Lakṣmī is said to dwell in the heart of the worshiper, she should be worshiped with mental sacrifice (spiritual offerings), such as relating to the supreme goal (*pāramārtha*).[130] This idea of Śrī-Lakṣmī dwelling in the heart of the worshipper echoes the familiar Śrīvaiṣṇava concept of Lord Viṣṇu as *antaryāmin,* which actually is one of the five forms of God according to the Pāñcarātra tradition. In the *Lakṣmī Tantra*, however, Śrī-Lakṣmī herself is

---

125. *LT*. 22:32-36. It is interesting to note the attitude of the *Lakṣmī Tantra* toward the Vedas and the Tantras. It obviously places the *mantra*-s of the Vedas and the Tantras on a lower status while making it clear that Pāñcarātra is different from the Tantra system. This is probably the clearest statement regarding its concern to claim a superior status in relation to both the Vedas and the Tantras. This statement also makes an important distinction between the Tantra system and the Pāñcarātra system.

126. *LT*. 23:3-4.

127. *LT*. 23:21 ff.

128. *LT*. 24:6-8.

129. *LT*. 35:80 (*aham sa bhagavān viṣṇuraham lakṣmīḥ sanātanī*| *ityevaṃbhāvavān yogī bhūyo naiva prajāyate*||). Here it is clear that in the context of ritual, Śrī-Lakṣmī's status is on a par with Viṣṇu.

130. *LT*. 36:1.

depicted as *antaryāmin*. The mental sacrifice, or internal worship, consists of various images with which the worshipper meditates upon Śrī-Lakṣmī. In the process of this mental worship, the worshipper conceives Śrī-Lakṣmī in various ways (for example, Lakṣmī arising out of Viṣṇu, Lakṣmī seated on the lap of the Lord, and so forth.). Thus, the images that result from the mental conceptions are said to be products of thought that are identical with Śrī-Lakṣmī herself. In other words, these products of thought are considered as manifestations of Śrī-Lakṣmī.[131] Further, these mental conceptions are not only objects of worship but also are considered as forms of offering. At the end of the mental worship, the worshipper must surrender all mental rites to Śrī-Lakṣmī.[132] According to the *Lakṣmī Tantra*, this mental worship should be continued by the worshipper throughout his life. The main thrust of the mental sacrifice is surrender (*prapatti*)—

> Having properly known the previously mentioned power of Tārikā, conceiving (Lakṣmī) with the idea of her being gracious (the worshipper) should surrender (*prapadyeta*) the fifth *ṛc* (of the *Śrī Sūkta*).[133]

Strange as it may seem, the *Lakṣmī Tantra* introduces external rites after the internal rituals (mental sacrifice), thereby reversing the usual order followed in the Tantric practice.[134] These external rites consist of finding an appropriate site, constructing a pavilion (*maṇḍapa*) and a platform (*vedī*) at the center (*brahmasthāna*) as well as a *maṇḍala* of lotuses, etc.[135]

In the external worship, the symbolism of lotus seems to become a dominant mode in the process of visualizing Śrī-Lakṣmī. The site chosen for the ritual is divided into sixteen parts. Subsequently, nine lotuses must be drawn in the areas as follows: one lotus with eight petals at the center, then four lotuses in each direction—east, west, etc., the other four lotuses are drawn in the four corners—northeast, etc. This square diagram of nine lotuses must have gates on the outside along with *śobha*-s and *koṇa*-s.[136] The significance of the *maṇḍala* of nine auspicious lotuses lies in the context of internal sacrifice. Every time the worshipper worships the deity he should call

---

131. *LT*. 36:147. Also see f.n., 4 in S. Gupta, *LT*. p. 226.

132. *LT*. 36:146.

133. *LT*. 36:122 (*pañcabhyā ca prapadyeta prasannāṃ bhāvayan dhiyā*| *jñātvā pūrvoktasāmarthyaṃ tārikāyā yathārthataḥ*||). (Translation mine). Also see S. Gupta, *LT*. p. 224. f.n. 1; *LT*. 36:146.

134. *LT*. 36:137. In the Śrīvaiṣṇava tradition external rituals are of great significance since they are done as eternal service (*nityakaiṇkarya*) to the Lord. The significance of the notion of eternal service to the Lord may be seen in light of Rāmānuja's *Nitygrantha* in which he describes the details of the daily worship of the Lord and his consorts.

135. *LT*. 37:3-7, 17-19 ff. See *Hayaśirṣa Pāñcarātra*, 5:1-53.

136. *LT*. 37:13-19; Also see *Jayākhya Saṃhitā*. 13:24 ff. For the meaning of *śobha* and *koṇa* see the diagram III in S. Gupta. *LT*. Also see *J.S*. 13:31-40, which has detailed description of the *maṇḍala*.

to mind the *maṇḍala* of nine lotuses. Further, it is stated that the noblest of those who possess knowledge of the *mantra* should worship the *maṇḍala* of nine lotuses by visualizing it in their mind. One should meditate on the *maṇḍala* since it is the visual representation of the basis of the entire cosmos and represents the abode of the gods. It is the supreme abode (*purottamam*).[137]

The significance of the symbolism of the lotus (*padma*) is further emphasized when the worshipper is directed to worship Śrī-Lakṣmī as the one who holds the lotus in her hand, and also as the one who stands on the lotuses.[138] In other words, she is within it and above it. Inasmuch as the lotus symbolizes the basis of the entire cosmos, Śrī-Lakṣmī is within it and at the same time she is visualized as surpassing all the cosmos. If the nine-lotus *maṇḍala* (*navapadmamaṇḍala*) is seen as representing the entire cosmos, then Śrī-Lakṣmī, holding as she does the lotus and standing on the lotuses, clearly represents her power (*śakti*) of transcendence. This idea of transcendence is further reinforced by visualizing the pericarp of the central lotus of the *maṇḍala* as the seat of the spiritual realization (*bhāvāsana*) on which both the lotus-eyed Viṣṇu and the lotus-goddess Śrī-Lakṣmī are located.[139] The central lotus also symbolizes the *vyūha*-s. While Vāsudeva is visualized as seated on the eastern petal of the central lotus, Saṃkarṣaṇa, Pradyumna, and Aniruddha are visualized as seated on the southerly petal, the westerly petal, and the northerly petal, respectively. In other words, the *navapadmamaṇḍala* is also a visual representation of the pure creation (the unmanifest creation).

The symbolism of the lotus is further extended to the bell that produces *mantra*-s by its very sound. In the sound of the bell all the *mantra*-s are produced, and as such the bell becomes the mother of all the *mantra*-s. Therefore, in visualizing Śrī-Lakṣmī the worshipper should visualize the handle on the upper side of the bell as the stem which supports the eight petalled lotus. Thus, the bell becomes the visual symbol of Śrī-Lakṣmī with eight arms. In that visualization, Śrī-Lakṣmī is perceived as seated in the posture of the lotus and as having large eyes shaped like the lotuses and a complexion like the color inside of a lotus.[140]

The lotus symbol is also identified with the seat of unmanifested consciousness. Thus, the worshipper in the context of worshipping the Tārikā *mantra*, should first visualize the form of the lotus in which the *tattva*-s exist. Then, the stem of the lotus is visualized as representing the unmanifest time (*kāla*), the individual self (*jīva*), and the imperishable being (*akṣara*). Then, under the stem of the lotus, the Śakti called Aniruddha is to be visualized; under that the Śakti called Pradyumna, and under that the Śakti of Saṃkarṣaṇa; and finally, under

137. *LT.* 37:20-25.
138. *LT.* 37:45.
139. *LT.* 38:29.
140. *LT.* 40:22-29.

all of that, Vāsudeva as the couple (Lakṣmī-Nārāyaṇa) in gross, subtle, transcendent, and supratranscendent forms are visualized.[141]

Although the external rites are quite elaborate, the symbolism that is associated with them is profound. During the external ritual the worshipper is led into a deeper level of mental process whereby he should visualize the *mantra* form of Śrī-Lakṣmī. For instance, the symbolism of lotus helps the worshipper to visualize Śrī-Lakṣmī as the supreme pure consciousness, as Brahman consisting of Lakṣmī-Nārāyaṇa. The external ritual is not completely devoid of mental worship but rather includes both. Every ostensible external ritual act is imbued with a deeper level of internal meditation with the sole purpose of pleasing Śrī-Lakṣmī, who then bestows her grace upon the devotee.

Śri-Lakṣmī as Goddess of Beauty

Although Gonda rejects the æsthetic categories such as "beauty" as unimportant in understanding Śrī-Lakṣmī in the Vedic tradition, his arguments seem to ignore an important aspect that becomes significant and meaningful to understanding Śrī-Lakṣmī in the Pāñcarātra tradition. Perhaps, even in the Vedic tradition Śrī-Lakṣmī's nature as "inconstant," and her role in relation to Indra, etc., gods who fail to retain her, may have to be seen in light of the enchanting beauty and charm with which she delights them.

In the Pāñcarātra tradition, the æsthetic categories seem to be structurally related to the understanding of Śrī-Lakṣmī. In the context of creation, she is described as beautifully formed (*cārusarvāṅgī, sarvāṅgasundarī*), with large eyes and a complexion like refined gold, lotus shaped eyes and so on. She manifests herself as the substratum of the universe.[142] Again, when Viṣṇu descends to the earth in his various *avatāra*-s in order to reassure the living beings, Śrī-Lakṣmī also takes a corporeal form and descends along with him. Her corporeal form is described as "with proportioned limbs beautiful in every lineament."[143] The descriptions of Śrī-Lakṣmī in terms of "beautiful," and so on, in both these contexts seem to carry the idea of perfection. In a similar context elsewhere, the terms such as "perfectly formed and beautiful" (*sarvāvayavasaṃpannaḥ sarvāvayavasundaraḥ*)[144] are used. These terms seem to imply that perfection and beauty go together. At a micro level, as a goddess worshipped by the devotee, she is perfectly shaped. At the macro level, that is, at the cosmic level, Śrī-Lakṣmī's perfect form has to do

141. *LT.* 43:7-13. Note that the lotus described here is to be pictured as if it is facing downward like a bell. Conversely, if the lotus is turned upward again, the place of Vāsudeva Śakti will be the central place at the pericarp of the lotus.

142. *LT.* 4:37, 38, 64; 5:6-8.

143. *LT.* 17:7-8.

144. *LT.* 17:29 (One of the manuscripts reads "*sarvāvayava saṃpūrṇaḥ,*" which seems to be better suited to the context here, as it indicates wholeness and completeness).

with cosmic perfection in every way. She is comparable to Viṣṇu in form (beauty), virtue, and age.[145]

The structural relationship between perfection and beauty has further implications: as an embodiment of beauty and perfection, Śrī-Lakṣmī symbolizes auspiciousness and luck. It is for the same reason that Śrī-Lakṣmī is visualized as having four arms endowed with matchless beauty.[146] The following passage eloquently brings out the motif of auspiciousness and its structural relation to beauty and perfection. Śrī-Lakṣmī says:

> The one with handsome face, beautiful eyes, two arms (adorned with) pretty earrings, the one whose splendor is like the inside of the lotus, wearing a chained girdle; the one who is wearing a white garland and clothes, necklace, and armlets, who is the embodiment of (auspicious) signs, with round, high, and firm breasts; the one with wide-open, large eyes, with smiling face, with her locks resembling a mass of moving black bees; the one wearing a charming, flowing and beautiful spot on the forehead, with gem-like red lips, superior pearl-like teeth; with forehead shaped like half-moon, with dark and curly hair, holding a noose and a goad, the bestower of *dharma*, *kāma*, *artha*, and *mokṣa*; the goddess seated in the lotus posture, shining with the most excellent diadem— thus I am worshipped as Lakṣmī, Satī, and the Ruler who is seated in the *vyūha*.[147]

The goddess who is visualized as such is also the one who bestows *dharma, kāma, artha*, and *mokṣa*. By visualizing Śrī-Lakṣmī as the embodiment of beauty (for example, in a beautiful woman), one should transcend sensual thoughts, like an ascetic, and contemplate her beauty with a mind free from lust.[148] Thus, in the context of worshipping the Tārikā *mantra*, and even in the process of mental sacrifice, Śrī-Lakṣmī is conceived as beautiful with large eyes, possessing a deep navel, a lean belly adorned with three lines, and so on.[149] The erotic symbolism rooted in the æsthetic conceptions here seems to become a structure for ascetic fulfilment and a means to transcend the mundane world. The polarized conceptions of eroticism and asceticism seem to be held in a transcending balance. By

---

145. *LT*. 17:35.

146. *LT*. 42:67-68; 40:3-4.

147. *LT*. 45:16-21. *saumyavaktrā saumyanetrā dvibhujā cārukuṇḍalā*| *padmagarbhopamā kāntyā mekhalādāmamaṇḍitā*|| *śvetamālyāṃbaradharā hāra-keyūramaṇḍitā*| *sarvalakṣaṇasaṃpannā pīnatuṅgaghanastanī*|| *prabuddhotpala-vistīrṇalocanā susmitānanā*| *caradvirephapaṭalatulyairyuktā tathālakaiḥ*|| *lalāṭe tilakaṃ citraṃ vahantī ca manoharam*| *āraktādhararatnā ca vaṃśa-muktāphaladvijā*|| *ardhacandralalāṭā ca nīlakuñcitamūrdhajā*| *pāśāṅkuśadharā devī dharmakāmārthamokṣadā*|| *baddhapadmāsanā caiva makuṭottamaśobhitā*| *evaṃ dhyeyāhamīśānā lakṣmīvyūhasthitā satī*||(translation mine).

148. *LT*. 43:73-77.

149. *LT*. 36:122-31; S. Gupta points out that "three horizontal shallow lines across the lower part of the abdomen are a sign of perfection in the female body." S. Gupta, *LT*. p. 224. f.n.5.

affirming erotic and æsthetic conceptions, the ascetic conceptions are also affirmed simultaneously.

There is also another kind of polarity that is emphasized in the context of visualizing Śrī-Lakṣmī as beautiful. On the one hand she looks beautiful, but at the same time dons a ferocious form with a dual purpose, namely, to protect the sages and to devour the demons.[150] In the context of the churning of the ocean, however, Śrī-Lakṣmī appears to the demons as an enchantress in her most beautiful form in order to distract them from the nectar. She misleads the demons with her beautiful form and then devours them in her ferocious form. But to the devotee she appears in her most graceful form to bestow grace upon him, and to enable the worshipper to realize her transcendent form as Brahman, which consists of Lakṣmī-Nārāyaṇa. Thus, visualizing Śrī-Lakṣmī in all these polarities, related to æsthetic and ascetic conceptions, one should ultimately meditate on her as one who is with form and without form (*dhyāyet rūpavantam arūpiṇam*).[151] The æsthetic conceptions are structurally related not only to auspiciousness and luck but also to the very liberation process and the ultimate goal of pleasing the deity. The devotee should, therefore, perform internal and external rites and through the *mantra* form visualize Śrī-Lakṣmī as the most beautifully and perfectly formed.

In concluding this chapter, it is important to underline two essential points that will have a bearing on the next chapters. Firstly, although there is divergence of opinion among the various Pāñcarātra texts in dealing with various aspects that we have discussed thus far, there is unanimity on the question of Viṣṇu's essential nature being characterized by six auspicious qualities. In this regard there is continuity between the older and the later texts. Secondly, both the older texts and the later texts agree on the essentially inseparable relationship that exists between Viṣṇu and his divine consort both at the level of ritual and also at the ontological level. Although the older texts do not specifically talk about Śrī-Lakṣmī's essential nature being characterized by the six auspicious qualities, the *Lakṣmī Tantra*'s endevor to attribute those qualities to her as well need not be seen as discontinuous from the older ones. If one accepts the essential oneness of the Lord and her consort at the ontological level, it is only natural to assume that they both share the six auspicious qualities. And it is this point that the *Lakṣmī Tantra* states without any uncertainty.

150. *LT*. 9:8-11, 39-41.
151. *LT*. 36:9.

CHAPTER FOUR

ŚRĪ-LAKṢMĪ IN THE WRITINGS OF YĀMUNA AND RĀMĀNUJA

In view of the relative brevity of material in their writings dealing with Śrī-Lakṣmī, both Yāmuna and Rāmānuja are being considered together in the same chapter. Besides, the two *ācārya*-s are very close in their understanding of not only the Pāñcarātra tradition in general but also the divine consort. In that sense, there is a great deal of continuity of thought between the two *ācārya*-s. Both of them represent the early developments in the interpretive process of the tradition and give shape and orientation to the subsequent develop-ments in the overall understanding of the Śrīvaiṣṇava tradition. While Yāmuna laid the foundation, Rāmānuja raised the superstructure and Bhaṭṭar consolidated the tradition firmly.

In the interpretive process of the Śrīvaiṣṇava tradition, both Yāmuna and Rāmānuja took the Pāñcarātra Āgamas seriously. For Nāthamuni, the first *ācārya* of the tradition, the challenge to the Pāñcarātra tradition perhaps did not arise because he was primarily preoccupied with the compilation of *Nāḷāyira Divyaprabandham* (Tamil—*Nāḷāyira Tiviya Piripandham*), which became the major source of the Śrīvaiṣṇava tradition. Obviously Nāthamuni did not develop a systematic philosophical framework for the Āḷvār tradition. He is, however, said to have left a tradition of logic and epistemology in his *Nyāyatattva* and a tradition of Yoga in his *Yogarahasya,* both of which are no longer extant. But the two works, as Neevel points out, provided Yāmuna with the necessary skills to integrate the Vedānta and the Pāñcarātra traditions.[1]

Both Yāmuna and Rāmānuja made significant attempts to defend the Pāñcarātra tradition. Yāmuna wrote an entire work called *Āgamaprāmāṇya* defending the Pāñcarātra tradition while Rāmānuja supplemented it by discussing the same subject in his *Śrībhāṣya* (2:2:40-43). Both have made attempts to integrate the Pāñcarātra tradition into the Vedāntic tradition. Through the integration of the Pāñcarātra and the Vedānta, the Śrīvaiṣṇava tradition assimilated

1. Walter G. Neevel, *Yāmuna's Vedānta and Pāñcarātra: Integrating the Classical and the Popular* (Montana: Scholars Press, 1977), p. 11. According to the hagiographical information, Yāmuna missed his chance at learning the secret teaching on Yoga from Kureśa and thereby lost the tradition of Yoga that Nāthamuni developed in his *Yogarahasya*. Garuḍavāhana Paṇdita, *Divya-sūricaritam*, with Hindi rendering by Pt. Mādhavācārya, ed. T. T. Sampath Kumārācārya and K. K. A. Venkatācāri (Bombay: Anantācārya Research Institute, 1978), p. 351 (sl.16:87-94).

significant Āgamic elements, especially into their ritual practice.[2] According to the tradition, Rāmānuja himself went from place to place visiting Vaiṣṇava temples and establishing ritual tradition on the basis of the Pāñcarātra Āgamas. One of the significant ways in which the Pāñcarātra Āgamas influenced the Śrīvaiṣṇava tradition is by their inherent emphasis on the female deity, Śrī-Lakṣmī. Although different Āgama texts project her status variously, she undoubtedly remains an important theme in almost all the texts. She is not only an aspect of Viṣṇu but also a deity in her own right. As presented in the previous chapter, while the entire *Lakṣmī Tantra* is devoted to the understanding of Śrī-Lakṣmī, other important Āgama texts such as *Pauṣkara Saṃhitā, Ahirbudhnya Saṃhitā, Īśvara Saṃhitā, Śrīpraśna Saṃhitā*, among others, have important accounts of Śrī-Lakṣmī, either in relation to the rituals connected to her or in relation to her association with the Lord Viṣṇu.[3]

My attempt in this chapter is to explore the understanding of Yāmuna and Rāmānuja of Śrī-Lakṣmī and to see how much of their understanding has been influenced by the Pāñcarātra tradition. One point that needs to be clarified at this point is that, although I wish to show the Pāñcarātra influence on Yāmuna and Rāmānuja, I do not imply that they were necessarily influenced by the *Lakṣmī Tantra* as such. However, it would be worth noting how much of their ideas correspond with those of the *Lakṣmī Tantra*. In a certain sense Śrī-Lakṣmī does not figure in the Vedāntic philosophy, since the chief subject of inquiry is Brahman. For the Śrīvaiṣṇava tradition, Brahman is none other than the Lord Nārāyaṇa, who is characterized by infinite auspicious qualities. Besides, he is always accompanied by his consort. The Pāñcarātra Āgamas provide ontological status to Śrī-Lakṣmī by conceiving of her and Viṣṇu as eternally inseparable, and sharing essentially the same auspicious qualities. Both pure creation and the nonpure creation proceed from them. Both the older Pāñcarātra texts (such as *Sāttvata-* and *Jayākhya Saṃhitā*) and the *Lakṣmī Tantra* agree that Viṣṇu is characterized by his six auspicious qualities, and secondly that Śrī is always present in the Lord.

Although both Yāmuna and Rāmānuja have vigorously defended the Pāñcarātra Āgamas in the course of integrating them into the

2. Note that both Yāmuna and the subsequent commentator Veṅkaṭanātha defended the Pāñcarātra from the standpoint of the ritual. See Yāmuna's *Āgamaprāmāṇya* and Veṅkaṭanātha's *Pāñcarātrarakṣa.* Both Neevel and van Buitenen make similar points for different reasons. While Neevel wants to show that Yāmuna was defending Pāñcarātra against the Mīmāṃsakas (See Neevel, op.cit., chap. 2), van Buitenen, in order to show that the meaning of Pāñcarātra has to do with *pañcakālika* rituals, argues that both Yāmuna and Veṅkaṭanātha, emphasized rituals rather than philosophical matters (See J. A. B. van Buitenen, *Yāmuna's Āgamaprāmāṇya* (Madras: Rāmānuja Research Society, 1971), pp. 6-7.

3. For detailed references on Śrī-Lakṣmī in Pāñcarātra texts, see H. Daniel Smith, *A Descriptive Bibliography of the Printed texts of the Pāñcarātra Āgama*, vol. 2 (Baroda: Oriental Institute, 1980), p. 94.

Vedānta, they seem to be selective in incorporating the Pāñcarātra elements into their Vedāntic framework. In both of them reference to Śrī-Lakṣmī is made in the context of ritual and not so much in the context of their philosophical discussions. As mentioned elsewhere, *Jayākhya Saṃhitā* discusses the role of Lakṣmī in the context of ritual. (JS. chs. 6, 15, and 27) While both Yāmuna and Rāmānuja seem to have taken her ontological status for granted, they do not, however, interpret Śrī-Lakṣmī as Prakṛti, as is the case in the *dvaita* system of Madhvācārya.[4] For the purpose of my analysis of Yāmuna and Rāmānuja, I shall take both their philosophical works and devotional works together, as they complement each other. I shall also rely on the traditional biographical materials, such as *Divyasūricaritam,* although these hiographical materials were prepared centuries after both these scholars passed away. The problem of devotional works, especially the *Gadya* works of Rāmānuja, has been discussed by scholars, such as Agnihothram and Lester, who have tended to see a division between the philosophical works and the devotional works of both Yāmuna and Rāmānuja. Both Carman and Vasudha Narayanan, in their respective works, responded to the discussion of the problem of the two kinds of works of Rāmānuja, and as such I shall not elaborate on that debate except to draw the attention of the reader to those discussions.[5] Regarding the question of the biographical materials, although the *Divyasūricaritam*, a biographical account of the early teachers of the Śrīvaiṣṇava tradition, was written centuries after the early teachers, I have chosen to utilize the materials from this account not so much because of their historical accuracy, but mainly because of the importance given to it within the traditional circles and also more recently among modern scholars. The question for me is not so much whether the account of the traditional biography is historically accurate or not; rather, in understanding the tradition, it is important to note how the subsequent generation remembers the teachers. And, as I mentioned in the introductory chapter, my purpose in this book is primarily to layout as faithfully and clearly as possible the community's understanding of the question of the goddess. The fact that Rāmānuja gave imprtance to the Pāñcarātra ritual tradition (of which we have direct evidence from the Śrībhāṣya) and the fact that there exist devotional works attributed to him by the tradition can only be reconciled by listening to the traditional biographical accounts such as the *Divyasūricaritam*. What is significant in this regard is that both the

4. E. J. Lott points out that Madhva takes the principle of māyā to mean the female power who is called Durgā. In fact, Śrī, Bhū, and Durgā are all identified with *māyā*, in the.sense that they are the Prakṛti's aspects as the pure (Śrī), vigorous (Bhū), and dark (Durgā). See E. J. Lott. *Vedantic Approaches to God* (London: The Macmillan Press, Ltd., 1980), p. 117.

5. J. B. Carman. *Theology of Rāmānuja*, pp. 240ff. V. Narayanan. *The Way and the Goal* (Washington, D.C.,: The Institute for Vaishnava Studies, and Center for the Study of World Religions, Harvard University, 1987), pp. 88ff.

sects agree on the traditional biographical accounts and no divergence of opinion has been noted as far as I am aware.

Śrī-Lakṣmī in the Writings of Yāmuna

Before we embark on exploring Yāmuna's understanding of Śrī-Lakṣmī, it may be useful to outline some aspects of Yāmuna's background in order to understand him in proper perspective. In his study of Yāmuna's Vedānta and Pāñcarātra, Neevel considers Yāmuna as follows : 1) as a Vedāntin who integrated the Pāñcarātra and the Vedānta; 2) as a dialectician who was influenced by his grandfather Nāthamuni's *Nyāyatattva*; 3) and as the defender of the Pāñcarātra tradition mainly against the Mīmāṃsaka-s, because the Mīmāṃsaka-s rejected Pāñcarātra ritual tradition as an alternative to the Pūrvamīmāṃsā ritual tradition. In his critique of Neevel's study of Yāmuna, R. Mesquita points out first that Yāmuna in fact supported the validity of the Pāñcarātra tradition, not on the basis of the inferential argument (*parataḥprāmāṇyam*) adopted by Pāñcarātrika Nyaiyāyika, but on the basis of self validation (*svataḥprāmāṇyam*) principle of the Vedānta Pāñcarātra tradition; secondly, that there is continuity of tradition between both Nāthamuni and Yāmuna in that Nāthamuni also belongs to the Pāñcarātrika Vedānta tradition. On this second point Mesquita differs from Neevel who tended to show that only in so far as the Nyāya tradition is concerned was Yāmuna influenced by Nāthamuni, but he departed from him in his pursuit of Pāñcarātrika Vedānta.[6]

According to the *Divyasūricaritam*, Yāmuna is supposed to have written eight works, namely, *Saṃvit Siddhi, Ātma Siddhi, Īśvara Siddhi, Āgamaprāmāṇya, Stotraratna, Catuśślokī, Gītārthasaṃgraha* and *Puruṣanirṇaya*.[7] There is another work, namely, *Kāṣmīr Āgamaprāmāṇya*, which is attributed to Yāmuna by some traditional scholars.[8] Western scholars[9] in this field in general, and some traditional scholars as well are not inclined to accept it as being the

6. For a detailed discussion on this, see R. Mesquita. "Yāmuna's Vedānta and Pāñcarātra: A Review," in *Wienner Zeitschrift für die Kunde Südasiens* (Wien), Sonderabdruck aus band 24 (1980): 199-224. Also see Roque Mesquita. "Zur Vedānta und Pāñcarātra-Tradition Nāthamunis," in *Wienner Zeitschrift für die Kunde Südasiens* (Wien), Sonderabdruck aus band 23 (1979): 163-93.

7. *Divyasūricaritam*, 16:83.

8. M. Narasiṃhācāri, editor of *Āgamaprāmāṇya*, tends to believe that since the reference to *Kāṣmīrāgamaprāmāṇya* in *Āgamaprāmāṇya* is similar to the reference in *Puruṣanirṇaya*, it is possible that Yāmuna could have written it. He, however, makes his tentative conclusion pending further evidence to disprove his hypothesis. (M. Narasiṃhācāri, *Āgamaprāmāṇya of Yāmunācārya* (Baroda: Oriental Institute, 1976), p. 4. f.n. 3). R. Rāmānujācāri, however, does not think it was written by Yāmuna.

9. J. A. B. van Buitenen seems to accept Yāmuna's authorship of *Kāṣmīr-āgamaprāmāṇya* even though he does not give any reasons for doing so. See J. A. B. van Buitenen, *Āgamaprāmāṇya*, pp. 1 and 4.

authentic work of Yāmuna not only because the reference to it in the *Āgamaprāmāṇya* is ambiguous but also because both the *Rahasyatrayasāra* of Veṅkaṭanātha as well as *Divyasūricaritam* do not make any mention of it.

Among all the eight works, it is only in *Stotraratna* and *Catuśślokī* that Yāmuna makes clear mention of Śrī-Lakṣmī. While *Stotraratna* is intended to be a hymn of praise for Lord Viṣṇu, *Catuśślokī* is clearly intended as a hymn of praise for Śrī-Lakṣmī. We shall return later in the chapter to the important question as to why Yāmuna was silent about Śrī-Lakṣmī in his other works. First it may be useful to lay out the understanding of Yāmuna about Śrī-Lakṣmī in so far as he speaks about her in his two above-mentioned devotional works. On the basis of the ritual procedure that Śrī-Lakṣmī is approached first and then Lord Viṣṇu, R. Rāmānujācāri thinks that Yāmuna might have written *Catuśślokī* first, and then *Stotraratna.*[10] In so far as this argument is based on a certain theological conviction and not on historical evidence, it is difficult to accept it *in toto,* although Yāmuna does indicate such ritual priority to Śrī-Lakṣmī in his *Catuśślokī*. Whether or not Yāmuna wrote *Catuśślokī* first, one has to take both *Catuśślokī* and *Stotraratna* together in order to understand his position on Śrī-Lakṣmī. In order to do that, I shall quote the entire *Catuśślokī* and the relevant verses from *Stotraratna* that deal with Śrī-Lakṣmī. Then I shall make an analysis of the contents of both the texts to provide a fuller understanding of Yāmuna on two major issues: a) the ritual priority of Śrī-Lakṣmī; b) Śrī-Lakṣmī's ontological status in relation to Viṣṇu.

Text of Catuśślokī[11]

O Bhagavatī, the Supreme Puruṣa [Viṣṇu], is your husband, the lord of snakes [Śeṣa] is your couch, the lord of the birds [Garuḍa], who is the soul of the Vedas, is your vehicle. Māyā, which deceives the world, is your curtain. The gods, i.e., Brahmā, Īśa, and others, along with their wives, are your male and female servants. But Śrī alone is your name.[12] How can we address you?[13] (v1)

The Lord, even though he is your husband, is unable to measure on his own such glory of yours, which is overflowing and always accessible by itself. I, a servant, the one who has sought refuge, praise you without fear. The only ruler of the world, the consort of the Lord, the patient one, they know you as merciful. (v2)

10. Although *Catuśślokī* is the more popular name of this work its actual title is *Śrīstuti*. In *Divysūricaritam* it is called *Māstotra* (Praise of the Mother) 16:83.

11. For the Sanskrit text see appendix 1. Translation is mine.

12. Although Śrī-Lakṣmī has other names, for Yāmuna and for the Śrīvaiṣṇavas the name Śrī has special significance.

13. The name Śrī is auspicious and the poet expresses the unworthiness of the devotees to even mention her name. Her glory is beyond that which any name can express, so the poet exclaims that he cannot even speak of her.

The three worlds, which were formerly dissolved [in the course of *mahāpralaya*] and which are now infinitely recreated, are protected by just a momentary, compassionate, nectar-like glance[14] of yours. There is no better grace than that of the consort [Śrī] of the one [Viṣṇu], whose mind is immersed in the lotus-eyed one. Everything belonging to the humans is brought about in the course of the imperishable world of Viṣṇu. (v3)

Just as the Brahman form of Hari is peaceful, everlasting, and of great power, the incarnate form of Brahman is also more pleasing and wonderful. All those other forms are said to be concealed together separately by your appropriate manifestations.(v4)

Text of Stotraratna[15]

Who [else] is the prosperity of Śrī? Who [else] is the support of the supreme *suttva*? Who [else] is the lotus-eyed one? Who [else] is the Highest Person? [Who else is he] in a subdivision of whose billionth part, the wonderful universe, which is divided into sentient and nonsentient beings, revolves? (v.12)

And you [Viṣṇu] have made your breast place her palace; your beloved abode her birthplace. The entire universe takes refuge in her side-long glance. And for her sake the ocean was churned and bound. (v.37)

She [Śrī] is always experienced by your own cosmic form, and she causes unprecedented delight by her qualities, form, and acts of pleasure, and she is always an appropriate support for you. (v.38)

[Viṣṇu] is seated on the infinite enjoyer [Ananta, the Serpent] in the unique abode of excellent knowledge and strength, and in the divine abode, the inside of which is illumined by the circle of luster emanating from the cluster of gems on his [Ananta] hoods. (v.39)

The long-armed one [Viṣṇu] thrills the queen [Śrī] with diverse sentiments and feelings of exceedingly bonded, and with lovely and skilful sports, and by causing time to pass away as a fraction of a second. (v.44)

[Viṣṇu] is the ocean of nectar consisting of the nature of beauty, which is unthinkable, divine, wonderful, and eternally youthful. He is the support of Śrī, the sole life of the devotees, suitable aim, friend in need, and the bestower of gifts for those who request him. (v.45)

In the first *śloka* of *Catuśślokī*, Yāmuna makes the following points: 1) Śrī-Lakṣmī's consort is the Highest Puruṣa (Viṣṇu); 2) her locus is the same as that of Lord Viṣṇu (sleeping couch and vehicle); 3) she is above all gods including Brahmā and Īśvara (Śiva); 4) although the goddess has other names, by emphasizing her name as Śrī alone, Yāmuna makes reference to her auspicious qualities such as *jñāna, aiśvarya, śakti, bala, vīrya* and *tejas*; 5) by exclaiming "*brūmaḥ kathaṃ tvāṃ vayam*" he indicates that Śrī-Lakṣmī is beyond all speech.

---

14. The verse here is loaded with similes. I have labored to bring out the idea in English. The idea that is conveyed here is that the three worlds are protected by the Goddess' compassionate glances, which are like sweet nectar. Furthermore, words such as *sandhukṣaṇāt* emphasize that the mere glance of the Goddess is sufficient to protect the entire universe.

15. For text in Sanskrit see appendix 2. Translation is mine.

In the second *śloka*, Yāmuna makes the following points: 1) the Lord himself is unable to measure the glory of Śrī-Lakṣmī. However, by adding "like himself" (*ātmana iva*)—(just as he is unable to measure his own glory) Yāmuna avoids any misunderstanding that the Lord is incapable of "measuring" and further reinforces the point that both the Lord and his consort are beyond measure; 2) Śrī-Lakṣmī is the only ruler (*Īśvarī*) of the world and she is merciful—"they know you as merciful"; 3) by referring to himself as servant (*dāsa*) and *prapanna*, Yāmuna contrasts his own lowliness with the supremacy of Śrī-Lakṣmī. Furthermore, his fearless praise of her is only due to her compassion.

In the third *śloka*, Yāmuna makes the following points: 1) Śrī-Lakṣmī protects the three worlds with her compassionate glances; 2) there is no better grace than that of the goddess.

Finally, in the fourth *śloka*, he makes the following points: 1) he describes the supreme Brahman form of Viṣṇu, which is full of auspicious qualities; 2) Śrī-Lakṣmī's form is considered even more pleasing and wonderful; 3) and by referring to all the other forms which are hidden in her, Yāmuna seems to make reference to her corresponding *vibhava* forms, which she takes along with Viṣṇu to please her devotees.

Then, in *Stotraratna* he makes the following points: 1) the Lord Viṣṇu himself is the support of Śrī-lakṣmī (v. 12); 2) the abode of Śrī-Lakṣmī is the chest of the Lord; 3) the universe is protected by the side-long glances of Śrī-Lakṣmī (v. 37); 4) the Lord Viṣṇu is seated always with Śrī-Lakṣmī; 5) Śrī-Lakṣmī, with all her attributes, is an equal match for the Lord; 6) she creates delight for the Lord; 7) she is comprehended eternally in the cosmic form of the Lord (vv. 38-39); 8) Viṣṇu himself delights Śrī-Lakṣmī by his lovely and skilful sports (v.44), and Viṣṇu is the support of Śrī.

In both *Catuśślokī* and *Stotraratna*, Yāmuna affirms that Śrī-Lakṣmī is the consort of Lord Viṣṇu and that she is inseparable from him. While in *Catuśślokī* Śrī-Lakṣmī shares the same locus with Viṣṇu, in *Stotraratna* she finds her abode in the chest of the Lord himself. Again, in both texts Yāmuna affirms her lordship over the universe and the fact that she protects the three worlds through her side-long glances.[16] In *Catuśślokī* she is placed above all gods including Brahmā and Śiva and is beyond speech, while in *Stotraratna* Śrī-Lakṣmī, with all her attributes, is an equal match for Viṣṇu and she is comprehended eternally in the cosmic form of Viṣṇu.

Further, Yāmuna, while on the one hand, affirming the supremacy of Viṣṇu in *Stotraratna*, says that the Lord himself is the support (*āśraya*) of Śrī-Lakṣmī, on the other, affirming Śrī-Lakṣmī's glory in *Catuśślokī*, he exclaims that even the Lord himself is unable to measure her glory. Yāmuna seems to hold the status of both the Lord

16. Yāmuna, *Stotraratna*, v. 37.

and his consort in perfect balance so that they do not constitute a duality but perfect unity.

Again, in *Catuśślokī*, Yāmuna speaks of Śrī-Lakṣmī as mediatrix between the Lord and his devotees.[17] But, on the other hand, in *Stotraratna*, he speaks of the Lord as the "sole sustenance of the devotee" (*bhaktajanaikajīvitam*).[18] It appears that, in his poetic language, Yāmuna wrestled with maintaining the unity of the Lord and his consort, in order to avoid any duality in the ultimate reality. By elevating the divine consort to a position above the gods, including Brahmā and Śiva, Yāmuna seems to avoid the duality in the ultimate reality. He also tries to avoid any misconception that she is a mere attribute of the Lord. The idea that the Lord exhilarates Śrī-Lakṣmī with his skilful sports[19] and that she in turn delights him with her attributes and beauty[20] is certainly indicative of their harmoniousness in a unitive vision. The idea that Śrī-Lakṣmī is an equal match to Viṣṇu and is comprehended in the cosmic form of Viṣṇu, reinforces the Pāñcarātra notion that Śrī-Lakṣmī and Viṣṇu share the same auspicious qualities. This idea, though not clearly present in the early Pāñcarātra texts, is substantially developed in the later Pāñcarātra text, viz., the *Lakṣmī Tantra*. In other words, although it is clear that Yāmuna did not derive this idea from the *Lakṣmī Tantra* (for it is certainly post Yāmuna), it is interesting to see the correspondence of ideas between Yāmuna and the *Lakṣmī Tantra* on the issue of the divine consort.

In his *Ātma Siddhi,* Yāmuna begins with a prayer to the Supreme Puruṣa, whom he describes as Śrīmān.[21] However, except in his above mentioned two hymns, Yāmuna does not speak about Śrī-Lakṣmī in his philosophical works such as *Siddhitrayam* and *Āgamaprāmāṇya*. The two hymns were recited by Yāmuna basically in the context of ritual. The absence of a discussion of Śrī-Lakṣmī in his philosophical works may, perhaps, be attributed to the fact that in his philosophical works he was involved in polemics primarily with the Mīmāṃsaka-s, the Nyaiyāyika-s, and the Advaitins, in which context the issue has to do not so much with Śrī-Lakṣmī as with the Lord and his relationship with the world and the *jīva*-s.[22] The inspiration for his philosophical works as well as his devotional hymns nevertheless comes from the

---

17. Yāmuna, *Catuśślokī*, v. 3.

18. *Stotraratna*, v. 45.

19. Ibid., v. 44.

20. Ibid., vv. 38-40.

21. Yāmuna, *Ātmasiddhi* (in *Siddhitrayam*), p. 1.

22. In his *Ātmasiddhi* Yāmuna tries to clarify matters concerning the finite self and the infinite Self: "There are many conflicting views concerning the finite self and the infinite Self. With a view to making the matter clear, the determination of the real nature of the soul is [here] undertaken." See *Siddhitrayam*, p. 1. Then in his *Īśvarasiddhi* he tries to "establish the truth that the universe runs its course under the control of some one person." See *Siddhitrayam,* p. 153.

Pāñcarātra Āgamas. In his philosophical works, he gives evidence to the fact that he was loyal to the doctrinal system and the ritual tradition of the Pāñcarātra. It is noteworthy to recognize that Yāmuna's own understanding of Īśvara, the main topic in all his three *Siddhi*-s, is substantially influenced by the Pāñcarātra tradition. True to the spirit of the Pāñcarātra tradition, he understands Īśvara (Viṣṇu) as "the treasure of *jñāna* etc., six *guṇa*-s" (*jñānādiṣāḍguṇyanidhi*).[23] In Pāñcarātra Āgamas including the early ones, Viṣṇu is depicted as possessing the six auspicious qualities, namely, *jñāna, aiśvarya, śakti, bala, vīrya,* and *tejas*.

Yāmuna's defense of the Pāñcarātra tradition reflects his concern with preserving the Āgamic ritual tradition within the Vedāntic tradition. He also attempts, however, to show that there is no conflict between the doctrinal system of the Pāñcarātra and the philosophical tenets of the Vedānta. His philosophical works in fact reflect the extent to which he assimilated the Pāñcarātra doctrinal system. van Buitenen, discussing the meaning of "*Pāñcarātra,*" points out that Yāmuna does not emphasize the philosophical content of the Āgamas but rather the ritual aspects of the Pāñcarātra tradition. He says that Yāmuna

> . . . does not accent on this philosophical content at all in the *Āgamaprāmāṇya*, and that he understands Pāñcarātra principally as a tradition of ritual worship. What Pāñcarātra signifies for him is *dīkṣā* and the other sacraments; *ārādhana* and various aspects of the ritual worship of the God; *pūja*, devotion to the *arcā*, function and use of *nirmalya* and *naivedya*; and rites like the *pañcakālika*.[24]

As pointed out earlier, Neevel also shows that Yāmuna's defense of Pāñcarātra has to do with the ritual tradition because his chief opponents were the Mīmāṃsaka-s. While both scholars are right in emphasizing the ritual aspects, it would be misleading and perhaps missing the point if one did not recognize how much Yāmuna owes to the philosophical system of the Pāñcarātra in developing the main tenets of the Viśiṣṭādvaita system. His understanding of the three *tattva*-s, namely, *Īśvara, Cit,* and *Acit*, and their relationship, seems to be substantially informed by the Pāñcarātra. In other words, Yāmuna tried to preserve not only the ritual tradition of the Pāñcarātra but also its doctrinal system. It is in his attempt to preserve both the philosophical and the ritual tradition that one needs to see the significance of his two hymns: the hymns are not disconnected from his overall philosophical position but rather form part of his total theological position. What Yāmuna says in his philosophical works is reflected also in his two hymns, which are used in the context of the ritual.

---

23. Yāmuna, *Siddhitrayam* (*Saṃvit Siddhi*), p. 178.
24. van Buitenen, *Yāmuna's Āgamaprāmāṇyam*, p. 7.

In his *Siddhitrayam*, Yāmuna writes at great length, defending and clarifying his position on *Īśvara*. His own theological position is stated succinctly in the *maṅgalaśloka*[25] of *Ātma Siddhi*:

> May I have the highest *bhakti* to that Supreme Puruṣa to whose will matter (*prakṛti*), bound souls (*puruṣa*), time, manifest nature, released souls, and innumerable eternally perfect souls always conform, to that *Śrīmān*, who is ever in bliss along with many eternally perfect souls whose sole enjoyment is in rendering service to Him.[26]

The Śrīvaiṣṇava teachers consider the *maṅgalaśloka*-s as significant statements of their faith. In the *maṅgalaśloka*-s, the Lord Viṣṇu is almost always referred to as Śrīmān. As we shall see later in the writings of the subsequent teachers, the significance of the epithet of Viṣṇu as Śrīmān becomes more and more clear. The *Puruṣa* or *Īśvara* that Yāmuna speaks of here is the one who is also called Śrīmān (the one who possesses Śrī). In other words, Yāmuna does not think of the Lord apart from his beloved consort, who is always seated with him. The Pāñcarātra Āgamas depict Viṣṇu in the same way: he is always inseparable from his consort, Śrī-Lakṣmī. It is noteworthy, again, to recognize that in the Pāñcarātra Āgamas the six auspicious qualities are attributed to both the Lord and his divine consort. This idea of an eternally inseparable relation between the Lord and his divine consort is of great significance to Yāmuna in affirming the oneness of the ultimate reality. In his *Catuśśloki*, he affirms that Śrī-Lakṣmī always accompanies the Lord in her corresponding *vibhava* forms. Yāmuna also speaks of Viṣṇu, in his *Stotraratna*, as one who is always seated with Śrī-Lakṣmī and is an equal match for him with all her attributes and beauty. In other words, Yāmuna, both in the context of ritual as well as in his ontological scheme, a significant place to Śrī-Lakṣmī. Therefore, all that he says about Śri-Lakṣmī in his hymns must be seen in relation to his overall philosophical position. Defending the Viśiṣṭādvaita position against the Advaitins, he makes an important statement affirming the oneness of the ultimate reality. He says:

> The phrase 'The absence of a second' does not mean Brahman itself nor an attribute thereof. For it is essentially negative, while Brahman is really not negative. Nor could it be an attribute of Brahman (for according to the opponent, Brahman is devoid of qualities). Thus the existence of the world is not contradicted by scriptural texts speaking of reality as nondual. The existence of the world is established by the sources of knowledge—(*pramāṇas*) relevant—thereto. Their verdict is further confirmed by scriptural testimony.

---

25. *maṅgalaśloka* is a verse at the beginning of a work. It is called auspicious because in it the author praises the god/goddess that is worshipped in that tradition. It contains the core of the author's understanding of that deity. For this reason, the Śrīvaiṣṇava tradition considers the *maṅgalaślokas* as very significant in interpreting their tradition.

26. Yāmuna, *Siddhitrayam (Ātmasiddhi)*, *sloka* 1. (Translation mine)

> The real significance of the text—"Reality exists as one only and without a second (*advitīya*)"—may now be explained. The person who is considered *advitīya* is one who neither has, nor had, nor will have an equal or superior capable of being counted as second. How could a small fraction of the entire collection of entities that constitute His possessions and that are under His sway (*vibhava*)? The statement—"The paramount ruler of the Coḷa country now reigning is without a second in this world"—is intended to deny the existence of a ruler equal to him. It does not deny the existence of his servants, sons, consort, and so on. Similarly, the whole host of *devas*, *asuras*, and men, the four-faced Brahmā and the cosmic egg, form but a small part of a drop from the ocean of the greatness (*mahimā*) of the possessions (*vibhūti*) of the Lord Viṣṇu, who is the Lord of all, who is touched neither by sorrows (*kleśas*) nor by merits, demerits (*karma*), or (*vipāka*) and so forth, and who is the seat of the sixfold qualities of knowledge (*jñāna*) and the like, and whose greatness cannot even be conceived by the mind.[27]

If the reality is ultimately one, then Śrī-Lakṣmī must be inseparably one with the Lord. In the above statement, Yāmuna admits the existence of the physical universe and the *jīva*-s, etc., while at the same time seeing all as part of God's reality. Nevertheless, while all that is only a fraction of the Lord Viṣṇu, the divine consort, as referred to in the hymns, is seen as an equal match and inseparably one with him. The last part of the statement gives evidence to the fact that Yāmuna understands the Lord in terms of the Pāñcarātra categories. Yāmuna identifies the Lord as one who is the seat of the six-fold qualities of knowledge, etc., all of which means he accepts the Pāñcarātra notion of the Lord whose auspicious qualities are also shared by his divine consort. In that sense, the Lord and his consort are inseparably one.

In his overall philosophical position, Yāmuna rejects any duality in the ultimate reality and affirms that Brahman (the Lord Viṣṇu) is the only ultimate reality. It is interesting to note that even though Yāmuna speaks of the physical universe, the *jīva*-s, and gods (including Brahmā and Śiva) as only a small part of God's reality, he speaks of the divine consort as the equal match of the Lord and as sharing the same auspicious qualities, such as *jñāna*, etc. In the context of ritual he approaches Śrī-Lakṣmī for refuge and mediation. Thus, unless the ritual side and the doctrinal side are brought together, it is difficult to see what Yāmuna is really affirming. When the ritual dimension and the doctrinal dimension are placed together, Yāmuna seems primarily to see both Śrī-Lakṣmī and the Lord Viṣṇu as one single reality. In the context of ritual his hymns reflect the compassionate side of the Lord expressed through the divine consort. In his philosophical discussions, however, he affirms only one reality, namely, Brahman.

The following points may be identified in Yāmuna's overall position: 1) Yāmuna affirms that ultimately Brahman is the only reality; 2) Brahman is perceived as the "seat of sixfold qualities" such as *jñāna*, etc.; 3) the world and the *jīva*-s are also real, but only a small

---

27. Yāmuna, *Siddhitrayam* (*Samvit Siddhi*), pp. 177-78. (Translation mine)

part of God's being; 4) Śrī-Lakṣmī is not merely a small part of God's reality, but rather is placed above all other gods and entities; 5) she is depicted as an equal match of the Lord, sharing, as she does, the same auspicious qualities with him, and is thus comprehended in God's cosmic form. Both in the Pāñcarātra and in Yāmuna's hymns, God and his consort are described as mutually interdependent and inseparably one, forming harmonious parts of a whole. Her status is not like any other entity that is part of God: her being an equal match does not necessarily cause a duality in the ultimate reality since Yāmuna maintains in his philosophical discussions that there is only one reality in the ultimate sense. The relationship between God and his divine consort, in Yāmuna's view, seems to be quite in line with the Pāñcarātra tradition, which characterizes the mutual relation in terms of "*sāmarasyatā*."[28] It is perhaps because of her special relationship to the Lord that Yāmuna speaks of her as the mediatrix between God and his devotees. However, he does not use the term "*puruṣakāra*," a term used later by Piḷḷān, the disciple of Rāmānuja who wrote a commentary on *Tiruvāymoḷi* of Nammāḷvār.

Śrī-Lakṣmī in the Writings of Rāmānuja

Rāmānuja appears in the Śrīvaiṣṇava history at a crucial time when the worship of Lord Viṣṇu (Lord Nārāyaṇa/Raṅga, the deity of Śrīraṅgam temple) is threatened not only from outside of Hinduism (that is, the Jain tradition) but also from within—from the Śaiva tradition, which was certainly at loggerheads with the Vaiṣṇava faith. During the Vaiṣṇava and Śaiva conflict Rāmānuja was forced to flee from Śrīraṅgam which was part of the Coḷa kingdom, where he was spreading the Vaiṣṇava faith and worship quite vigorously.[29]

There is no doubt about the magnificent achievements of Rāmānuja in developing the Viśiṣṭādvaita philosophy, and establishing it on a firm Vedāntic ground. His *Śrībhāṣya*, *Gītābhāṣya*, *Vedārtha-saṃgraha*, *Vedāntasāra*, and *Vedāntadīpa* are all fine examples of his philosophical achievements. Nonetheless, his *Śaraṇāgatigadya*, *Śrīraṅgagadya*, and *Vaikuṇṭhagadya* (together called *Gadyatraya*) are basically statements of his profound faith in Lord Raṅga. His *Nityagrantha* is a significant manual of Vaiṣṇava rituals.

The biographical materials depict Rāmānuja as a devout worshipper of Lord Raṅga, whose worship gave him much happiness. In fact, as *Divyasūricaritam* describes, the Lord Raṅga himself commanded Rāmānuja to undertake his service at Śrīraṅgam, which he is said to have performed happily.[30] Further, in order to facilitate the

---

28. The word means "mutuality" (lit. *samarasa* = having equal feelings). See chap. 2 of this work.

29. *Divyasūricaritam*, 18:71-89; also see J. B. Carman, *Theology of Rāmānuja* (New Haven & London: Yale University Press, 1974), p. 44.

30. *Divyasūricaritam*, 17:79-80.

service of Lord Raṅga by all castes, including the Brāhmins and the Śūdras, he divided their ritual activities into ten respective subcategories.[31] He is said to have gone from place to place recruiting disciples and establishing the Vaiṣṇava faith and practice.[32]

According to *Divyasūricaritam*, for Rāmānuja the Lord who is obtained through *śruti* is none other than the Lord who is bedecked with his consort, Śrī-Lakṣmī,[33] who herself is merciful and who resides in Śeṣācala (Nāgendrālaya/Tirupati). Rāmānuja is thus depicted in the biographical materials not only as a Vedāntic teacher who spread the Viśiṣṭādvaita teaching but also as a profound devotee of Lord Raṅga, whose worship was of paramount significance for him. It was not merely the philosophical differences with the Advaitins that caused his exile from the Coḷa kingdom; what was at stake was his profound faith in Lord Raṅga over against Śiva. The Coḷa king, who enjoyed the support of the Śaiva priests, perpetuated the worship of Śiva, and it was in this context that Rāmānuja was demanded to recant his faith in Lord Raṅga and affirm the worship of Śiva.[34] Having fled to Nārāyaṇapuri (Melkote in Karnataka State) Rāmānuja established the worship of Lord Viṣṇu in the name of the local deity, Lord Saṃpatkumāra, and placed fifty two of his disciples at the service of the Lord.[35]

By focusing on Rāmānuja's philosophical achievements within the Vedānta tradition, traditional scholars as well as Western scholars have tended to downplay his deep involvement in reforming the ritual tradition of the Śrīvaiṣṇavas. This other side of Rāmānuja's intense devotional and ritual life needs to be explored in order to focus properly on his understanding of Śrī-Lakṣmī. Besides, in developing an understanding of Rāmānuja, the distinction between his philosophical and devotional works is misleading. Some scholars, such as Lester, have tended to view the devotional works as secondary when compared with the philosophical works. Such a distinction is not only artificial but gives a one-sided understanding of Rāmānuja. Unless one seriously doubts the authenticity of his authorship of those devotional works, there is no reason why one could not regard both the philosophical works and his devotional works as equally significant and mutually complementary. In other words, there is continuity between the philosophical works and the devotional works in the sense that the devotional works often provide the missing connections in our understanding of the tradition. They do not contradict the philosophical works but affirm the same teaching by providing the other dimension. In view of this, I have taken the philosophical works and the

31. Ibid., 17:84-85.
32. Ibid., 18:12, 20, 21, 36.
33. Ibid., 18:32.
34. Ibid., 18:72-74.
35. Ibid., 18:89; also see Carman, *Theology of Rāmānuja*, p. 44.

devotional works together, in order to gain a fuller understanding of the tradition.

Further, his deep involvement in transforming the Vaiṣṇava rituals must be seen in light of the influence of the Pāñcarātra tradition. When Rāmānuja interprets the metaphysical notions pertaining to *jīva*'s ultimate union with Brahman, he deals with a range of beliefs that have ritual significance. For instance, there is the belief that when a man dies either at night or during the southern progress of the sun, the soul does not reach Brahman. While interpreting the *sūtra* 4:2:18 and 19 in *Śrībhāṣya*, Rāmānuja rejects that belief system, and affirms that for a wise man, the one who has knowledge of Brahman, there is no difference, whether he dies at night or during the southern progress of the sun. Rāmānuja cites the example of Bhīṣma and points out that Bhīṣma postponed his death not to determine the proper time of dying but rather to "proclaim before the world the excellence of the season and thus to promote pious faith and practice."[36] Even the *Gītā* passages 8:23-27 do not set the proper time of dying but only mention the two paths—the path of light and darkness. Thus, Rāmānuja tries to reinterpret the ritual tradition in light of the Pāñcarātra.

The major systematic discussion that Rāmānuja provides in defense of the Pāñcarātra Āgamas is in his *Śrībhāṣya*,[37] which is in keeping with Yāmuna's *Āgamaprāmāṇya*. A closer look at his argument in the *Brahma Sūtras*, in the context of the *Adhikaraṇa*—"*vipratiśedhāt ca*"[38]—reveals that his basic understanding of Brahman is deeply influenced by the Pāñcarātra tradition. He incorporates the Pāñcarātra understanding of Lord Viṣṇu into the Upaṇiṣadic understanding of Brahman. Following the line of Yāmuna's defense of the Āgamas in his *Śrībhāṣya* 2:2:43, he makes the following points:

1) the Pāñcarātra doctrine manifestly rejects the idea that *jīva* originates (i.e., *jīva* has no beginning); 2) the Pāñcarātra doctrine is expounded "to facilitate the understanding of the sense of the Veda." The Lord Hari who is called Brahman in the Upaniṣads, out of mercy for his devotees, condensed the essential meaning of the Veda; 3) the worship of Mādhava (Lord Viṣṇu) must be performed by all castes;[39] 4) the Lord Nārāyaṇa, who is none other than Brahman himself, is the promulgator of the Pāñcarātra doctrine, and 5) this doctrine teaches the very nature of Brahman and the proper way of worshipping him. Rāmānuja points out that

> the Sāṅkhya explains the twenty five principles, the Yoga teaches certain practices and means of mental concentration, and the Āraṇyakas teach that all the subordinate principles have their true Self in Brahman, that the mental concentration enjoined in the Yoga is a mode of meditation on

---

36. Rāmānuja, *Śrībhāṣya*, trans. by George Thibaut, SBE. 48 (Delhi: Motilal Banarasidass, 1966), p. 742.
37. Rāmānuja, *Śrībhāṣya*, 2:2:40:43.
38. Ibid., 2:2:43. (Thibaut. p. 528).
39. Ibid., 2:2:43. (Thibaut. p. 528).

> Brahman, and that the rites and works which are set forth in the Veda are means to win the favor of Brahman—thus giving instruction as to Brahman's nature. Now all these elements, in their inward connection, are clearly set forth in Pāñcarātra by the highest Brahman, i.e., Nārāyaṇa himself.[40]

This passage illustrates Rāmānuja's open admission of Pāñcarātra teachings. Furthermore, he sees those teachings as being perfectly in harmony with the teachings of the Veda. The highest Brahman that he mentions is none other than Vāsudeva, who has for his body "the complete aggregate of the six qualities," namely, *jñāna, aiśvarya, vīrya, śakti, bala*, and *tejas*.[41] Inasmuch as Yāmuna also incorporated this doctrine in his *Saṃvit Siddhi*, Rāmānuja was continuing the same line of teaching in his *Śrībhāṣya*.

In light of his open defense of the teachings of the Pāñcarātra tradition and in light of the obvious presence of those teachings in both his philosophical and devotional works, they must be taken together in order to explore his understanding of Śrī-Lakṣmī.

Unlike Yāmuna, Rāmānuja did not write any specific work either in the form of poetry or prose in praise of Śrī-Lakṣmī. Nor did he make any explicit philosophical statements about the divine consort. Nevertheless, his own understanding on this subject can be gathered through several implicit statements that he makes about Brahman, who, for him, is Lord Raṅga himself. In taking those statements as keys to Rāmānuja's understanding of Śrī-Lakṣmī, my own assumption is that if Rāmānuja is largely in agreement with the Pāñcarātra understanding of Lord Viṣṇu, and perpetuated a ritual tradition that is in line with the Pāñcarātra tradition, then it is difficult to accept that Rāmānuja had ignored the place of Śrī-Lakṣmī in the context of ritual. His relative silence about Śrī-Lakṣmī in his works does not necessarily mean that he gave no importance to the role of Śrī-Lakṣmī in the ritual context. Neither traditional scholars nor Western scholars in this field have shown any evidence that Śrī-Lakṣmī is of no significance to Rāmānuja.

Carman rightly points out in his *Theology of Rāmānuja* that Rāmānuja makes scant references to Śrī-Lakṣmī in almost all his works. Apart from the references in his *maṅgalaśloka*-s at the beginning of his three commentaries on *Vedāntasūtra*-s (*Brahma Sūtra*-s), namely *Vedāntadīpa, Vedāntasāra*, and *Śrībhāṣya*, Rāmānuja mentions Śrī-Lakṣmī both in his *Bhagavadgītābhāṣya* and *Vedārthasaṃgraha*. In his *Gītābhāṣya*, Rāmānuja indeed makes some explicit statements on Śrī-Lakṣmī. However scanty these references are, it would be useful, nonetheless, to make an analysis of them in order to gain an insight into Rāmānuja's perception of Śrī-Lakṣmī. Furthermore, it would be important in order to judge how much scope there is for the later commentators in the tradition to develop the

---

40. Ibid., 2:2:43. (Thibaut. pp. 530-31).
41. Thibaut. p. 525.

doctrine of Śrī-Lakṣmī, a doctrine which became a sensitive point in their doctrinal reflections, especially during the thirteenth century.

To begin with, the references to Śrī-Lakṣmī in his three commentaries on *Brahma Sūtra*-s are rather indirect—"*Śrīnivāsa*" (the abode of Śrī-Lakṣmī);[42] "*Śrīmate*" (Viṣṇu, who is associated with *Śrī-Lakṣmī*);[43] "*Śriyaḥ kāntaḥ*" (*Nārāyaṇa*, the consort of *Śrī-Lakṣmī*).[44] In the *Gītābhāṣya*, Rāmānuja uses expressions such as "*Śriyaḥ Patiḥ*" (Lord of *Śrī-Lakṣmī*), "*Śrīvallabhaḥ*" (beloved of *Śrī-Lakṣmī*),[45] "*Śrīmat*" (*Nārāyaṇa*, who is associated with *Śrī-Lakṣmī*).[46] Then in the *Gītābhāṣya* 10:34, Rāmānuja's comment simply restates the verse as "*Śrīraham,*" etc.[47] In this verse Lord Viṣṇu identifies himself with Śrī-Lakṣmī, Kīrtī, Vāk, Smṛtī, Medhā, Dhṛtī, and Kṣamā, all of whom also figure in various Pāñcarātra texts as the female partners of Lord Viṣṇu. While avoiding any additional comment by way of explanation, Rāmānuja seems to accept and state the prevailing Śrīvaiṣṇava understanding of Śrī-Lakṣmī. In other words, the Pāñcarātra way of identifying Śrī-Lakṣmī with Lord Viṣṇu seems to have been accepted by Rāmānuja. Śrī-Lakṣmī essentially shares the same auspicious qualities and is considered inseparable from Lord Viṣṇu to the extent that they are no longer seen as two entities but form one reality. This seems to have been no accident in view of Rāmānuja's description of Lord Viṣṇu and of Śrī-Lakṣmī as possessing exactly the same auspicious qualities. In *Gītābhāṣya*, he describes the Lord as Śrīvallabhaḥ,

> ...the multitude of whose unlimited, unsurpassed, and innumerable auspicious qualities such as sovereignty and graciousness and whose nature, form, and (its) excellences and whose glory are dear to and worthy of Him and are eternal and faultless.[48]

Again in his *Śaraṇāgatigadya*, Rāmānuja uses exactly the same compound to describe Viṣṇu. Interestingly enough, at the beginning of *Śaraṇāgatigadya*, Rāmānuja also uses the very same compound to describe Śrī-Lakṣmī. Whereas the compound that describes the Lord begins with "*svābhimata,*" the compound that describes Śrī-Lakṣmī begins with the statement "*Bhagavannārāyaṇābhimata*" indicating that both these descriptions are in consonance with the Lord's mind.[49]

---

42. *Śrībhāṣya*, 1:1:1 (Thibaut. p. 3).
43. *Vedāntasāra*, 1:1:1.
44. *Vedāntadīpa (maṅgalaśloka)*.
45. *Gītābhāṣya*, 1:1 (trans. Sampatkumaran, p. 1).
46. Ibid., 7:1.
47. Ibid., 10:34.
48. Ibid., 1:1 (Sampatkumaran, p. 2).
49. *Gītābhāṣya*, 1:1—*svābhimatānurūpa nityaniravadyasvarūparūpa guṇavibhavaiśvarya śīlādy anavadhikātiśayāsaṃkhyeya kalyāṇaguṇa śrīvallabhaḥ*|| cf. *Śaraṇāgatigadya*. 7 where Rāmānuja uses the same qualities to describe Śrī-Lakṣmī—*bhagavannārāyaṇābhimatānurūpasvarūpa guṇavibhavaiśvaryaśīlādy*

Among the more philosophical works, it is in the *Vedārthasaṃgraha* that Rāmānuja makes much more explicit statements about Śrī-Lakṣmī. The first reference is to mention her as one of his two consorts.[50] The second announces Śrī-Lakṣmī as the "Queen of this world."[51] In his third reference, he speaks of the inseparability of the Lord and his consort. Lord Viṣṇu is described as eternally associated with Śrī-Lakṣmī (*Śrīvatsavakṣaḥ nityaśrīḥ*).[52] His fourth statement on Śrī-Lakṣmī suggests more than merely the idea of inseparability. He says:

> This Śrī, the Mother of the universe, is eternal and knows no separation from Viṣṇu. Even as Viṣṇu is all-pervading, she is all-pervading. When he becomes *deva*, she assumes the *deva* form. She makes her form conform to the form of Viṣṇu.[53]

In a typically Pāñcarātra fashion, Rāmānuja affirms that Śrī-Lakṣmī is the Mother of the universe and that she is all-pervading like her consort. In other words, Śrī-Lakṣmī is with the Lord both during the creative process as well as during the period of sustenance in her corresponding *vibhava* forms. She accompanies the Lord everywhere, not merely as another attribute but as one who shares in his auspicious qualities and as one who is the Mother of the universe. Here, Rāmānuja's idea of Śrī-Lakṣmī and Viṣṇu corresponds with that of the *Lakṣmī Tantra*. Rāmānuja's seems to be aware, though not through the *Lakṣmī Tantra*, of the general sense in which Viṣṇu and his consort are understood in the Pāñcarātra tradition. The older Pāñcarātra texts (for example, Jayākhya Saṃhitā) have already established that association between Viṣṇu and Śrī-Lakṣmī. Furthermore, if one accepts Schrader's dating of the *Ahirbudhnya Saṃhitā* (around 8th century C.E.), then even if Rāmānuja does not mention it, it is more than likely that with his scholastic backround he was certainly aware of texts that discussed the association of Viṣṇu with Śrī-Lakṣmī.

In Rāmānuja's thought, the Lord, accompanied by his consort, does not constitute a duality in God's reality. In fact, Rāmānuja affirms the multiplicity of reality within Brahman in that Śrī-Lakṣmī herself is a reality within Brahman who is Lord Viṣṇu himself. As far as her reality is concerned, Śrī-Lakṣmī is as real as any of the aspects of Brahman, namely, the *jīvas* in which God dwells as the *antaryāmin*.[54] But while

---

anavadhikātiśayāsaṃkhyeya kalyāṇaguṇagaṇāṃ padmavanālayāṃ bhagavatīṃ sriyaṃ. . . . Here "*svābhimata*" is replaced by "*bhagavannārāyaṇābhimata*."

50. Rāmānuja, *Vedārthasaṃgraha*, trans. S. S. Raghavachar (Mysore: Sri Ramakrishna Ashrama, 1968), p. 109, v. 135.

51. Ibid., p. 161, v. 202.

52. Ibid., p. 170, v. 216.

53. Ibid., pp. 170-71, v. 217—*nityaivesā jaganmātā viṣṇoḥ śrīḥ anapāyinī| yathā sarvagato viṣṇuḥ tathaiveyaṃ dvijottama|| devatve devadeveyaṃ manuṣatve ca mānuṣī|*

54. Ibid., p. 176, v. 225.

all the sentient and insentient entities constitute only a billionth part of Brahman who is their inner ruler,[55] Śrī-Lakṣmī pervades the whole universe just as the lord does. Furthermore, Rāmānuja affirms that

> ...sentient selves and non-sentient existents and the Lord are mutually distinct in their substantive nature and attributes and there is no mutual transportation of their characteristics.[56]

In other words, the lower reality does not share in the Lord's auspicious qualities and in his perfection. Even Brahmā is understood by Rāmānuja as a creature in whom *sattva, rajas*, and *tamas* predominate.[57] Thus, all creatures (gods, including Brahmā) are subject to material properties constituted by the three *guṇa*-s. But with regard to the divine consort, Rāmānuja thinks of her as the mother of the universe, who is not subject to the variegations of the three *guṇa*-s. The culmination of this understanding of Śrī-Lakṣmī may be noted in his *Śaraṇāgatigadya*. In the very first *śloka* he prays to Śrī-Lakṣmī in the following way:

> With no other help to resort to I seek Thee, Śrī Devī, full of all beneficent qualities, seated in a forest of lotus flowers. (Thou art) the refuge of all the helpless; (Thou art) my Mother, indeed the Mother of the whole world. The crowned divine queen of the Lord of the Devas, the pure and unsullied, never separated from the Lord. Thy self, Thine form, its qualities, and the most wonderful limitless innumerable collection of auspicious qualities of Thine, such as Greatness, Rulership, and high Virtues, all to His liking and worthy of the natural form and qualities of Bhagavān Nārāyaṇa.[58]

In this profound personal statement, Rāmānuja gives evidence to his own perception of Śrī-Lakṣmī as the mediatrix between the Lord and the devotee. He perceives her as the resort of all helpless people. Note that Rāmānuja refers to himself when he says that there is no other help except Śrī-Lakṣmī. The language of this prayer is very similar to the language in the Pāñcarātra Āgamas. Furthermore, the descriptions of Śrī-Lakṣmī in the prayer of Rāmānuja fit very well with the Pāñcarātra notions of Śrī-Lakṣmī. Here Rāmānuja undoubtedly regards Śrī not only as means (*upāya*), but also as the goal (*upeya*). It is significant to note that the later commentators, especially, Śrutaprakāśikācārya and Sudarśana Bhaṭṭa, who are respected by both sects of the Śrīvaiṣṇava community, certainly take this text in particular, and the entire *Śaraṇāgatigadya* in general, as propounding the doctrine of Śrī-Lakṣmī as the mediatrix. In fact, Śrutaprakāśikācārya takes the word "*astute,*" at the end of second

55. Ibid., p. 82, v. 105.
56. Ibid., p. 90, v. 117.
57. Ibid., p. 105, v. 132.
58. Rāmānuja, *Śaraṇāgatigadya* (with commentary by Śrutaprakāśikācārya) translation by K. Bhashyam (Madras: Viśiṣṭādvaita Pracāriṇī Sabha, third edition, 1970), pp. 1-2, v. 1.

śloka, as a word of blessing by Śrī-Lakṣmī.[59] Whether it comes from Śrī-Lakṣmī herself or not, the point is clear that according to the tradition, Rāmānuja felt the assurance of the divine consort. The Śrīvaiṣṇava community traditionally believes that the historical context for *Śaraṇāgatigadya* was set in Śrīraṅgam, where Rāmānuja is said to have performed *śaraṇāgati* before Lord Raṅga and his consort. It is believed that both the Lord and his consort spoke to Rāmānuja and granted his prayers. Rāmānuja's prayer to the divine consort has undoubtedly become a *locus classicus* for the later Śrīvaiṣṇava theologians to develop a more elaborate doctrine of Śrī-Lakṣmī as the mediatrix.

Again, while in *Vaikuṇṭhagadya* Rāmānuja speaks of Lord Viṣṇu as seated with Śrī-Lakṣmī (*śriyaṃ sahāsīnam*),[60] in his *Nityagrantha* he clearly provides a place for the worship of Śrī-Lakṣmī. Although in the ultimate metaphysical sense there is only one reality, namely, Brahman, in the context of ritual, however, Rāmānuja clearly sees the significance of the worship of Lord Viṣṇu along with his divine consort and a host of his attendants.[61] In his *Nityagrantha* he describes the ritual procedure in the following way:

> Then, [standing] on the right side of the Lord, [the devotee must] salute with "*auṃ Śrī*, salutation to Śrī." Thus Śrī is to be invoked and saluted. (Then standing) on the left side, [the devotee must] salute with "*auṃ bhūṃ*, salutation to Bhūdevī." Thus Bhūdevī is to be invoked, and there itself (that is, in the same direction) [the devotee must] salute with "*auṃ nīṃ*, salutation to Nīlā." Thus Nīlā is to be invoked . . . .[62]

Thus, the procedure continues and includes all the other aspects of the Lord—his ornaments—in a specific order that seems to indicate a particular ritual procedure. The order in which each aspect is worshipped seems to have some significance to Rāmānuja and provides us an insight into his perception of the divine consort, Śrī-Lakṣmī. The sequence of the ritual acts is indicated by Rāmānuja's use of "gerunds" (e.g., *śriyam āvāhya, praṇamya* etc.,).[63] One ritual act leads to the next one. The procedure, which Rāmānuja sets, begins with the Lord and then he mentions Śrī-Lakṣmī and others. Whether a clear hierarchy in the ritual procedure is intended by him is not very clear. What is clear, however, is that one ritual act follows the other in a systematic way. Even today, in the Śrīvaiṣṇava temples, the ritual order is meticulously followed.

Yāmuna and Rāmānuja—A Comparative Perspective

---

59. Ibid., p. 8.
60. Ibid., p. 13.
61. Rāmānuja, *Nityagrantha*, in *Rāmānujagranthamālā* (Kāñcīpuram: Granthamālā office, 1956), pp. 186-87.
62. Ibid., p. 184. (Translation mine).
63. Ibid., p. 184.

Having surveyed both Yāmuna's works and those of Rāmānuja, it will be useful to discuss some of the issues that have emerged. Both of them defended the Pāñcarātra Āgamas vehemently and saw themselves as part of the ritual tradition of the Pāñcarātra. While Yāmuna was basically involved in integrating the Pāñcarātra and the Vedānta, Rāmānuja, while developing the philosophical framework for the Śrīvaiṣṇava tradition, systematized the ritual tradition along the lines of the Pāñcarātra. In the midst of their philosophical achievements, both remained intense devotees of Lord Raṅga and his divine consort. Both performed their daily rituals in Śrīraṅgam before the divine couple. Although neither provides elaborate information on Śrī-Lakṣmī, they do, however, provide significant insights on which later theologians and commentators developed substantial doctrines of Śrī-Lakṣmī. Both Yāmuna and Rāmānuja make some explicit statements about Śrī-Lakṣmī in their devotional works.

As pointed out earlier in this chapter, taking the philosophical works as primary and the devotional works as secondary would not only be inadequate for developing an overall perspective of their teachings but also comes into conflict with their actual lives and practices, especially as remembered in the tradition. Biographical materials reveal that both Yāmuna and Rāmānuja followed and perpetuated the Pāñcarātra ritual tradition. Rāmānuja made special efforts to establish the Pāñcarātra ritual tradition in all the Śrīvaiṣṇava temples.

In view of their own lives and practices, both their philosophical as well as devotional works must be viewed together, to develop a coherent understanding of Śrī-Lakṣmī. Besides, there seems to be no conflict between the two types of works in their basic understanding of God. Both types of works understand God as possessing auspicious qualities, free from all imperfections. Both speak of God as transcendent (*para*) but at the same time accessible (*saulabhya*) to the devotees. In other words, the God of Yāmuna and Rāmānuja combines in himself the two natures, namely, the transcendent and the immanent (*paratva* and *saulabhya*). It is precisely because of this affirmation of unity in God's nature that scholars like Carman tended to see Śrī-Lakṣmī as problematic to the unity in God's nature. As a result of this, Carman relegates Śrī-Lakṣmī to the status of a divine attribute who accompanies God everywhere—in the divine realm as well as in the human. He argues:

> The later commentators have interpreted the prayer of surrender to Śrī at the beginning of the *Śaraṇāgatigadya* as clear indication of such a distinct function, one of which is suggested by the title "Mother." One first performs the act of surrender to Śrī and prays for her blessing on one's act of surrender to the Lord, Sudarśanasūri suggests, because the Lord is difficult to approach because he has a father's sternness. Śrī, on the other hand, is full of forgiving love (*vātsalya*) and is thus intercessor (*puruṣakāra*) for approaching the Lord. Sudarśanasūri also notes an alternative explanation; it is enjoined that we should first approach Śrī and secure surrender to the

> Lord. It is the first explanation that was generally accepted by the Śrīvaiṣṇavas of his own time and thereafter, and they therefore put a great deal of emphasis on the function of the goddess as the intercessor between men and God, as the forgiving mother who can persuade the sterner father to forgive.[64]

He further argues:

> It is unnecessary, however, to assume a distinction between a mother's easy forgiveness and a father's stern justice in order to explain the presence of a prayer to the Divine Consort at the beginning of the *Śaraṇāgatigadya*.[65]

Carman wants to locate both the polarities in Lord Viṣṇu himself. Further, he sees the Lord and his consort as separate entities and therefore finds it difficult to divide the two natures of God—God as the stern and just father and the divine consort as loving mother. But neither the Pāñcarātra Āgamas nor Yāmuna and Rāmānuja see the Lord and his divine consort as separate entities. Therefore, it is not difficult for them to see the role of Śrī-Lakṣmī as the mediatrix. In fact, one of the most important points made repeatedly by all the *ācārya*s, including Yāmuna and Rāmānuja, is the essentially inseparable nature of God and his divine consort.

While Rāmānuja emphasizes the reality of the divine consort,[66] he also equally emphasizes the point that she is "eternal and knows no separation from Viṣṇu."[67] In the Pāñcarātra, the Lord and his divine consort are mutually interdependent and form two aspects of the same reality. This interdependence is not like God's dependence on *jīvas* for his body but rather the two natures of God are in perfect equilibrium by virtue of mutual interdependence of God and his consort. In other words, in the ultimate metaphysical sense, there is only one reality, namely Brahman or Lord Nārāyaṇa, and that reality affirms multiplicity. While the sentient and nonsentient entities constitute only a billionth part of God, Rāmānuja makes it clear that Śrī-Lakṣmī, unlike even the creator Brahmā, pervades the whole universe and is always inseparable from him. That is to say, Śrī-Lakṣmī's reality is none other than God's essential reality because she, unlike the lower entities, shares in God's essential qualities and perfection. It is precisely for this reason that God and the divine consort are intrinsically one. When Rāmānuja calls her the "Mother of the universe"[68] and "Queen of this world,"[69] he does not radically separate her reality from God's essential reality. It is because Śrī-Lakṣmī is inseparable from Viṣṇu that Rāmānuja thinks of the Lord as both mother and father—(*mama*

64. Carman, *The Theology of Rāmānuja*, p. 240.
65. Ibid., p. 240.
66. Rāmānuja, *Vedāthārthasaṃgraha*, p. 176, v. 225.
67. Ibid., p. 171, v. 217.
68. Ibid., p. 171, v. 217.
69. Ibid., p. 176, v. 225.

mātaram, mama pitaram).[70] Further, it is because Śrī-Lakṣmī is inseparable from Viṣṇu that both *paratva* and *saulabhya* natures can fully exist in God. In affirming his *śaraṇāgati* in Śrī-Lakṣmī, Rāmānuja in no way contradicts his *śaraṇāgati* in Lord Nārāyaṇa. In fact, in his *Śaraṇāgatigadya*, Rāmānuja's *śaraṇāgati* is immediately followed by his *śaraṇāgati* to Lord Nārāyaṇa.[71] This means that in the ritual context Rāmānuja sees no contradiction in invoking Śrī-Lakṣmī prior to his *śaraṇāgati* to Lord Nārāyaṇa. It appears that Śrī-Lakṣmī is none other than the accessible nature of God worshipped in the form of God's consort in the ritual context.

It seems that it is on the basis of the inseparable nature of the relationship between God and his divine consort that both Yāmuna and Rāmānuja maintained the tension between the two natures of God. Thus, Śrī-Lakṣmī and the Lord together form the *śeṣin* side of the equation, and the sentient and nonsentient beings, including the gods and the attendants of God and his various other attributes, form the *śeṣa* side of the equation. Carman, however, is quite right in maintaining that

> Both Yāmuna and Rāmānuja wanted to guard against the Consort being conceived as the immanent power in material nature who is in some sense over against the transcendent Deity. Their successors in the Śrīvaiṣṇava tradition remained faithful to their teaching at this point, for they never accepted the Tantric view that the Consort of Nārāyaṇa was the active principle in Her own right, the Śakti.[72]

This, in effect, raises the question as to how much Yāmuna and Rāmānuja accepted from the Pāñcarātra Āgamic tradition, especially, in relation to Śrī-Lakṣmī. Both of them admit Brahman (Nārāyaṇa) as both the material as well as instrumental cause of the universe and assert that there is none who is greater than he. The Pāñcarātra Āgamas themselves in general do not contribute to the Tantric view of Śakti as the creative principle, although the *Lakṣmī Tantra* provides an explicit role for Śrī-Lakṣmī in the process of creation, maintenance, and dissolution. In other words, the *Lakṣmī Tantra*, with its clear emphasis on the role of Śrī-Lakṣmī, does not fully share the Tantric viewpoint but rather attempts to see her and Lord Viṣṇu as inseparable from each other and mutually interdependent. Śrī-Lakṣmī does not become an independent Śakti on her own. Her role is tied up with the role of Viṣṇu.

While incorporating the Āgamic elements, both Yāmuna and Rāmānuja accept the inseparable relation of the Lord and his consort, but do not admit Śrī-Lakṣmī as God's creative principle. Also, in the context of refuting the Sāṅkhya view of Pradhāna as the material

---

70. Rāmānuja, *Vaikuṇṭhagadya* in *Stotramālā* (Kāñcīpuram: Granthamālā Office, 1958), p. 13.

71. Rāmānuja, *Śaraṇāgatigadyam*, 1-2.

72. Carman, *The Theology of Rāmānuja*, p. 243.

cause of the universe, Rāmānuja, by quoting the Bhagavad Gītā 7:4-7, affirms that Brahman alone is the cause of the universe, both the material and instrumental cause, and that there is nothing higher than he. The Gītā passage (7:4-7) that he quotes says:

> Remember that all beings spring from this. I am the origin and the dissolution of the whole universe. Higher than I there is none else. All this is strung on me as pearls on a thread.[73]

By rejecting the view of the theistic Sāṅkhya that Pradhāna, superintended by the Lord, constitutes the material cause,[74] Rāmānuja also takes the precaution to protect his position from the Bhedābhedavādins (Madhva) who interpreted *prakṛti* as Śrī-Lakṣmī. In other words, for Rāmānuja, *prakṛti* (*pradhāna*) is neither the material cause nor is it to be interpreted as the female aspect of God as Madhva interpreted it. But, in some Śruti texts where *prakṛti* is declared to be the eternal and material cause of the world, Rāmānuja takes *prakṛti* in such passages as referring to Brahman himself.[75]

Thus, Śrī-Lakṣmī is not understood in terms of *prakṛti* but only as his divine consort who exists in him because he is her abode. Rāmānuja makes a distinction between the way Śrī-Lakṣmī is perceived and the way other attributes of God are perceived. He further makes a distinction to show that Śrī-Lakṣmī is certainly higher than the gods, and so forth. By elevating her to a place higher than the gods, he seems to favor a special place for the divine consort who mediates between God and his devotees. Attributing the accessible nature of God to the divine consort does not seem to be problematic to the unity in the divine nature, since Śrī-Lakṣmī is not seen by Yāmuna and Rāmānuja as a separate entity but as part of God's *śeṣin* side. Rāmānuja seems to follow closely the understanding of Yāmuna in affirming the inseparable relation of the Lord and his consort and the mediatorial role of the consort. By affirming the inseparable nature of the relationship between the Lord and his consort, both Yāmuna and Rāmānuja seem to be quite in line with the teaching of the Pāñcarātra Āgamas. Seetha Padmanabhan says:

> According to the Āgamas, Brahman and Śakti are inseparables (sic), and the two together form a single deity without losing their individuality.[76]

Although both Yāmuna and Rāmānuja do not use the term "*puruṣakāra*" as used by Piḷḷān,[77] the cousin of Rāmānuja, there are,

---

73. Rāmānuja, *Śrībhāṣya* (Thibaut), p. 359.

74. Ibid., p. 397 (*SB.* 1:4:23).

75. Ibid., p. 399.

76. Seetha Padmanabhan, *Pādma Saṃhitā*, pt. 2 (Madras: Pāñcarātra Pariśodana Parishad, 1982), Introduction, p. xiii.

77. Both Carman and Narayanan show that Piḷḷān first used the term "*puruṣakāra*." See Carman, *The Theology of Rāmānuja*, p. 240f; Vasudha

however, clear indications as to their perception of Śrī-Lakṣmī as the "mediatrix." In her historical study of all the early *ācārya*-s of the Śrīvaiṣṇava tradition, Nārāyanan points out, "Beginning with Yāmuna, all the *ācārya*-s also surrender themselves to Śrī and seek her compassion."[78] Furthermore, she points out that Yāmuna and Rāmānuja did not use the term "*puruṣakāra*" but agrees that the mediating aspect of Śrī-Lakṣmī is implied in their writings. She points out:

> A prayer to Śrī is at the beginning of the *Śaraṇāgatigadya*. Rāmānuja surrenders to Śrī but does not call her mediatrix. To the best of my knowledge that term "*Puruṣakāra,*" is used for the first time in the Śrīvaiṣṇava tradition by Rāmānuja's cousin Piḷḷān. Rāmānuja's surrender to and glorification of Śrī seem similar to Yāmuna's expressions in *Four Verses*. The only difference I note is that in *Four Verses* Yāmuna calls himself *prapanna*, or one who has already surrendered himself to Śrī, and in the *Śaraṇāgatigadya* we witness Rāmānuja in the act of surrendering. In *Four Verses* Yāmuna hails Śrī as the beloved of the Lord, and in the *Gadya* Rāmānuja describes her nature and qualities as being appropriate for and pleasing to the Lord. Rāmānuja asks Śrī to bless his surrender to the Lord; thus the mediating aspect of Śrī is implied in the *Gadyas* as it was in *Four Verses*.[79]

Narayanan's work also reiterates the point that both Yāmuna and Rāmānuja were influenced by the Pāñcarātra tradition. One of the most important Pāñcarātra categories that both of them explored is the category of "inseparability." Śrī-Lakṣmī is described by them as "*anapāyinī*." Thus, in exploring the understanding of Śrī-Lakṣmī in the works of Yāmuna and Rāmānuja, both the devotional works and the Pāñcarātra tradition need to be taken seriously. They cannot be seen as less significant than the philosophical works of the two *ācāryas*.[80] In my view, the contribution of both Yāmuna and Rāmānuja to our understanding of the Lord and his divine consort need to be based on two important aspects: 1) that both the older Pāñcarātra Āgamas (for example, *Sāttvata*, *Jayākhya*) and the later texts (for example, *Lakṣmī Tantra*) characterize Viṣṇu with the six auspicious qualities; 2) both the older and the later texts agree on the inseparabile nature of the Lord and his consort. This is to suggest that Śrī-Lakṣmī must essentially share in the divine auspicious qualities of the Lord. The

---

Narayanan, *The Way and the Goal: Expressions of Devotion in the Early Śrīvaiṣṇava Tradition* (Published jointly by the Institute for Vaiṣṇava Studies, Washington, D.C. and the Center for the Study of World Religions, Harvard University, 1987), p. 89.

78. Vasudha Narayanan, *The Way and the Goal*, p. 148.

79. Ibid., pp. 89-90.

80. Both van Buitenen and Narayanan agree that philosophical and devotional works cannot be separated. Carman's work also demonstrates that the two types of works cannot be separated. Cf. van Buitenen, *Rāmānuja's Vedārthasaṃgraha*, pp. 32-33. Also see Vasudha Narayanan, *The Way and the Goal*, p. 91.

Jayākhya Saṃhitā in fact mentions it quite clearly when it says that just as the sun's rays reflect in the ocean Lakṣmī (Kamalā) is always present in the Lord. (JS 6:77ff). The *Lakṣmī Tantra*, of course, unequivocally attributes the divine auspicious qualities to Śrī-Lakṣmī inasmuch as it does to the Lord. And both Yāmuna and Rāmānuja, by agreeing on the above two important aspects of the Lord and his consort, seem to indicate the equal status of the two both in the context of ritual as well as in the context of doctrine.

CHAPTER FIVE

ŚRĪ-LAKṢMĪ IN THE WRITINGS OF PARĀSARA BHAṬṬAR

In his *Śrī Viṣṇusahasranāma Bhāṣya,* Bhaṭṭar identifies himself as Raṅga, son of Śrīvatśaṅka, and a disciple of Rāmānuja.[1] The Śrīvaiṣṇava community believes that Bhaṭṭar was a gift to his parents by the divine couple and was, in fact, adopted by them and raised in the temple of Śrīraṅgam. He was a man of unusual poetic talents. He is said to have mastered all the *śāstra*-s at a very young age and made a strong impact on both his *guru*, Rāmānuja, and on his own students. His mastery over Tamil and Sanskrit languages was well demonstrated through his discourses. In fact, his *Bhāṣya* on *Śrī Viṣṇusahasranāma* is full of grammatical points that exhibit not only the depth of his knowledge of Sanskrit grammar but also his uncanny ability to interpret the tradition coherently and systematically. It is said that Rāmānuja himself was so deeply satisfied by his

> ... *jñāna, anuṣṭāna* and *pravacana* that he appointed Bhaṭṭar as the Pontifical Head of the Vaiṣṇavas in the presence of all his disciples.[2]

As in the case of his predecessors, there are conflicting views about his age. Some biographical accounts accord to him a long life of 100 years (1106-1206); other accounts place him at 97 (1078-1175); and some other accounts give a very short span of 28 years (1123-1151). While no definite information is available, Raghavan places Bhaṭṭar in the first half of the twelfth century of C.E.[3] We may say, nevertheless, with some certainty that he was a younger contemporary of Rāmānuja.

Bhaṭṭar is said to have written nine works: 1) *Śrī Viṣṇusahasranāma Bhāṣya* (also called *Bhagavadguṇadarpaṇa*); 2) *Aṣṭaślokī*; 3) *Śrī Raṅga Aṣṭaka*; 4) *Śrī Raṅgarājastava*; 5) *Śrī Guṇaratnakośa*; 6) *Tattvaratnākara*; 7) *Nitya*; 8) *Ādhyātma-khanḍadvaya*; and 9) *Lakṣmīkalyāṇa*. He also wrote two works in

---

1. Parāśara Bhaṭṭar, *Śrī Viṣṇusahasranāma Bhāṣya*, with translation in English by H. Srinivasa Raghavan (Madras: Śrī Viśiṣṭādvaita Pracāriṇi Sabha, 1983), p. 2—"*Bhāṣya upodgāta,*" *śloka* 4. In the same *śloka,* Bhaṭṭar alludes to the fact that "Parāśara Bhaṭṭar" is the title given to him by Lord Raṅga of Śrīraṅgam.

2. Ibid., p. xi.

3. Ibid., p. ix. Vasudha Narayanan seems to accept the short age; See her, *The Way and the Goal: Expressions of Devotion in the Early Śrīvaiṣṇava Tradition (*Institute for Vaiṣṇava Studies, Washington, D.C. and Center for the Study of World Religions, Harvard University, 1987), p. 131.

Maṇipravāḷa (a form of Tamil modified to write Sanskrit)—one is an exposition on a chapter in Varahapurāṇa, and the other is a commentary on the verse of Tirumaṅgai Āḷvār that is called "*Tiruneḍum Taṇṭakam.*"[4] Of the above eleven works only the first five are available in full, the rest being extant only in fragments.[5] For the purposes of this study I will be using mainly the *Śrī Viṣṇusahasranāma Bhāṣya*, *Śrī Guṇaratnakośa*, and *Aṣṭaśloki* in which he deals with Śrī-Lakṣmī quite substantially. *Śrī Viṣṇusahasranāma Bhāṣya* is a commentary on the thousand names of Lord Viṣṇu. *Śrī Guṇaratnakośa* is a hymn of praise to Śrī-Lakṣmī, and *Aṣṭaśloki* contains eight *śloka*-s on the meaning of the three *mantras*, namely, *Aṣṭākṣara Mantra*, *Dvaya Mantra*, and *Carama Śloka*.[6] Unlike Yāmuna and Rāmānuja, Bhaṭṭar is very clear and unambiguous about his understanding of Śrī-Lakṣmī. His philosophical position is presented coherently and clearly in his *Bhāṣya* on *Śrī Viṣṇusahasranāma*.

Among the disciples of Rāmānuja, Piḷḷān and Bhaṭṭar stand out uniquely for their contributions to the ongoing interpretive process of the Śrīvaiṣṇava tradition. Piḷḷān, who was also a cousin of Rāmānuja, wrote a commentary on the *Tiruvāymoḷi* of Nammāḷvār[7] and was the first of the *ācarya*-s who explicitly stated the position of Śrī-Lakṣmī by calling her "mediatrix" (*Puruṣakāra*). Although a study of Piḷḷān's work would further illuminate the subject matter in this work, in view of the fact that I limit the present study to the Sanskritic side of the tradition, I will confine myself to the writings in Sanskrit and pursue the study of Piḷḷān's material at a later time in another study. For the purposes of this chapter I will only consider the Sanskrit writings of Bhaṭṭar. His works reflect the views of Piḷḷān, especially, on the divine consort. Also, by virtue of the fact that Bhaṭṭar was the chief priest in the temple of Śrīraṅgam and held a unique position in the community, expounding his views on Śrī-Lakṣmī will certainly reflect the general understanding of the community during his time and after Rāmānuja.

Some of the issues that I shall be focusing on in this chapter are: 1) the question of Śrī-Lakṣmī as "mediatrix;" 2) the question of the nature of her relationship to Lord Viṣṇu; 3) the question as to how far Bhaṭṭar's thought was continuous with that of his predecessors; and, 4) to what extent Bhaṭṭar incorporated Pāñcarātra views in his interpretation of Śrī-Lakṣmī. Before expounding on the views of Bhaṭṭar it would be useful to look at the sources of his understanding of the tradition in general and of Śrī-Lakṣmī in particular.

---

4. *Viṣṇusahasranāma Bhāṣya*, trans. H. Srinivasa Raghavan, pp. xvi ff.

5. Ibid., p. xv.

6. Note that in the Śrīvaiṣṇava ritual tradition the *carama śloka* of the *Bhagavad Gītā* (18:65) is treated as an important *mantra*. It is of great significance in developing the notion of *prapatti mārga* in Rāmānuja's *Gītābhāṣya*.

7. Rāmānuja is said to have entrusted to Piḷḷān the responsibility of writing a commentary on *Tiruvāymoḷi* of Nammāḷvār to keep his promise to his predecessor, Yāmuna, at the time of the latter's death.

Sources of Bhaṭṭar

Bhaṭṭar certainly inherited a rich tradition from his predecessors, namely, Yāmuna and Rāmānuja, and from his own father, Śrīvatśaṅka. His works are largely in the nature of hymns (*stotra*-s). His commentary on *Śrī Viṣṇusahasranāma* is, nonetheless, a coherent articulation of his theological position. In his commentary, he largely draws his material from the Purāṇic and epic sources. It is from the time of Bhaṭṭar that the Purāṇic and epic materials begin to play a major role in shaping the interpretive process of the tradition. By writing a commentary on *Śrī Viṣṇusahasranāma*, he affirms the significance of *Mahābhārata* as an authoritative scripture. He quotes various Purāṇic texts, such as *Bhaviṣyat Purāṇa*, *Matsya Purāṇa*, *Viṣṇu Purāṇa*, and *Mārkaṇḍeya Purāṇa* to stress the significance of the *Mahābhārata*. His commentary on *Śrī Viṣṇusahasranāma* must also be seen in light of the already existing commentary by Śaṅkara, who gives an Advaitic understanding of the same text. Thus, Bhaṭṭar's commentary, at least in terms of the Śrīvaiṣṇava tradition, comes as a corrective to Śaṅkara's interpretation while at the same time articulating the Śrīvaiṣṇava position.

The significance of the *Mahābhārata* for Bhaṭṭar may be seen in the following:

> In the *Mahābhārata* itself, it is stated that a Brāhmin who is not versed in this Itihāsa but only in the four Vedas, Vedāṅgas, and Upaniṣads is not learned.[8]

He also stresses that the Vedas must be understood through the Itihāsas and the Purāṇas. The basic reason for accepting the *Mahābhārata* as central to his theological position is that the text contains the thousand names of Lord Viṣṇu and the recitation of those names has crucial ritual significance for Bhaṭṭar. For Bhaṭṭar, the text not only affirms the supremacy of Viṣṇu but lays great emphasis on the path of devotion. The most effective way to approach the Lord is to recite the thousand names of God. He also accepts the significance of the *Rāmāyaṇa* and quotes extensively from it while interpreting the thousand names of God.

By his greater dependence on the epic material, namely, the *Mahābhārata* and the *Rāmāyaṇa*, in interpreting the tradition, Bhaṭṭar moves in a remarkably new direction, taking the tradition from the hitherto Vedāntic framework to the epic framework. Thus, he provides a popular appeal by making the tradition more easily understandable and accessible to the ordinary devotees. It must, however, be pointed

---

8. *Viṣṇusahasranāma Bhāṣya (*trans. H. Srinivasa Raghavan), p. 7.—*yo vidyāt caturo vedān sāṅgopaniṣadān dvijāḥ| na cākhyānamidaṃ vidyāt naiva sā syāt vicakṣunaḥ||*

out, as Narayanan points out in her work,[9] that his interpretation is continuous with that of his predecessors. He does not depart from his predecessors' essential teachings.

His interest in the epic material must also be seen in light of the devotional elements that those texts present. Furthermore, much of his understanding of Lord Viṣṇu and his divine consort, Śrī-Lakṣmī, though rooted in the Pāñcarātra Āgamas, finds concrete expression in the epics. His understanding of Śrī-Lakṣmī is derived largely from the epic character of Sītā in the *Rāmāyaṇa*. Both in his *Śrī Viṣṇusahasranāma Bhāṣya* and in *Guṇaratnakośa* the figure of Sītā becomes a major theme. It will be worth exploring the range of images of Śrī-Lakṃī that he develops.

Sītā in the Rāmāyaṇa

For Bhaṭṭar, Sītā is synonymous with Śrī-Lakṣmī. Introducing his *Guṇaratnakośa*, he points out that he is attempting to praise the glory of Śrī-Lakṣmī that Brahmā and other gods themselves began a long time ago at the beginning of creation: "Therefore we desire to praise your glory with appropriate hymns that the former Brahmā, and other gods long ago began."[10] For him, Sītā is none other than Śrī-Lakṣmī who is discussed in the Śruti-s, Itihāsa-s, and the Purāṇa-s by the sages of the past.[11]

Further, he perceives Śrī-Lakṣmī in very concrete terms and refers to her concrete acts of compassion. He speaks of the necessity for Śrī-Lakṣmī to become incarnate with her corresponding forms along with the Lord, and refers to her as the one who protected Vibhīṣaṇa, the brother of Rāvaṇa.[12] The significance of the concreteness of the divine reality is further seen in his conception of Lord Viṣṇu in the form of Rāma. He constantly recounts the events related to Sītā in the *Rāmāyaṇa*—that she left the supreme abode to live in the forest, to go through all the shame, for the sake of the devotees:

> Mother (*Jananī*), the eternal helper of the Ruler (*Netā*), you came here into the world to save us, and received much rejection (hostility) from those who are deaf to the knowledge of your glory. Having left the delicate abode of the jasmines you were born and lived in the forest on hard stones. The freedom of both of you cannot be controlled. Have mercy on (us).[13]

---

9. Vasudha Narayanan, *The Way and the Goal,* chap. 6.

10. Parāśara Bhaṭṭar, *Guṇaratnakośa,* v. 5. *yadyāvat tavavaibhavaṃ taducitastotrāya dūrespṛhā stotum ke vayamity adaś ca jagṛhuḥ prāñco viriñcadāyaḥ*| (Translation mine)

11. Ibid., vv. 10 and 14.

12. Ibid., v. 50.

13. Ibid., v. 53. *netur nityasahāyinī janani! nastrātuṃ tvamatragatā; loke tvanmahimāvobodha badhire prāptā vimardaṃ bahu*| *kliṣṭaṃgrāvasu mālatīmṛdupadaṃ viśliṣya vāsovane; jāto dhikkaruṇaṃ dhigastu yuvayos svātantryam atyaṅkuśam*|| (Translation mine).

He identifies Ayodhya, the capital city of Rāma, with Śrī-Lakṣmī's supreme abode.[14] He says:

> The ruler (Lakṣmī) who commands and bestows grace, who is fearful and soft, and who divides the fruit, who is said to be in the undefeated Ayodhya, is known as seated beyond the heavens. O Lakṣmī in the house of the Lord of Śrīraṅgam, the people know the capital of both of you by the feelings, by the thick, impenetrable places of enjoyment, and by the streams of nectar.[15]

Furthermore, that very Ayodhya is identified with the town of Śrīraṅgam where the Lord and his consort are eternally present, for the sake of the devotees, as Lord Raṅga and Raṅganāyakī.[16] Time and again, he dwells on the concrete forms of Śrī-Lakṣmī in the house of Lord Raṅga. In his *Śrī Raṅgarājastava,* Viṣṇu is presented as Lord Raṅga, and in his *Guṇaratnakośa*, Śrī-Lakṣmī is presented as Raṅganāyakī. Thus, there is a gradual concretization of Śrī-Lakṣmī—from the one who dwells in the eternal and supreme abode of Viṣṇu (*Vaikuṇṭha*) to the one who dwells in the forest (in the *Rāmāyaṇa*) and further down to Śrīraṅgam in the house of Lord Raṅga.

This down-to-earth image of Śrī-Lakṣmī is very crucial for him as a devotee who constantly rejoices in serving at her feet and as one who considers himself to be the dust of her feet.[17] In other words, his devotion to Śri-Lakṣmī is not simply intellectual but very real and concrete, since she is present before him in very concrete form as Maithilī and Raṅganāyakī. She is not only the one who contemplates on the Vedānta (*vedāntatattvacintām*),[18] but also the one who dwells on the chest of the Lord and, more importantly, dwells in the house of Lord Raṅga in Śrīraṅgam (*śrīraṇgadhāmamaṇimañjarī*).[19] On the one hand, he thinks of her in transcendental categories, but on the other, he praises her in very concrete forms. He pays obeisance to she who supervises the entire creative process through her sidelong glances: "Salutations to Śrī, who oversees the whole process of creation of sentient and nonsentient beings by her purposeful and consenting glances."[20] He thinks of her as the ruler of the universe;[21] he perceives her as the source of pleasure, thought, learning, courage, plenty and

---

14. Ibid.; v. 23.
15. *Viṣṇusahasranāma Bhāṣya*, trans. L. Venkataratnam Naidu (Tirupati: Tirupati Devasthanams, 1965), p. 49, v. 16.
16. The process of concretization of Lord Viṣṇu and his consort as Raṅga and Raṅganāyakī reinforces the Pāñcarātra concept of *Arcā*, one of the five manifestations of God. In the context of Śrīvaiṣṇava ritual tradition which is derived basically from the Pāñcarātra Āgamas the *Arcā* form of God becomes extremely significant. Even the Āḷvārs also paid great attention to the *Arcā* form of God. Bhaṭṭar speaks about it in *Viṣṇusahasranāma Bhāṣya*, v. 640.
17. *Guṇaratnakośa*, v. 61.
18. Ibid., v. 4.
19. Ibid., v. 47.
20. Ibid., v. 1.
21. *Viṣṇusahasranāma Bhāṣya*, v. 610.

perfection,[22] and yet he says that that very Śrī-Lakṣmī rejoices in the house of Lord Raṅga, protecting the devotees.

By locating the Lord and his consort in the epic stories and perceiving them in concrete forms in the temple of Śrīraṅgam, Bhaṭṭar develops a profound sense of immediacy and accessibility to them.[23] In almost all his works the epics and the temple of Śrīraṅgam become the hub around which his poetic theology revolves. By combining his concern for the epic-centered devotion on the one hand with a concern for temple-centered worship on the other, he draws together the Āḻvār tradition and the Pāñcarātra tradition, and provides a unique synthesis of the two streams.

Śrī-Lakṣmī as Mediatrix

Bhaṭṭar's contemporary, Piḷḷān, without any ambiguity, calls Śrī-Lakṣmī "mediatrix" (*Puruṣakāra*).[24] Bhaṭṭar, however, does not use the term in any of his *stotras* or in the *Śrī Viṣṇusahasranāma Bhāṣya*, except in his comment on Tirumaṅgai Āḻvār's verse, i.e. *Tiruneḍum Taṇṭakam,* written in the Maṇipravāḷa language.[25] Nevertheless, all his works clearly show that he understands Śrī-Lakṣmī not only as the Universal Mother but also as the "mediatrix" between the Lord and his devotees. The word "mother" occurs in his works several times when he refers to the divine consort. Some of the words he uses are "*aṃbā*," "*mātā*," and "*jananī*."[26]

In his *Śrī Viṣṇusahasranāma Bhāṣya*, while commenting on the epithet "*Mādhava*" of Lord Viṣṇu, he lays out his position quite clearly by quoting various texts such as *Viṣṇu Purāṇa*, *Brahma Purāṇa*, *Śrī Lakṣmīsahasranāma* and others. It will be useful to look at the entire passage in order to gain an insight into Bhaṭṭar's perception of Śrī-Lakṣmī. He comments:

> He is so called (*Mādhava*) because He is the Lord of Śrī or Lakṣmī. "Śrī, the consort of Viṣṇu, rules the Universe. Hṛī and Lakṣmī are his wives." Like her personality, her form which is eternally pure, her riches which are supreme and immeasurable, her Universal Motherhood, her natural relation with Bhagavān, her eternity and imperishability are explained in detail in the *Śāstras* dealing with the Supreme Truth. In Vedic literature, Śrī Sūktam,

---

22. *Guṇaratnakośa*, v. 17.

23. *Viṣṇusahasranāma Bhāṣya*, v. 640.

24. *Puruṣakāra*—literally means human effort, as opposed to the divine effort or fate. But in the context of the Śrīvaiṣṇava tradition, the term has taken on a technical meaning in the sense of a mediator. Śrī-Lakṣmī provides the effort on behalf of human beings in the process of their salvation. Thus, she replaces human effort by her involvement, and becomes the mediator between God and human beings.

25. I did not have access to *Tiruneḍu Taṇṭakam* of Bhaṭṭar. But see Vasudha Narayanan, *The Way and the Goal*, p. 140.

26. In *Guṇaratnakośa* the word "*mātā*" occurs 6 times, "*aṃbā*" 3 times, and "*jananī*" 3 times.

Śraddhā Sūktam, Medhā Sūktam, Uttara Nārāyaṇam, and Kausītakī Brāhmaṇam etc. In *Viṣṇu Purāṇa* "She is Eternal, Universal Mother, the wife of Viṣṇu and Imperishable. O! Great Brāhmin, as Viṣṇu is pervading the entire Universe so also She is pervading." After this the churning of the ocean for ambrosia and the praise by Indra, etc., are described in detail. In the *Brahma Purāṇa* "that Śakti is invincible, terrible, and is considered as the Śakti of Viṣṇu. She is supreme, endowed with manifold forms and remains in the lotus-like hearts of all beings of the universe. She is the mother of *mantras*, the mother of the universe. She is eternal." She is again styled as "goddess, dark as the mixed collyrium, colorless like the void space." "Similarly she is styled the only Supreme Śakti and is the receptacle of the compassion of the Supreme. She is the embodiment of the six qualities like knowledge etc. His only Śakti, Lakṣmī, moves as his second. She is eternal and moves about with Him, taking all forms, high and low. She has innumerable names and is the Nāyikā or Queen of the wheel of Śakti. She remains pervading this entire universe of moving and unmoving." She is eternal Queen of Bhagavān Vāsudeva, the Lord of the universe, with infinite riches and the embodiment in full of all six auspicious qualities (knowledge, power, etc.,). "She remains pervading the entire universe as the very embodiment of all Śaktis. She is endowed with all prosperity and qualities and is always the consort of the Supreme Viṣṇu. In short she is the source of all Śaktis, beside being the finer element of all of them." You can gather some more particulars from "*Lakṣmīsahasra*" to supplement what has been stated above. From this book, "All the Śaktis are the emanation of Śrī or Lakṣmī, always pervade the entire universe, and remain in it as the prime cause under the ordinance of Śrī. Therefore, Śrī, the Universal Mother and the beloved of *Acyuta*, is highly pleased, and the Śaktis of Śrī themselves well pleased bestow prosperity pleasing to Him." The same topic is detailed at length in Vaiṣṇava Smṛti and *Dharma Śāstras* Even the *Rāmāyaṇa* corroborates the same idea. The entire poem *Rāmāyaṇa* is nothing but the mighty story of Sītā. "The Supreme gets His Supreme nature by virtue of His association with Śraddhā or Lakṣmī." This is the secret truth about Śrī.[27]

In the above passage, Bhaṭṭar affirms: 1) the universal motherhood of Śrī-Lakṣmī; 2) that she is spoken of in the Vedic literature (*Śrī Sūkta*, et al.); 3) that she is the consort of Lord Viṣṇu and pervades the whole universe; 4) that she is the embodiment of six auspicious qualities such as *jñāna, aiśvarya*, etc., referred to in the Pāñcarātra Āgamas; 5) that she is the receptacle of the Lord's compassion; 6) that she moves about always with him taking corresponding forms; 7) that she is the life-giving Śakti of the Lord and source of all Śaktis and *mantra*-s; 8) and finally, he closes with the comment connecting the Lord's supremacy with Śrī-Lakṣmī.

Although Bhaṭṭar seems to have depended for his material on the *Lakṣmīsahasranāma*, the passage reflects the Pāñcarātra Āgama texts very closely. The language of the *Lakṣmīsahasranāma* and the *Lakṣmī Tantra* seem so close that the notions related to Śrī-Lakṣmī seem to be from the same origin. In other words, Bhaṭṭar's conception of Śrī-Lakṣmī seems to have heavily depended on the Āgamic notions.

27. *Viṣṇusahasranāma Bhāṣya* (trans. L.Venkataratnam Naidu), pp. 66-67.

Bhaṭṭar's appropriation of Āgamic notions becomes even more evident in another passage that he quotes in expounding the name of the Lord, "*Lakṣmīvān.*" While Rāmānuja clearly made attempts to avoid the identification of Śrī-Lakṣmī with Prakṛti, Bhaṭṭar, in his comment on "*Lakṣmīvān,*" includes the following passage, which is similar to the one found in the *Lakṣmī Tantra*:

> During my embrace with *devī* (Lakṣmī) I consigned to her playfully the *mantra* known as *Dvaya*, thereby making plain that she is without a beginning like Myself and Prakṛti. This Prakṛti is entwined with my hands and I with Prakṛti's (hands). I am Her follower and Her form rests in Me." She is Prakṛti the Universal Mother and Śrī.[28]

Apart from this one instance, I did not come across any other insance where Bhaṭṭar makes such an identification of Śrī-Lakṣmī and Prakṛti. Therefore, it is perhaps superfluous to draw the conclusion that Bhaṭṭar makes such an identification. Even in the above comment he speaks of Śrī-Lakṣmī as different from Prakṛti and yet makes a statement that identifies Śrī-Lakṣmī with Prakṛti. One way of overcoming this seemingly inconsistent position is, perhaps, to see this passage in light of the other passage to which I referred earlier. In that passage, Bhaṭṭar clearly speaks of the ultimate reality in two aspects, namely, Lord Viṣṇu and his Śakti (Śrī-Lakṣmī). Since the Śakti of the Lord is often spoken of as Prakṛti even in the Pāñcarātra Āgama texts, Bhaṭṭar refers to the same idea. For Bhaṭṭar, this dual aspect of the ultimate reality is not problematic because he affirms the inherent oneness of the Lord and his consort in spite of the ostensible dual roles they seem to be playing at the functional level.[29]

In very clear terms, he speaks of the Lord as the Universal Father and Śrī-Lakṣmī as the Universal Mother. It is through his divine consort that the Lord bestows his compassion and blessings on the *jīva*-s. Commenting on the epithet of Lord Viṣṇu—"*Samitiñjaya*"—he says:

> It is through Lakṣmī that the Universal Father who, like a father, bestows happiness, and conquers the trouble of *jīvātmas* about the dispute whether they are servants or not.[30]

This mediatory role of Śrī-Lakṣmī is upheld by Bhaṭṭar because he understands her as "receptacle of the Lord's compassion." Time and again he dwells on the theme of Śrī-Lakṣmī's compassion—he speaks

28. Ibid., p. 114; cf. *Lakṣmī Tantra*, 11:38.

29. This idea of the essential oneness of Viṣṇu and his consort is also reflected in *Śrīstava* of Kureśa. It is conceivable that Bhaṭṭar is simply following the line of interpretation that has already been established (whether implicitly or explicitly) before him by the Śrīvaiṣṇava teachers. Cf. Kureśa's *Śrīstava*, v.1., and also see my footnote 2 in my appendix 2.

30. Venkataratnam Naidu, op.cit., p. 114, v. 364.

of her as the Mother full of compassion,[31] her looks overflowing with compassion,[32] she is excellent in generosity, compassion, and affection for those who resort to her[33]—and so on.

At the beginning of *Śrī Guṇaratnakośa* Bhaṭṭar, speaks of Śrī-Lakṣmī as his refuge and takes refuge in her. He invokes her grace to complete the hymn of praise that he is about to write. He further states that Śrī-Lakṣmī herself collects all the hymns by her sweet grace: "Lakṣmī, the Queen of the Lord of Śrīraṅgam, herself collects our sayings by her sweet grace."[34]

In appealing to Śrī-Lakṣmī's mediatory role, Bhaṭṭar quite frequently uses metaphors such as "queen" (*mahiṣī*), "lover" (*priyā),* "beloved" (*praṇayinī*), and "companion" (*sakhī*), in relation to Lord Viṣṇu, indicating a special privilege that she holds in order to be able to intercede between the Lord and his devotee. He speaks of Sītā who protected and enabled Vibhīṣaṇa to join Rāma. Bhaṭṭar further invokes her to protect him through her "sudden (ungrounded) forgiveness" (*kṣāntiḥ tava ākasmiki*).[35] He does not use the conventional term "*nirhetuka kṛpa,*" but his idea of "sudden (ungrounded) forgiveness" seems to carry the same force of meaning. By becoming conscious of himself as a great sinner (*mahā āgasaḥ*) Bhaṭṭar seeks Śrī-Lakṣmī's "sudden (ungrounded) forgiveness." This seeking of Śrī-Lakṣmī's forgiveness need not be construed as an act in itself because in the succeeding *śloka* he speaks of envisioning the Lord Hari. In other words, Śrī-Lakṣmī's intervention is seen as a means to envision Viṣṇu. He says that "on account of your relationship may we see Hari."[36] This is to suggest that Bhaṭṭar seeks Śrī-Lakṣmī's forgiveness as a means of access to the Lord's presence. For him she is such a mother who, having forgotten their sins, accepts the devotees by appropriate means: "You are that Mother who, having forgotten (our sins), makes us your own by appropriate means."[37] In this sense, Bhaṭṭar perceives Śrī-Lakṣmī as the eternal helper of the Lord (*netur nityasahāyinī*).[38]

---

31. *Guṇaratnakośa,* v. 38.
32. Ibid., v. 41.
33. Ibid., v. 57.
34. Ibid., v. 1, 7. *sūktiṃ samagrayatu naḥ svayameva lakṣmīḥ; śrīraṅgarāja-mahiṣī madhuraiḥ kaṭākṣaiḥ*| (Translation mine).
35. Ibid., v. 50.
36. Ibid., v. 51.
37. Ibid., v. 52. *tvamucitair upāyair vismārya svajanayasi mātā tadasi-naḥ;*(Translation mine).
38. Ibid., v. 53.

Lord Viṣṇu as the Ultimate Reality

Bhaṭṭar's conception of Śrī-Lakṣmī as the mediatrix between the Lord and his devotees cannot be fully explained without expounding his understanding of the Lord and his divine consort. Without any ambiguity Bhaṭṭar upholds the supremacy of the Lord. The Lord is the only object of attainment. Having made references to Yāmuna and Rāmānuja, he quotes his own father (Śrīvatśaṅka) saying,

> My revered father says "We arrive at the decisive conclusion that thou art the Supreme Lord through hundreds of Vedic texts relating to the truth and its reality, through Smṛtis and other similar texts, through *Sāttvika* and good Purāṇas dealing with the Supreme Truth, and even through great men who have realised the Supreme." "Great men confirm thy overlordship by thy supremely beautiful form, thy great lustre, by thy various and notable actions in the *Avatāras*, by thy unique symbols and by other undeniable things."[39]

Further, explicating Viṣṇu's epithet "*bhūtabhavyabhāvāt prabhu,*" Bhaṭṭar says, "He (Viṣṇu) is the Lord of all that exists in all the three periods of time, present, past and future, i.e., the over-lord, the Master."[40] Speaking of the abode of Lord Viṣṇu he says:

> In Ṛg Veda, this *sthāna* or *loka* is the prior cause of all effect, the superior objective of all words, the highest seat. In *Araṇya Parva* it is declared "who is described as the external prime cause of all beings, the divinity which knows no beginning or end, the Lord Nārāyaṇa, the Supreme abode is far more brilliant than the *loka* of Brahmā."[41]

Furthermore he says:

> Addressing Agastya, Bhagavān says: "See this world which is mine and which is not seen by the Vedas. For your benefit this *loka* has been shown to you."[42]

By pointing out that even the Vedas did not perceive the abode of the Lord but only the devotee of Bhagavān, Bhaṭṭar places the path of devotion above Vedic knowledge. Both in his introduction and also in the first few passages, while commenting on various epithets of Viṣṇu in his *Śrī Viṣṇusahasranāma Bhāṣya*, he tries to emphasize the efficacy of the path of devotion, especially by singing and meditating on the thousand names of God.

For Bhaṭṭar, both the object of attainment (*upeya*) and the means of attainment (*upāya*) are the Lord himself. He considers devotion to

---

39. Venkataratnam Naidu, op.cit., p. 30, vv. 45, 48; also see p. 57, v. 43, pp. 58, 59.

40. Ibid., p. 40, cf. vv. 663, 665, 669; also see pp. 159-60.

41. Ibid., p. 48.

42. Ibid., p. 48.

the Lord as the best and the highest means. For him, service (*sevā*) and meditation (*upāsana*) are synonymous with *bhakti*. Referring to *Viṣṇu Tattva* (Viṣṇu Smṛti), he points out that "*Sevā*, when done with true understanding (that the soul is servant and Bhagavān is the master), is *Bhakti*...."[43] He further notes:

> In both cases of *Upāsana* and *Bhakti*, the form to be meditated upon is only that of *Puṇḍarīkākṣa* (the Lotus-eyed Brahman), *Chodana* (injunction) is "*upasva*," "*bhajasva*," which are identical in meaning. The terms *upasti* and *bhajati* are forms of service. Hence, the lexicographers write *Sevā, Bhakti,* and *Upasti* as synonymous. In *Liṅga* and *Mārkaṇḍeya Purāṇas* "this root '*Bhaja*' is explained in terms of '*Sevā*.' Therefore it is that the wise have largely used the term *Bhakti* to denote *sevā*." The selfsame term *Upāsana* is explained in terms of *Bhakti* when it is in the form of unlimited affectionate devotion towards Bhagavān on account of His being possessed of innumerable faultless qualities, and produces in the *Upāsaka* the taste for service unto Him alone on account of being the undisputed Lord.[44]

Over and over again Bhaṭṭar makes it clear that Lord Viṣṇu is the Supreme reality and the Supreme goal of human beings. When he understands '*sevā*,' '*upāsana*' and '*bhakti*' basically as '*vedana*' (which is understood as reciting the names of God), what he really emphasizes is that the recitation of the names of God is done primarily because the Lord himself is the means and the goal and that the Lord is accessible at all times and at all places. It is precisely because the singing of the names of God does not require any special time and place, and so forth, that Bhaṭṭar considers it the superior means. There is no danger of sacrilege, even if some were to sing in a place that is not considered ritually pure. By the same token, even if a ritually impure person sings these praises, there is no impurity attributed to the Lord. He says, "There is nothing unclean about singing indiscriminately as Bhagavān is purity embodied." He further points out that the Lord's capacity to bestow favor is not diminished because of the person's impurity, as the Lord's purity itself will cleanse the impurities of people and make them acceptable to God.[45] Again, as the Lord himself is both *upeya* and *upāya,* he makes himself accessible to the devotees, and therefore the Lord's compassion does not depend on the human capacity to please him. In other words, he discredits all human effort to please God.

Thus, Bhaṭṭar speaks of the Lord as being the highest goal and the highest means and as accessible to his devotees because of his own compassion for them. He also speaks of the Lord as the "Father of the Universe." Expounding the auspiciousness of the Lord (*maṅgalānāṃ ca maṅgalam*), he says:

---

43. Ibid., p. 16.
44. Ibid., p. 16.
45. Ibid., p. 22.

He is the most auspicious of all that is auspicious in the universe, He is full of sweet-smelling garments, sandal paste, divine damsels, ambrosia, sweet drinks, etc., as He is completely free from all bonds of material existence, and is saturated with pure and boundless knowledge and bliss, and besides, He is very much desired by the pure soul (soul free from the bonds of *saṃsāra*). He is therefore *Paramaṃ Prāpyam* (the greatest object to be attained).

Having declared that the one with these qualities is the greatest object to be attained, to repeat it as if it has been established shows the high celebrity attained in the *Śāstras*.

Who is the God of gods and is the eternal Father of all beings in the universe, from whom all beings are born at the beginning of the age (*yuga*) and in whom all those beings merge at the end of the world or deluge?

Further:

He is the Supreme Deity over all deities like Brahmā, Śiva, Indra etc., Why? He is the Father, the cause of existence of all of them and the epithet *Avyaya* (imperishable) distinguishes Him from their immediate fathers. Being fathered by Him the most ancient, none is fatherless. The fatherhood of the Lord is now explained. "*yataḥ sarvāni bhūtāni*"— from whom all creatures are born, "from whom"—indicates He is the *Nimittakāraṇa* (rudimentary cause) of all objects from Brahmā down to the tree from the beginning, when the creator (Brahmā) was created. Although after the creation of Brahmā by Bhagavān and during the intermediate creations, beings are created through the agency of Brahmā, it is not so during the first creation (after *Mahāpralaya*). This is indicated by the word "*Ādiyugagame*."

He is also the material cause of the universe for the reason that all these created beings go back to Him at the end of the *yuga* and obtain "*laya*" in Him. By the conjunction "*ca*" (and) in "*yasmiṅś ca*" it is suggested that He is also the accessory cause of creation and primary cause of the existence and activity of all beings.

Further, His being the threefold cause of creation (*Nimitta, Upādāna, and Sahakāri*) is shown in the illustration: "He is the Brahmā forest where the tree of Brahmā is grown." This is proved in *Brahma Sūtra* (1:4:23): *Adhikaraṇa*: "*prakṛtiś ca pratijña dṛṣṭāntānuparodāt.*" Therefore the theory that Bhagavān is the material cause and Maheśvara is the rudimentary cause is not based on Vedic texts.[46]

I quoted the above, rather long passage to show the range of things that Bhaṭṭar says about the Lord. He makes it clear that the Lord as the Father of creation is the threefold cause. He also tries to remove the misunderstanding that either Brahmā or Śiva is in any sense causally related to creation. Thus, it is clear that Bhaṭṭar calls the Lord the Father of the Universe in order to uphold his supremacy and his overlordship. In another place Bhaṭṭar speaks of the Lord both as 'Father' and 'Mother' as well as 'Brother' and so on:

Nārāyaṇa is the Universal Mother, Father, Brother, the abiding place, the refuge, friend and final goal.[47]

---

46. Ibid., pp. 28-29.
47. Ibid., p. 35.

This passage, however, must be seen in the context of God's accessibility and compassion for the *jīvas*. For Bhaṭṭar the Lord is everything. The metaphors "Mother," "Father," "Brother," and "Friend" all seem to indicate that the Lord himself is accessible to his devotees. Bhaṭṭar often speaks of the Lord's eagerness to embrace the devotees:

> He shows Himself to His devotees in His haste to embrace them, though He is ordinarily hidden like the treasure in the bowels of the earth.[48]

Bhaṭṭar thinks of the Lord as the one who himself causes devotion in the devotees by his self-giving nature. By descending into the world in his many *avatāra*-s, he enables the devotees to reach him. He says,

> He enriches the devotion of His devotees by giving Himself up to them.[49]

Further he says:

> Thus He causes happiness to the beings of the earth by manifesting His own beauty, easy accessibility, and other qualities.[50]

Bhaṭṭar also stresses the extent to which the Lord makes himself accessible. He says:

> He does not exercise His Lordship over persons solely devoted to Him. He is in the hands of His devotees with regard to bath, decoration, and the concourse of people on the occasion of His worship.[51]

Thus, on the one hand he speaks of the Lord as the ultimate, supreme reality above all the gods, including the creator god Brahmā, whereas on the other he speaks of the Lord as both the means and the goal, saying that he, the Lord, himself causes devotion and is accessible to his devotees of his own accord. This dialectical perception of the Lord in Bhaṭṭar's thought is certainly continuous with that of his predecessors.

Essential Nature of the Relationship between Śrī-Lakṣmī and Viṣṇu

It is interesting to note that even though Bhaṭṭar speaks of the Lord in terms of both supremacy and accessibility, as discussed earlier, he also speaks very clearly and specifically of the divine consort, whom he clearly projects as the mediatrix between the Lord and his devotees. This raises the essential question of how Bhaṭṭar relates Śrī-

48. Ibid., p. 53.
49. Ibid., p. 53.
50. Ibid., p. 55.
51. Ibid., p. 154, v. 632.

Lakṣmī to Lord Viṣṇu. In other words, if the Lord is accessible to the devotees on his own initiative without the help of a mediator, why does Bhaṭṭar speak of the divine consort as the mediatrix? The answer seems to be more than a play of language or rhetoric.

It is perhaps useful to refer again to the passage that we referred to earlier, namely, the comment of Bhaṭṭar on Lord Viṣṇu's epithet, "*Mādhava*."[52] There Bhaṭṭar speaks of Śrī-Lakṣmī as the "Śakti of Viṣṇu," the "Mother of the *mantra*-s," and the "Mother of the Universe." He further says that she is eternal, and is the "embodiment" of all *śakti*-s, and is the life-giving Śakti of the Lord and source of all *śakti*-s. In all these abovementioned aspects of Śrī-Lakṣmī, Bhaṭṭar gives clear evidence of the extent to which the Pāñcarātra Āgama perception of Śrī-Lakṣmī has been incorporated into his own understanding of Śrī-Lakṣmī. Besides, his understanding of Lord Viṣṇu also gives evidence of the fact that he was using Pāñcarātra categories to expound the supremacy of the Lord. He thinks of Viṣṇu primarily in terms of *Para, Vyūha, Vibhava, Arcā*, and *Antaryāmin*. To the extent that he incorporated Pāñcarātra elements in his understanding of the Lord and his divine consort, he presents both of them in a unity characterized by its dialectical nature.

One of the points he makes about Śrī-Lakṣmī is that she is a suitable companion of the Lord not only in the *avatāra*-s but even in the *Para* aspect and during the *Vyūha*-s. He affirms the inseparable nature of their relationship. He speaks of the Lord's perpetual embrace with Śrī-Lakṣmī. By virtue of the embrace of the Lord she is perceived as having no beginning. She is eternal and incarnates with her corresponding forms along with him.[53] The Lord always entertains her and therefore she is never separate from him.[54]

This view of Bhaṭṭar fits in with the Pāñcarātra assertion that Lord Viṣṇu and his Śakti are never separable, even though at the time of creation she becomes distinguished. Both in the Pāñcarātra tradition and in Bhaṭṭar's perception, Bhagavān's Śakti (Śrī-Lakṣmī) is distinguished for the purpose of creation, which in turn becomes the basis for her being distinguished in the ritual context, where she is perceived as a "receptacle of the compassion of the supreme."

The affirmation of the inseparability of the Lord and his divine consort is crucial for Bhaṭṭar not only because of his conception of the goddess as the mediatrix, but also to avoid an ontological dualism, just as his predecessors did.[55] On the one hand, it was important for Bhaṭṭar to affirm the reality of both God and his consort; on the other hand, the goddess is an essential part of the total reality of God. The presence of the goddess is significant both in the context of ritual and

---

52. Ibid., p. 66, v. 73.

53. Ibid., p. 67, v. 73; also cf. *Guṇaratnakośa*, 48.

54. Ibid., p. 116, v. 378.

55. The Pāñcarātra also avoids this kind of dualism at the ontological level to maintain their *ekāntika* philosophy. I tried to show this in chap. 2.

in the ontological scheme. This is why Bhaṭṭar perceives the entire *Rāmāyaṇa* as centered around Sītā. He says: "The entire poem *Rāmāyaṇa* is nothing but the mighty story of Sītā."[56]

The inseparable nature of the relationship of the Lord and his divine consort is stated in such dialectical terms in order to indicate not only the two complementary aspects of the same ultimate reality but also the ritual distinction between the Lord and his consort. And this ritual distinction has an ontological basis because at the ontological level God's Śakti, Śrī-Lakṣmī, is distinguished at the time of the creative process.

In *Guṇaratnakośa,* Bhaṭṭar says that the Lord is the auspiciousness of Śrī-Lakṣmī (*śriyaḥ śrī*).[57] Further, in *Śrī Viṣṇusahasranāma Bhāṣya*, he elaborates that the Lord is the one

> who bestows on Śrī (Lakṣmī) the happiness of his great, eternal, ever fresh and spontaneous affection. In other words, He is Lakṣmī's very life. Lakṣmī gets her name Śrī only by virtue of His protection.[58]

Then Bhaṭṭar quotes from *Rāmāyaṇa*, wherein Lakṣmaṇa tells Rāma:

> Oh Rāma, neither Sītā nor myself (sic) can live without you for a moment, like fish taken out of water.[59]

He continues further:

> Such is the nature of Sītā. "She (Lakṣmī) will never remain without Viṣṇu," "Sītā is not separate from me as the sun and its luminosity have no separate existence." "I cannot be separate from Rāghava."[60]

In the same vein he continues again:

> "He (Lord) is the cause of the prosperity of Lakṣmī." She owes her prosperity to Him.[61]

Thus, while Bhaṭṭar speaks of the Lord as the source of Śrī-Lakṣmī both in terms of her existence and beauty, as well as her prosperity, he also stresses the other side of Śrī-Lakṣmī. In contrast to what he said about the Lord in the above statements he says about Śrī-Lakṣmī:

> It is Śrī (Lakṣmī) that brings Him (Viṣṇu) into relief. She is the cause of His greatness being manifested. "His brilliance is beyond comprehension, as He is the Lord of Sītā, the daughter of Janaka."[62]

---

56. Venkataratnam Naidu, op.cit., p. 67, v. 73.
57. *Guṇaratnakośa,* 9.
58. Venkataratnam Naidu, op.cit., p. 151. v. 612.
59. Ibid., p. 151.
60. Ibid., pp. 151-52; also see p. 114, v. 363.
61. Ibid., p. 152, v. 613.
62. Ibid., p. 152, v. 616.

In *Guṇaratnakośa,* he points out that the independent form of the Lord exists because of her embrace;[63] that she is the soul of the Lord.[64] Describing the form of the Lord as "*Lakṣmīvān*," he makes the point:

> "I am Her follower and Her form rests in me." She is Prakṛti, the Universal Mother and Śrī.[65]

The above reference clearly follows the line of the *Lakṣmī Tantra* in describing Śrī-Lakṣmī. Moreover, since Bhaṭṭar sees the entire Rāmāyaṇa from the point of view of Sītā, it becomes important for him to make the statement that the Lord broke the bow of Śiva for the sake of Sītā.[66] In other words, in Bhaṭṭar's view Śrī-Lakṣmī's significance lies in the fact that she is the purpose and object of the Lord's deeds. He seems to establish a special relationship between the Lord and his divine consort that provides meaning to all of existence. Everything, including the liberation of the *jīva*-s, is seen in the context of their mutual association and mutual enjoyment. It is through her touch that the Lord can be experienced by the devotees,[67] and it is because of her relationship with the Lord that Bhaṭṭar prays that the devotees might be able to see the Lord.[68]

It is, thus, in the context of their dialectical relationship that Bhaṭṭar sees the totality of the reality. In that reality Śrī-Lakṣmī forms part of the *śeṣitva* of the Lord. It is important to recognize again the metaphors that Bhaṭṭar uses. They indicate a mutuality and an innate relationship and interdependence:

> (The Lord is the one) who bears Lakṣmī as a natural part of Himself, like the lustre of a gem, the smell of a flower, the moonlight of the moon, and the sweetness of ambrosia. "As fame cannot be separated from a famous person she (cannot be separated from Rāma)."[69]

It is quite possible to argue that the attribute is secondary to the subject. The question here is not whether the subject or the attribute is more important; rather, what is significant for Bhaṭṭar is to recognize the reality in its oneness and inseparability. That is why the Lord and his consort together form the *śeṣitva* side of the ultimate reality. For the same reason, he again points out that the divine attendants, namely, Ādiśeṣa, Garuḍa, and others, were devoted to both the Lord and his divine consort.[70] In his theological exposition, it becomes important for him to affirm that "one should meditate on the Supreme,

63. *Guṇaratnakośa*, 28.
64. Ibid., 46.
65. Venkataratnam Naidu, op.cit., p. 152, v. 617.
66. *Guṇaratnakośa*, 54.
67. Ibid., 29.
68. Ibid., 51.
69. Venkataratnam Naidu, op.cit., p. 152, v. 617.
70. Ibid., p. 153, v. 625.

the Lord of Lakṣmī, shining like Brahmā and bearing in his two hands Lakṣmī and the wheel."[71] In clear terms, he states again:

> Along with her, the Universal Mother, He as the Father is the refuge of all—"You (Śrī) are the Mother of all beings in the universe and Bhagavān Hari, the Lord of all gods, is the Father."[72]

Thus, the ultimate reality for Bhaṭṭar is the inseparable unity of the Lord and his divine consort. The unity is so integral that he makes no ontological distinction between the two. Even at the ritual level, at times, he addresses the Lord as "*Father*" and "*Mother*" and Śrī-Lakṣmī as "*Mother*" and "*Father.*"[73] Thus, using the metaphors so fluidly and interchangeably, he affirms the ultimate oneness of the Lord and his divine consort, not in a *śeṣin-śeṣa* relation but rather as both belonging to the *śeṣin* side of the equation. Furthermore, there is a structural relationship between his perception of the Lord, and his perception of the consort. On the one hand, as pointed out earlier, he seems to be saying that the Lord is accessible on his own initiative; on the other, he emphasizes the role of Śrī-Lakṣmī as mediatrix. The structural relationship between these two ostensibly inconsistent positions becomes clear when the two positions are placed together in the context of Bhaṭṭar's overall metaphysics. In his *Aṣṭaślokī*, he quite characteristically sets these two positions together in one and the same *śloka*:

> Having taken refuge in Śrī, the beloved of the Lord of the universe and of gods, the eternally inseparable (*anapāyinī*) one, I take refuge in Hari, the root of all qualities that are appropriate for accessibility (*āśrayānocita*); Along with Śrī who is the means of all desires I seek refuge in the Lord of the Self (Supreme Self); Indeed, having been completely freed, I perform service (to the Lord) without the feeling of I-ness (*nirmamaḥ*).[74]

In this *śloka,* Bhaṭṭar speaks of the accessibility of Hari; yet he also speaks of his taking refuge in Śrī-Lakṣmī before he takes refuge in the Lord. Nevertheless, he provides a clue in the word "*anapāyinī*"[75] to his ostensibly inconsistent position. The word indicates the inseparable nature of the relationship between the Lord and his divine consort. Thus, in the ultimate sense, his refuge in Śrī-Lakṣmī is synonymous with his refuge in the Lord.

---

71. Ibid., p. 114, v. 363.
72. Ibid., p. 153, v. 620.
73. *Guṇaratnakośa*, 61.
74. Bhaṭṭar, *Aṣṭaślokī*, 6 (Translation mine).
75. The adjective *anapāyin* means "to be constant in the same state." See Monier-Williams, op.cit., p. 25, col. 3.

CHAPTER SIX

ŚRĪ-LAKṢMĪ IN THE WRITINGS OF LOKĀCĀRYA

The Śrīvaiṣṇava tradition witnessed one of the most productive periods in its history during the thirteenth century C.E. The tradition not only faced controversial issues that eventually led to the division of the community into two sects; the Northern (Vaṭakaḷai) and Southern (Teṅkaḷai) cultures, but it also had to come to grips with some of the issues that the early *ācāryas* had dealt with somewhat vaguely. Two of the most important theologians of this period were Piḷḷai Lokācārya (1213-1323) and Veṅkaṭanātha (1268-1369), who were subsequently identified with the Teṅkaḷai and Vaṭakaḷai sects respectively. In the present chapter, I shall deal with the writings of Piḷḷai Lokācārya in order to explore his understanding of Śrī-Lakṣmī.

Background of Piḷḷai Lokācārya

Piḷḷai Lokācārya was the son of Vādukku Tiruvīthi Piḷḷai, who wrote a commentary on Nammāḷvār's *Tiruvāymoḷi*. According to the Teṅkaḷai counting, he occupies the seventh position in the line of Śrīvaiṣṇava teachers. As is the case with almost every single *ācārya* of the tradition, the Śrīvaiṣṇava community considers the circumstances in which Piḷḷai Lokācārya was born to be extraordinary. It is said that Vādukku Tiruvīthi Piḷḷai followed the life of a *brahmacārin* even after his marriage. His parents became anxious when they realized that he did not uphold the marital relationship with his wife and complained to his teacher Nampiḷḷai. Nampiḷḷai asked Vādukku Tiruvīthi Piḷḷai's parents to bring the girl to him, and he gently stroked her stomach and sent her home. Later he told his disciple, Vādukku Tiruvīthi Piḷḷai, to honor the usual marital relationship even while practicing *brahmacarya*. Eventually, Vādukku Tiruvīthi Piḷḷai's wife bore two sons—Piḷḷai Lokācārya and Alagīya Manavāla Perumaḷ Nayanar. It is said that both the brothers lived the life of a *brahmacārin* and dedicated their lives to the continuation of the tradition. Alagīya Manavāla Perumaḷ Nayanar is said to have written *Ācāryahṛdayam* and died at an early age. Piḷḷai Lokācārya (from now on I shall refer to him as Lokācārya) was a senior contemporary of Veṅkaṭanātha. Tradition says that during the Muslim invasion, when Śrīraṅgam was attacked, Lokācārya carried away with him the *utsavamūrti* of Śrīraṅganātha, and Veṅkaṭanātha carried with him Śrutaprakāśācārya's commentary on Rāmānuja's *Śrībhāṣya*. It is said that

Lokācārya died in a village called Jyotiṣkuḍi due to exhaustion from travel.

All together about eighteen works, called *Aṣṭādaśa-rahasya*-s (Eighteen Esoteric Teachings), were attributed to him. He wrote in Maṇipravāḷa (mixed Sanskrit and Tamil). It is clear from his writings that he drew his material from Vedānta and the Āḷvār tradition. Thus, he became known as the dual Vedāntist (*ubhayavedāntin*). He also drew his material from the Pāñcarātra Āgamas. Among Lokācārya's eighteen works, three are said to be of great significance for the Teṅkaḷai community: 1) *Tattvatrayam* (which deals with *Īśvara, cit*, and *acit*); 2) *Mumukṣuppaḍi* (which deals with the three *mantras*, namely, *Dvaya mantra, Tirumantra*, and *Carama śloka* of *Bhagavad Gītā* 18:66); and 3) *Śrīvacanabhūṣaṇa* (Ornament of Auspicious Sayings). *Tattvatrayam, Mumukṣuppaḍi*, and *Śrīvacanabhūṣaṇa* have been rendered into English.[1] In the present chapter I shall explore Lokācārya's understanding of the Lord and the *jīva,* and then relate it to his understanding of Śrī-Lakṣmī. I shall also try to relate his understanding to the Pāñcarātra tradition.

Sources of Lokācārya

Before attempting an understanding of Lokācārya it may be useful to look at the sources that he uses for his theological reflections. We have already noted in the fourth chapter the extensive use of the epic literature in the writings of Bhaṭṭar. Directly after Rāmānuja, we see a significant shift in terms of the use of scriptural sources. While Rāmānuja limited himself to the Upaniṣadic and some selected Purāṇic material with a few additional texts from the Pāñcarātra Āgamas, Bhaṭṭar added to that material an extensive selection from the epic literature. In the case of the thirteenth century theologian, Lokācārya, the use of *Rāmāyaṇa* and *Mahābhārata* is even more pronounced. It must be noted, however, that his background material largely comes from the hymns of the Āḷvārs and the Pāñcarātra Āgamas as well. Again, he uses less of the Āgamic material than he does of the hymns of the Āḷvārs. For instance, in his *Śrīvacanabhūṣaṇa*, he refers to two Pāñcarātra Āgama texts, namely, the *Ahirbudhnya Saṃhitā* and the *Lakṣmī Tantra*, only twice. But his use of Āḷvār hymns is very extensive. He uses *Tiruvāymoḷi* of Nammāḷvār, *Peria Tirumoḷi, Nācciar, Tirumoḷi*, and hymns of *Āṇṭāl*, among others. As per the Vedic material, while he makes a single reference to Kaṭhā Upaniṣad (2:23) in his *Śrīvacanabhūṣaṇa*, he understands the Vedas primarily in relation to the Itihāsa-s and the Purāṇa-s. He says: "The meaning of

1. *Tattvatrayam* and *Mumukṣuppaḍi* are trans. M. B. Narasimha Iyengar (Madras: Educational Review Book Depot, 1962, 1966). *Śrīvacanabhūṣaṇa*, trans. Robert C. Lester (Madras: The Kuppuswami Sastry Research Institute, 1979). My translations of *Śrīvacanabhūṣaṇa* in this chapter are based on Lester's translation.

the Vedas is brought to completion by means of the Smṛti-s, Itihāsa-s, and Purāṇa-s."[2] Between the Itihāsa-s and the Purāṇa-s, he considers the Itihāsa-s as more important.[3] Notice that he uses the *Bhāgavata Purāṇa* instead of the *Viṣṇu Purāṇa*, which was more acceptable to Rāmānuja.[4] Furthermore, between the two epics he seems to express favoritism toward the *Rāmāyaṇa*. He calls the *Rāmāyaṇa* "the most excellent Itihāsa" and refers to the other epic simply as "*Mahābhārata*."[5] In his use of the two epics, however, he does not make a radical distinction in terms of hierarchical status, although he sees the purpose of the two epics as distinct from each other. While the *Rāmāyaṇa* is used to expound the meaning of "mediator" (*Puruṣakāra*), the *Mahābhārata* is used to expound the meaning of "the means (*Upāya*) to *mokṣa*."[6] In clarifying the sources of Lokācārya, one point that must be made clear is that the content of his theology reflects the hymns of the Āḷvārs and the Pāñcarātra Āgamas. He draws his illustrations from the epic sources to explicate that content. In other words, the two epics do not provide any new material as such, but rather they provide the illustrations to explain the content that is already present in the hymns of the Āḷvārs and the Āgamas. Sītā of the *Rāmāyaṇa* illustrates the meaning of "mediator," while Kṛṣṇa of the *Mahābhārata* illustrates the meaning of "the means." Thus, Lokācārya's use of the epics is more as examples and analogies. Time and again he refers to Sītā and Lakṣmaṇa of the *Rāmāyaṇa*, and to Kṛṣṇa and Arjuna of the *Mahābhārata* to illustrate his points.

Lokācārya's Conception of the Lord and the Jīva

Like his predecessor, Rāmānuja, Lokācārya sees the relationship between the Lord and the *jīva* as master-servant (*śeṣin-śeṣa*). Nevertheless, what is distinctive about Lokācārya's conception of the Lord-*jīva* relationship is that he lays so much emphasis on the independent nature of God that the *jīva* is absolutely at the mercy of God, to the extent that it cannot even take the first step in the process of *prapatti*. The Lord himself takes the initiative and counts the "accidental good deeds" of the *jīva*, and provides an occasion for the *jīva* to approach the Lord. By such an interpretation, Lokācārya is attempting to affirm the radically independent nature of God's omnipotence and compassion on the one hand, and to radically eliminate *ahaṃkāra* in the *jīva* on the other. In the following discussion, I shall attempt to lay out the nature of the relationship between the Lord and the *jīva*, and show how he perceives the role of the mediator

2. Piḷḷai Lokācārya, *Śrīvacanabhūṣaṇa*, p. 15. v. 1.
3. Ibid., p. 15. vv. 3 and 4.
4. Ibid., p. 65.
5. Ibid., p. 15. v. 5.
6. Ibid., p. 16. v. 6.

(*Puruṣakāra*). In *Arthapañcakam*,[7] he describes the Lord as knowledge and bliss (*jñānānandamaya*).[8] He further explains the name, *Īśvara* in the following:

> By reference to *Īśvara*, when the appellation "Supreme" is give to Him, it means, "the Supreme Lord who resides in the highest Empyrean called *Vaikuṇṭha*. He is described in the *Upaniṣads* as *avākī*—speechless, and *anākāraḥ*— formless, incapable of being grasped by the inner senses and the senses of perception." He is the Prime Light and is distinguished from other forms of His by the name of Para Vāsudeva (*Cāndogya. Up*. 3. 4. 34).[9]

Both in his *Śrīvacanabhūṣaṇa* and *Arthapañcakam,* Lokācārya speaks of the Lord's five forms: in his *para* form, he is Para Vāsudeva; in his *vyūha* form, he is Vāsudeva, Saṃkarṣaṇa, Pradyumna, and Aniruddha; in his *vibhava* form, he is incarnated as Rāma and Kṛṣṇa; in the *antaryāmin* form, he resides in the *jīva*-s; and in the *arcā* form, he resides in the form given to him by the devotee. For Lokācārya, it is important, however, to emphasize the significance of the *arcāvatāra*. He says in his *Śrīvacanabhūṣaṇa*:

> The *antaryāmitva* (the Lord dwelling within the heart) is like waters deep in the earth (not easily accessible); the *Paratva* (the transcendent Lord) is inaccessible like the oceans surrounding the earth; *Vyūha* (fourfold manifestation as Vāsudeva, Saṃkarṣaṇa, Pradyumna, and Aniruddha) is (inaccessible) like the milk-ocean; the *Vibhava* (*avatāra*) is like rivers only periodically in flood (but now dry); *Arcāvatāra* is like the deep pools in such rivers, easily available for use at all times.[10]

The *arcāvatāra* is not only easily accessible, but is, indeed, at the disposal of the devotees. The transcendent Lord willingly confines himself to the shapes and forms given to him by the devotees. Lokācārya says:

> Arcāvatāra is that denomination of the Lord in which he assumes that form that is agreeable to His devotee, and holds that title that is given to Him by His devotee. He has no form or name for His own sake, but He transforms Himself into the shape liked by His devotee, and bears the name of his choice. Although He is omniscient, He behaves as though He were ignorant; though omnipotent He appears, as it were, without strength; though without desire unfulfilled, He remains as if in need; though the Savior of all, He demands protection. Thus reversing the relation of the owner and the owned (the order of the object (*sva*) and the subject (*svāmi*), He lets Himself (sic)

---

7. A Sanskrit work attributed to him, although there is no clear evidence to support it.

8. Piḷḷai Lokācārya, *Arthapañcakam*, v. 13.

9. Ibid., p. 28, v. 15. Note: *avākī* and *anādāraḥ* are used, perhaps, to indicate that in the manifestation of Viṣṇu in his Arcā form he does not seem to speak (*avākī*) and does not seem to appreciate (*anādāraḥ*) the devotee's devotion. See f. n. 1 on p. 28.

10. Piḷḷai Lokācārya, *Śrīvacanabhūṣaṇa*, p. 24, v. 39.

> to common perception and becomes accessible to all by dwelling in public temples, and in the private sanctums of those who adore Him.[11]

Even this reversal of the natural relationship between the Lord and the *jīva* demonstrates, for Lokācārya, the independent nature of God. The Lord is so independent that his accessibility does not need even the slightest initiative from the *jīva*. There is no way that the *jīva* can reach God unless he (God) makes himself accessible.

The significance of the *arcāvatāra* is enhanced on account of two important factors that Lokācārya cites: 1) the *arcāvatāra* reveals the fullness of the Lord;[12] 2) unmindful of both his fullness and independent nature, the Lord appears in his *arcāvatāra*.[13] In both these factors, the Lord's fullness and self-dependent nature are emphasized. In Lokācārya's conception, God's fullness and perfection are structurally related to his accessible nature. He says: "The perfection (of the Lord) is for the purpose of (His) descending upon (the soul); it is not to occasion the withdrawal (of the soul)."[14]

As opposed to the self-dependent nature of God, the *jīva*, says Lokācārya, is totally dependent upon the Lord—"Independence and all allegiance (*śeṣatva*) to another (other than the Lord) are foreign (to the soul)."[15] He explains this by saying "Independence obstructs allegiance (to the Lord); allegiance to another obstructs allegiance to That One (the Lord)."[16] In other words, while emphasizing the dependent nature of the *jīva,* he also emphasizes that the *jīva*'s allegiance is only to the Lord and to none else.

The dependent nature of the *jīva* is such that it is its very essential nature (*svabhāva/svarūpa*). He says, "When the bonds caused by pride (*ahaṃkāra*) are broken, the eternal name of the soul is 'servant' (Tamil—*aṭiyan*)."[17] Lokācārya stresses over and over again that this essential nature of the *jīva* as servant does not depend on God's attributes such as omnipotence and compassion. The *jīva* serves the Lord not because of God's accessible qualities but primarily because it is the very nature (*svarūpa*) of the *jīva* to perform service. He says, "It is not by seeing His qualities that one becomes involved with the Lord; it is due to the essential nature (*svarūpa*) (of the soul)."[18] The relationship between the Lord and the *jīva* is, thus, a natural one rather than consequential. Therefore he says, "Service motivated by (one's) essential nature is better than that arising from (seeing) the qualities (of the Lord)."[19]

---

11. Lokācārya, *Arthapañcakam*, p. 39, sl. 19.
12. Lokācārya, *Śrīvacanabhūṣaṇa*, v. 34.
13. Ibid., v. 38 .
14. Ibid., p. 47, v. 138.
15. Ibid., p. 31, v. 75.
16. Ibid., p. 32, v. 76.
17. Ibid., p. 32, v. 77.
18. Ibid., p. 40, v. 108.
19. Ibid., p. 41, v. 111.

On the one hand, he emphasizes that the *jīva* must continue to approach the Lord, but on the other, he stresses that the *jīva* approaches the Lord only due to its natural relationship. It is to maintain this natural relationship that the *jīva* must continue to serve and approach the Lord. The very existence of the *jīva* depends on this natural relationship. Stressing the *jīva*'s need to approach the Lord for its existence he says:

> If it be said "Is striving toward the Lord appropriate?" we answer that such striving springs from overpowering love; that (love) arises from the relationship (of the soul to the Lord); that (relationship) indeed, is not conditional; it is appropriate to the very existence (of the soul).
>
> There would be cessation of existence (of the soul) if there were no experience as the result of overpowering love; all efforts to maintain this existence are inevitable and appropriate; therefore, striving toward the Lord is appropriate.[20]

Note that here Lokācārya sees the basis of the "overpowering love" of God in the natural relationship between the Lord and the *jīva*. The *jīva* approaches God because of his "overpowering love," which in turn is derived from the relationship that exists between the *jīva* and the Lord. This relationship is a specific connection. This means that the Lord does not need any reason or cause other than this "specific connection" to shower his grace and love upon the *jīva*. This is why he speaks of "accidental good deeds" (*yādṛcchika sukṛta*) on the part of the *jīva*. God finds an excuse in those accidental good deeds of the *jīva* to shower his grace. He says:

> In the splendor of the three fourths (*Vaikuṇṭha*), where the experience of complete fullness is going on, that enjoyment does not take any shape since the divine mind is always with those in bondage, like a father, not sleeping, remembering a son who is in another country. As if fleeing from (His) house, the divine will, going to the side of those in *saṃsāra*, being unable to bear their being separate (from Him), grants them organs and bodies for exchanging (with Him) and power by which to perform with these. Not visible to the eye, lest being seen (by them) they curse Him, saying, "Go away!" He dwells within, embracing them unbeknown to them, like a mother embracing her sleeping child unbeknown to the child. Sharing her (sic) sorrows, protecting their being, not preventing their continuation in bad deeds, giving permission, standing as if indifferent, He searches for a way to rescue them. Without coming across even one defect that can be exaggerated into a virtue, He sheds tears just as a physician scratches the forehead (of a patient) to see if there is any blood, and loses all hope when no blood is seen. As He gets a chance, (sic) if He can find any excuse, imagining that, "you said the name of My place," "you spoke My name," "you protected My devotees," "you gave them shelter," then He grants them these qualities like a goldsmith testing gold on a touchstone and with the aid of wax, collecting a gram of gold from what is rubbed off, He imagines

20. Ibid., p. 41-42, vv. 113-14.

> distinctions of merit, however, incidental and unintentional, over a series of births and multiplies them tenfold.[21]

This passage of Lokācārya illustrates the "overpowering love" of God which has no basis other than the natural connection. In the protector-protected relationship, God's protection of the *jīva* is spontaneous, unconditional, and, thus, natural. God's protection does not depend on the condition that the *jīva* must approach God, but rather, God provides an occasion by finding an excuse on the basis of some accidental good deeds performed by the *jīva*. In this structure of relationship, while God alone takes initiative, the *jīva* must renounce all effort to reach God. Lokācārya draws his examples from the epics and the Āḷvārs and says: "The Goddess (Sītā) renounced her power, Draupadī renounced her shame; Tirukkannamaṅgai Āṇḍān renounced his self-exertion."[22] Even though Sītā had power, to destroy the demonesses (*rākṣasis*), she did not use her power but let Rāma come and rescue her. Again, when Draupadī was being derobed in front of all the court by Duśśāsana (brother of Duryodana), she did not have the power to protect her shame and only Kṛṣṇa could protect her. In a similar way, Tirukkannamaṅgai Āṇḍān renounced his self-exertion. It is said that

> Āṇḍān one day observed two dogs fighting. One dog became hurt and its owner killed the other dog. Āṇḍān concluded that if an owner of a dog will go to that extent to protect his dog, there is no limit to what the Lord will do to protect the soul. Thus, Āṇḍān removed all effort toward salvation.[23]

This self-exertion or self-effort is unnecessary for the *jīva* not by virtue of its surrender but by virtue of the fact that the *jīva* exists only on account of its dependence on the Lord, as it is in the analogy of *śeṣa-śeṣin*. Lokācārya says:

> The fruit of dependence (on the Lord) is the cessation of self exertion; the fruit of *śeṣa*-hood is the cessation of self-aim.[24]

In the above sense, then, *prapatti* on the part of the *jīva*, in Lokācārya's view, is only a natural relationship of the *jīva* to the Lord. It is precisely because of this natural connection that the Lord himself becomes the *Puruṣakāra* and *Upāya*—

> The greatness of *Upāya* is demonstrated in the Mahābhārata by Kṛṣṇa taking upon Himself the duty of *ācārya*, making known completely the

21. Ibid., p. 101, v. 381. Note: Lokācārya also quotes the story of Lalitā from the *Viṣṇu Dharma Purāṇa*. See p. 102, v. 382.
22. Ibid., p. 33, v. 82.
23. Ibid., p. 33, (notes by Robert C. Lester on v. 82).
24. Ibid., p. 31, v. 71.

meanings which were unknown and (showing Himself) as *Puruṣakāra* and *Upāya*.[25]

Since the Lord himself is the means, *prapatti* is performed to the Lord alone. Lokācārya emphasizes that there is no specific time, place, and other conditions necessary to perform *prapatti*.[26] The only condition is that "the Lord only is to be the object of *prapatti*."[27]

In order to make sure that even in the performance of *prapatti* there can be no element of *ahaṃkāra* on the part of the *jīva*, Lokācārya emphasizes the greatness and independence of God's mercy toward the *jīva*. God accepts the *jīva* not on account of *prapatti* but in spite of his defects. The greatness of *Puruṣakāra* and *Upāya* (here both *Puruṣakāra* and *Upāya* refer to the Lord) lies in not merely disregarding (the soul's) defects and lack of merit, but also in making these the very basis for the acceptance of the soul.[28] Elsewhere he refers to the examples of Bhārata and the chief Guha in the Rāmāyaṇa and points out that Rāma refused Bhārata's request although he performed *prapatti* and was defectless, but accepted Guha in spite of his defects. He says: "As for the blessed Bhārata, his very goodness was a fault; as for the Lord Guha, his very fault was goodness."[29]

In this radically new conception of *prapatti*, Lokācārya tries to eliminate the self-assertion on the part of the *jīva* and tries to emphasize God's initiative rather than the *jīva*'s. For this very reason, he does not consider *prapatti* as a means to God.[30] He does not recognize the need for the *aṅga*-s connected with *prapatti* as developed in the Pāñcarātra Āgamas.[31]

In the structure of the relationship between God and the *jīva*, where God's initiative, independent grace, and his overpowering love are greatly emphasized, there seems to be no logical need for a mediator (*Puruṣakāra*) other than the Lord himself. Nevertheless, Lokācārya does speak of the divine consort as a mediator. Against the background of the Lord-*jīva* relationship that I have tried to spell out so far, I shall now turn to Lokācārya's conception of the divine consort and her role in the scheme of salavation for the *jīva*-s.

Lokācārya's Conception of Śrī-Lakṣmī

As indicated in the earlier section, in Lokācārya's scheme, logically, there can be no other mediator (*Puruṣakāra*) than the Lord himself, since he is both the the goal to be attained (*Upeya*) and the means to

25. Ibid., p. 18, v. 14.
26. Ibid., p. 20, vv. 23, 26.
27. Ibid., p. 20, v. 24.
28. Ibid., p. 18, v. 15; also see vv. 16, 17.
29. Ibid., p. 48.
30. Ibid., p. 48, vv. 146, 147.
31. Ibid., p. 28, v. 56.

that goal (*Upāya*). Nevertheless, he seems to see the possibility of mediator/s other than the Lord in a certain qualified sense. Discussing the significance of the mediator, he attributes three essential qualities to the mediator: mercy (*kṛpā*), dependence on the Lord (*pāratantryam*), and non-subservience on another (*ananyārhatvam*).[32] He then applies these qualities to the divine consort and says,

> The Goddess' first separation revealed her mercy. Her dependence (on the Lord) is revealed in the middle separation. The final separation revealed her not being subservient to another.[33]

The commentator explains that according to Lokācārya, Sītā was separated from Rāma three times. First, when she was taken away by Rāvaṇa, she showed mercy for the demonesses; second, when she was sent to the forest to undergo a fire-ordeal, she displayed her dependence by obeying Rāma; third, when she finally left the earth and Rāma, she demonstrated that she was subservient to Rāma and to none else.[34] Thus, while accepting the mediatorship of the divine consort, he nonetheless affirms that the goddess mediates only by being dependent on the Lord. Moreover, the goddess mediates between the Lord and the *jīva*, both while she is separate as well as while she is in union with him. He says,

> In the state of union (of the Goddess and the Lord), there is rectification (Tamil—*tiruṭṭum*) of the Lord; in the state of separation, there is rectification of sentient beings.[35]

In other words, while in union, the goddess influences the Lord and while in separation, she influences and draws the *jīva* toward the Lord.

Lokācārya refers to the *karmic* relationship that exists between the Lord and the *jīva*. On the one hand, the *jīva* is bound by its good deeds (*karman)* and bad ones (*karman*), and on the other, the Lord is committed to reward the *jīva* for the good deeds and punish it for the bad deeds.[36] In other words, there are actually two kinds of relationships that exist between the Lord and the *jīva*-s—one is the natural relationship that is discussed in the earlier section and is referred to as the *śeṣa-śeṣin* relationship, which is eternal; the other is the *karmic* relationship which is conditional. Thus, Lokācārya says, "The dependence on each other of the two (the soul and the Lord) is both conditional and eternal."[37] This is explained by the commentator in the following:

---

32. Ibid., p. 16, v. 7.
33. Ibid., p. 16, v. 8.
34. See note by Lester, ibid., p. 16, v. 8.
35. Ibid., p. 17, v. 10, also see v. 9.
36. Ibid., pp. 50-52, vv. 15-21, 58.
37. Ibid., p. 50, v. 154.

> The dependence of the soul on the Lord is conditional in so far as it is determined by *karma*; the dependence of the Lord on the soul is also conditioned by *karma* in as much as the Lord cannot move except in accordance with the soul's *karma*. On the other hand, the relationship of *śeṣa-śeṣin* is eternal.[38]

In fact, the *karmic* relationship is a factor that comes as an obstruction in the way of the real and natural relationship. Nevertheless, this relationship, being conditional on account of the *Jīva*'s *karma*, is broken by the mediation of *Puruṣakāra*. By that (mediation), the dependence on each other which is noneternal (conditional) is destroyed. Lokācārya also points out that this conditional relationship cannot be broken without the mediator (*Puruṣakāra*). He says:

> As the Lord and soul have the (third factor) of a *sākṣi*, namely, *Puruṣakāra*, the two alone cannot bring to an end their mutual relationship of savior and the saved, and the doer of *karma* and the disposer of its fruit.[39]

Therefore, he says "The two (the soul and the Lord) invoke aid (i.e., seek a mediator) to make up for their faults."[40] This verse is again explained by the commentator:

> The soul needs a mediator because it is fearful of going before the Lord with all its faults; the Lord needs a mediator since He is committed to punishing bad deeds and finds it difficult to accept the soul with all its faults.[41]

In order to circumvent this problem, the divine consort mediates between the Lord and the *jīva*, and she does it by means of counsel (*upadeśa*). "By counsel, the dependence on *karma* of both (the Lord and the soul) is removed."[42] He also adds, "If not rectified by counsel, the soul is rectified by grace, the Lord is rectified by (the Goddess') beguiling charms."[43] If the *jīva* does not listen to the counsel, the divine consort showers her grace on the *jīva*, and if the Lord is intent on punishing the *jīva* for the bad deeds committed by it, then the goddess distracts the Lord's anger by her charming beauty.

Here, Lokācārya's notion that God is intent on punishing the *jīva* for its sins seems to be in conflict with his other notion that God himself becomes the mediator (*Puruṣakāra*), as in the case of Kṛṣṇa, and makes the very defects of the *jīva* the basis for his acceptance. On the one hand, he speaks of God himself as the mediator, who makes even the defects the basis for his mercy,[44] while on the other, he speaks of the divine consort as the mediator (*Puruṣakāra*) who

38. Ibid., p. 50, see also Lester's comment on v. 154.
39. Ibid., p. 51, v. 156.
40. Ibid., p. 50, v. 152.
41. Ibid., p.50, see Lester's comment on v. 152.
42. Ibid., p. 17, v. 12.
43. Ibid., p. 18, v. 13.
44. Ibid., p. 18, v. 15.

mediates between God and the *jīva*-s. He refers to Sītā in the Aśokavana: although she was tormented by the demonesses, she pleaded with Hanumān not to harm them. Lokācārya emphasizes that it is precisely the defects of the demonesses that became the basis for her mediation.[45]

Taking the two positions together, then, what seems to be emphasized here is not so much whether the Lord or the divine consort is the mediator (*Puruṣakāra*) as the fact that human defects or sins do not stand in the way of divine grace. As far as the notion of mediator (*Puruṣakāra*) is concerned, Lokācārya seems to see the possibility of both the Lord and the divine consort as mediators. He points out that in the Mahābhārata, Kṛṣṇa himself becomes the mediator, whereas in the Rāmāyaṇa, Sītā becomes the mediator. In other words, the materials that Lokācārya was using themselves seem to provide for this kind of dual position, and he simply adopts for his scheme the two positions presented by the epics about the mediator. Nevertheless, in the final analysis the two positions are not contradictory. Divine grace is mediated through different means appropriate to the occasion and to the experience of the *jīva*. For this very reason, Lokācārya speaks of other mediators such as one's own *ācārya*, as I shall point out later on in this chapter.

In this sense, the divine consort is not the only mediator (*Puruṣakāra*). Moreover, she mediates not as an equal partner of the Lord (as *śeṣin*), as Veṅkaṭanātha would prefer, but only as his dependent and subordinate (*śeṣa*), which, as pointed out earlier, are the essential qualities for the mediator.

The activity of the divine consort as mediator can only be understood in terms of her essential nature as the dependent of the Lord. In order to emphasize the essential nature of the divine consort as *śeṣa*, he points out the passive derivation of the term "*srī*" in the *Dvaya Mantra* : "The abundance of (Her) doership is to be understood from the essential nature and qualities indicated by the passive derivation."[46] This verse is further explained by his commentator as follows:

> One of the possible interpretations of the term, "*Śrī*," in the *Dvaya Mantra*, is the passive construction (*karmaṇi vyutpatti*), i.e., *śrīyate*, "one who is sought after." Thus is indicated her passive power—she is sought out by the soul due to its essential nature as *śeṣa* and sought out by the Lord as His affectionate wife. In this way, she influences both soul and Lord in her role as mediatrix.[47]

The important distinction that is made here between the Lord and his divine consort is that the Lord himself reaches out, as mediator, to find the *jīva* and to bestow his divine grace on it, whereas the divine

45. Ibid., p. 19, v. 18.
46. Ibid., p. 52, v. 158.
47. Ibid., p. 52, see Lester's comment on v. 158.

consort's power to mediate is seen only in a passive sense. That is to say, it is the *jīva* that seeks the mediation of the goddess, but she herself does not reach out to the *jīva*. This passive power of the divine consort is stressed in order to emphasize her subordination to the Lord. Furthermore, the subordination of the divine consort in the scheme of Lokācārya's theology is essential to maintain the independent nature of God. In the ultimate sense, divine grace is not consequent upon the mediator, although the mediator in some sense bridges the hiatus between the Lord and the *jīva*. In other words, as shown in the case of Kṛṣṇa of the *Mahābhārata* and Sītā of the *Rāmāyaṇa*, divine grace is mediated sometimes directly and sometimes through a mediator (i.e., the divine consort). It is important, however, to recognize that in Lokācārya's theological position, it is divine grace that provides the possibility of a mediator, and therefore even in the mediator's role, it is God's compassion that is operative. Thus, there is no such a thing as the grace of the goddess independent of God's own grace.

Speaking about the auspicious qualities of the Lord in his *Tattvatrayam,* Lokācārya places special emphasis on the goodness and the self-giving nature of God. He says:

> He gives away himself and all that He possesses to the devotees, so that they may use them in such a manner as they can use their own properties. He becomes satisfied only when His devotees attain their objects (of desire). He never thinks of the good acts done by Him, but always of the little good done by His devotees.[48]

The abundance of divine grace is illustrated in the way God is willing to give Himself up totally and without restrictions. His satisfaction lies in the satisfaction of the devotees. In Lokācārya's thought, God's attachment to the devotees is so great that he even opposes his divine consort and discards her. Unlike his usually short and cryptic verses, a rather lengthy passage describes how God's grace, his attachment to the *jīva*-s, is independent of any mediator. He says:

> Like a man who pretends not to observe the faults of his (beloved) wife and children, He does not think in His mind of their (i.e., His devotees') sins. Even if His consort, Lakṣmī, points out the faults (committed by His devotees), He opposes her firmly and protects His devotees. Like the lover who delights in the dirtiness (sic) of his lady love, He looks upon the sins of His devotees as enjoyable. He is sincere towards them with all the three instruments (of the soul, namely, mind, tongue and body). In case of their separation from Him, He is moved in such a way that their grief will be (insignificant) like a hoof mark (as compared with His own vast ocean of grief). He assumes a state wherein they (i.e., His devotees) can tie Him with a rope or beat Him (reference to the sports of Kṛṣṇa in Bhāgavata Purāṇa). His attachment to His devotees goes to the extent of His discarding His consort, Lakṣmī, and the eternally free souls (in their favor).

48. Piḷḷai Lokācārya, *Tattvatraya*, p. 19, v. 151.

> This is similar to the case of a cow that tries to serve its newborn calf by attacking with horns and hooves her earlier born calf and those who bring her grass.[49]

Reference to God opposing his divine consort in the above passage seems to be an imaginary situation that Lokācārya uses to stress the independent nature of God. In the reference to God discarding the divine consort, there is, perhaps, an allusion to Rāma sending Sītā to the forest to go through the fireordeal. Nevertheless, in both illustrations, Lokācārya emphasizes the independent grace of God.

Thus, while Lokācārya admits the role of the divine consort as mediator (*Puruṣakāra*), he does not, limit God's grace to the intervention of a mediator. Even when he admits the possibility of a mediatorship in order for the divine grace to be appropriated by the *jīva*-s, such a mediatorship does not seem to be exclusive to the divine consort. As I have already alluded to earlier, Lokācārya sees the possibility of such mediatorship even through persons other than the divine consort, such as one's own *ācārya*. He says that even service to a *Bhāgavata* (especially a lower class) can be instrumental in leading the devotee toward the Lord:

> The first step to the goal is service of the *ācārya*; the middle step is service to the Lord; the last step is service to *Bhāgavatas*.[50]

Notice that in this hierarchy of steps the divine consort is not mentioned at all. Moreover, he makes it clear elsewhere that the Lord can choose any one as his mediator. In other words, the devotees that the Lord accepts may be used by him as his mediators. Illustrating this idea, Lokācārya says,

> That those whom He (the Lord) accepts are used by Him as mediators when another seeks Him can be seen from the (episode of) the giving [of the] assurance of safety.[51]

The commentator explains the above verse saying:

> Rāma gave Vibhīṣaṇa assurance of safety after consulting Sugrīva. Sugrīva was acting on behalf of the Goddess, Sītā, as having found her jewels, he was living in her grace. In the case of Vibhīṣaṇa, as she was staying in Laṅka, she blessed him so that he might seek Rāma's protection.[52]

In this case, Vibhīṣaṇa received a double blessing before he was accepted by Rāma: one from the divine consort and the other from Sugrīva, whom Rāma had already accepted. It is not clear, however, whether the double blessing here necessarily implies the prior

---

49. Ibid., p. 20, v. 151.
50. Lokācārya, op.cit. (*Śrīvacanabhūṣaṇa*), p. 110, v. 412.
51. Ibid., p. 50, v. 151.
52. Ibid., p. 50, see Lester's comment on v. 151.

mediation of the divine consort before other mediations (e.g., other persons such as *ācārya*, etc.,). In any case, the point of Lokācārya, in the above passage is that the Lord can choose people whom he has already accepted and use them as his mediators in order to enable the *jīva*-s to approach him. In the final analysis, however, the mediator is necessary only at the level of "means" (*upāya*), and not at the level of attainment of the final salvation. Lokācārya makes this point very clearly when he says:

> At the time of the choice of means there is dependence upon the *puruṣa* (the devotee) and the *Puruṣakāra* (the mediator); at the time of accomplishment there is no dependence on these two.[53]

This verse is again explained by the commentator as follows:

> The fifth contestant (referring to five types of people that strive for salvation) is brought to favor by the mediator. Thus the question arises as to whether the mediator himself accomplishes grace. The answer is that the devotee and the mediator are active only at the stage of taking refuge in the Lord; the Lord is independent in accomplishing the salvation of the devotee.[54]

Thus, the divine consort and the *ācārya* are mediators in securing the grace of the Lord. The Lord, however, remains independent in conferring his grace on the *jīva*-s and finally saves them from their *karmic* bondage.

Moreover, Lokācārya also perceives the role of the divine consort in the overall scheme of the salvation of the *jīva*-s as one whose example is to be followed by the *jīva*-s. He cites examples of Sītā and Draupadī, saying that one should be like them with regard to the means (*Upāya*) to attain the grace of God. Just as Sītā renounced her power and Draupadī her shame, the *jīva*-s must renounce all effort to reach God.[55] At best, what the divine consort does is to set an example to the *jīva*-s and show the way. She is seen as the supreme example to be emulated by the *jīva*-s. At a higher level, i.e., when all the defects of the *jīva*-s are removed, the *jīva*'s nature, indeed, becomes like that of the divine consort "When rags (i.e., the body with its defects) are removed, all will come to the nature of the best of women (the goddess, Lakṣmī)."[56] Lokācārya further elaborates on this, saying that "Pure persons are equal to that one (Lakṣmī) in essential nature, in six ways."[57] The commentator explains the six ways:

> These six are: (1) having allegiance to no other (than the Lord) *ananyārhaśeṣatvam*; (2) taking refuge in no other *ananyaśaraṇatvam*; (3)

53. Ibid., p. 78, v. 268.
54. Ibid., p. 78, see Lester' comment on v. 268. Note: comment in parenthesis is mine.
55. Ibid., p. 33, v. 239.
56. Ibid., p. 69, v. 239.
57. Ibid., p. 70, v. 240.

being enjoyed by no other *ananyabhogyatvam*; (4) being composed while in union (with the Lord) (Tamil—*saṃśleṣattil ariyirukkai)*; (5) not being composed while in separation (Tamil—*viśleṣattil ariyirāmai)*; (6) being controlled solely by That One *tadekanirvahyatvam*.[58]

By equating the essential nature of the *jīva* with that of the divine consort, Lokācārya not only affirms the *śeṣatva* of the divine consort but also affirms the independent nature of God. God's independent nature is so fundamental to the overall framework of Lokācārya's theology that he does not even compromise it with the nature of the goddess, and in so doing he stands unique in the Śrīvaiṣṇava tradition.

58. Ibid., p. 70, v. 240.

CHAPTER SEVEN

ŚRĪ-LAKṢMĪ IN THE WRITINGS OF VEṄKAṬANĀTHA (VEDĀNTA DEŚIKA)

Veṅkaṭanātha (1268-1369), the junior contemporary of Piḷḷai Lokācārya, received the tradition from the hands of his maternal uncle, Ātreya Rāmānuja, also known as Appular, who was a grandson of Praṇatārtihara, a disciple of Rāmānuja.[1] Some of the biographical details of Veṅkaṭanātha, unlike those of other *ācārya*-s, are drawn from his own works. In his *Saṃkalpasūryodaya,* he mentions the names of his father and grandfather as Ananta Sūri and Puṇḍarīkākṣa respectively; that he belonged to the *gotra* of Viśvāmitra (and that the goddess, Gāyatrī (Lakṣmī) belongs to the same *gotra*); that he was honored with the titles of *Vedāntācārya* and *Kavitārkikasiṃha* (Lion of Logicians and Poets);[2] that he was an incarnation of the bell in the temple of Tirupati; that he mastered all branches of learning before he was twenty years old; and that he taught the *Śrībhāṣya* of Rāmānuja over thirty times.[3] These biographical details, though mentioned by Veṅkaṭanātha himself,[4] are of great significance in his claiming a special place for himself in the development of the Śrīvaiṣṇava tradition.

The community's belief that he was, indeed, the incarnation of the bell in the temple of Tirupati perhaps needs to be seen in light of his becoming spokesperson for the Viśiṣṭādvaita philosophy, as if he were

---

1. For the Northern Culture (*Vaṭakaḷai*), it is important to make the point that Veṅkaṭanātha received the tradition from his maternal uncle who was trained by none other than Rāmānuja's disciple because they uphold Veṅkaṭanātha as the true exponent of Viśiṣṭādvaita, and he was loyal to the teachings of Rāmānuja. See R. L. Narasimhan's Introduction in *Yādavābhyudayam*, with text and translation by K. S. Krishna Tatachariar (Madras: Vedānta Deśika Research Society, 1976), p. 20.

2. He also had other titles such as Vedānta Deśika, Vedāntācārya, Sarvatantrasvatantra (Master of all Crafts and Arts), etc.

3. Veṅkaṭanātha, *Saṃkalpasūryodayam*, trans. M. R. Rajagopala Iyengar (Madras: Deśika Research Society, 1977), pp. 30-31.

4. It is customary in the tradition of Sanskrit drama for the author of the drama to be introduced and his special place in the literary circles to be praised by the *Sūtradhāra* (lit. one who bears the thread/connects the thread, i.e., one who introduces the play to the audience). In other words, through the mouth of the *Sūtradhāra* the author speaks of himself. Such a personal glorification is not considered self-boasting but rather is in keeping with the time-honored tradition of letting the audience know the accomplished place of the author among literary scholars. Not only does Veṅkaṭanātha speak of his own greatness; the community also believes that he was indeed the incarnation of the bell in the Tirupati temple.

the "voice" of the community. This aspect of Veṅkaṭanātha becomes evident in the way he systematically refuted the positions of both *āstika* and the *nāstika vāda*-s. In his *Śatadūṣaṇi* he basically refutes the Advaita position, and in his *Paramatabhaṅga* he systematically refutes, among others, the Lokāyata, Yogācāra, Mādhyamika, Sautrāntika and Vaibhāṣika schools of the *nāstika* tradition.[5]

In the midst of such intense debates with the rival schools, Veṅkaṭanātha was also a poet of extraordinary talent. He not only produced hymns of praise (*stotra*-s) but also *kāvya*-s and *nāṭaka*-s. Narasimhan in his introduction to *Yādavābhyudayam*, classifies Veṅkaṭanātha's works in the following categories[6]: a) 28 *Stotra*-s in praise of the various deities; b) 4 *Kāvyas*; c) 1 *Nāṭaka*; d) 14 *Vedānta Śāstra*-s; e) 8 Commentaries; f) 2 Books on rituals; g) 32 Books on esoteric (*Rahasya*-s) texts; h) 24 *Prabandhams* in Tamil.

While most of these are extant, it may be useful to mention some significant works that speak not only for the greatness of the author but also for the works themselves. His *Nyāyapariśuddhi*, *Nyāyasiddhāñjanam*, and *Tattvamuktākalāpa* (with his own commentary, *Sarvārthasiddhi*) demonstrate his command of logic and dialectics; *Śatadūṣaṇi*, *Paramatabhaṅga*, and *Vāditrayakhaṇḍana* deal with the controversies with other systems of Indian philosophy and thought; in *Seśvaramīmāṃsā* he tries to show that both *Pūrvamīmāṃsā* and *Uttaramīmāṃsā* are in harmony with each other and therefore form one *śāstra* (*aikaśāstravāda*).[7] Further, he is said to have written three commentaries on the *Śrībhāṣya* of Rāmānuja, namely, *Adhikaraṇadarpaṇa* (not extant), *Adhikaraṇasārāvali* (metrical commentary), and *Tattvaṭīkā* (only a fragment of the first section is available—541 vv.). His *Tātparyacandrikā* is an extensive commentary on the *Gītābhāṣya* of Rāmānuja. In his *Īśāvasyopaniṣad Bhāṣya* he develops the synthesis of Upaniṣadic thought. He also commented on Yāmuna's *Gītārthasaṃgraha* in his *Gītārthasaṃgraharakṣā*. In his *Rahasyarakṣā*, he commented on Yāmuna's *Catuśślokī* and *Stotraratna*, and also on Rāmānuja's *Gadyatrayam*. Then, in his *Pāñcarātrarakṣā,* he defends the Śrīvaiṣṇava daily rituals from the standpoint of the Pāñcarātra Āgamas and also defends Rāmānuja's

---

5. While Lokāyata is a materialistic philosophy the other four are schools of Buddhism that perhaps were in vogue during the time of Veṅkaṭanātha and which were systematically refuted by him in order to place Viśiṣṭādvaita on a firm ground.

6. Veṅkaṭanātha, *Yādavābhyudayam*, p. iii. According to the list provided by V. K. S. N. Raghavan, Veṅkaṭanātha wrote 130 works. See V. K. S. N. Raghavan, *History of Viśiṣṭādvaita Literature*, (Delhi: Ajanta Publications, 1979), pp. 27-48. According to K. C. Varadachari the total number is 118. See Veṅkaṭanātha, *Īśāvasyopaniṣad Bhāṣya*, trans. K. C. Varadachari and D. T. Thathacharya, (Madras: Vedānta Deśika Research Society, 1975), p. 16.

7. Veṅkaṭanātha objects to Śaṅkara's radical division of the two *mīmāṃsās* and also Śaṅkara's rejection of the *karmamīmāṃsā* entirely. For Veṅkaṭanātha, the two *mīmāṃsās* are continuous with each other and thus form one *śāstra*.

Nityagrantha (a manual of daily rituals). Among his literary works, *Yādavābhyudayam*, *Saṃkalpasūryodayam*, *Haṃsasandeśa* (modeled on Kālidāsa's *Meghasandeśa*), and *Pādukāsahasra* are considered his literary masterpieces. Among his hymns of praise (*stotras*), we may mention *Acyutāṣṭaka*, *Abhītistava*, *Godāstuti*, *Daśāvatāra Stotra*, *Devanāyakapañcasat*, *Dehalīśastuti*, *Nyāsatilaka*, *Śrīstuti*, *Varadarājapañcasat*, *Hayagrīva Stotra*, *Dayāśatakam*, etc. Among his *maṇipravāla* works, *Tattvaratnāvalī*, *Tattvamātṛkā*, *Rahasyatrayasāra*, and *Paramatabhaṅga* (mentioned earlier) are significant. He also wrote *Dramiḍopaniṣad Tātparyaratnāvalī*—a summary of Nammāḻvār's *Tiruvāymoḻi*.[8]

In a unique way, Veṅkaṭanātha combined both philosophy and poetry in his works. If Rāmānuja wrote poetry in prose (*Gadyatraya*), Veṅkaṭanātha certainly wrote philosophy in poetry. Vaṭakalai scholars of the Śrīvaiṣṇava community uphold him as the true interpreter not only of Rāmānuja but also of the earlier *ācārya*-s including the Āḻvārs. The community believes that he achieved this task through a synthetic approach. K. C. Varadācāri, in his introduction to *Īśāvasyopaniṣad Bhāṣya*, points out

> that the great merit of Śrī Veṅkaṭanātha's writings lies in the synthesis and correlation that he has made between the several thinkers who preceded him. He has referred to almost all his predecessors and has criticized them or supplemented their views with arguments revealing wealth of understanding altogether unsurpassed.[9]

Even though such a large number of works is attributed to him, the continuity of thought and style in almost all his works makes it possible to accept the idea that he indeed was the author of all those works attributed to him. Besides, unlike the case of Rāmānuja, no attempt has been made so far by scholars to dispute the authenticity of his authorship on the basis of the division of philosophical and devotional literature. Nonetheless, it has been pointed out that at least two of the works attributed to him—*Sajjanavaibhava* (which praises the Vaikhānasa Āgamas) and *Daśadīpaka Nighaṇṭu*—may have actually been written by a later scholar or scholars.[10]

His poetics range from the highly philosophical and dialectical to ordinary topics, such as the dietary practices the Śrīvaiṣṇavas should follow (e.g., *Āhāraniyama*—a Tamil work). He seems to have functioned as an encyclopedia to his community. The intellectual activity of Veṅkaṭanātha is enriched by the devotional aspect that comes out quite strikingly in his *stotra* literature. Most of his *stotra*-s seem to have originated out of a specific context, such as when he visited a shrine or in the context of his travels through the South. Some

---

8. For a comprehensive list of Veṅkaṭanātha's works see Raghavan, op.cit., pp. 27-48.

9. K. C. Varadachari, et al. op cit., p. 13.

10. Ibid., pp. 47-48.

arose in the context of his individual experience of intense religiosity. The intensity of his devotion may be seen in such *stotra*-s as *Dehalīśastuti*, *Dayāśatakam*, *Varadarājapañcasat* and *Śrīstuti,* among others.

In all of his works, Veṅkaṭanātha combined Pāñcarātra tenets with Vedāntic thought on the one hand and *Āḻvār* devotion on the other. The three streams have culminated in his works in such a synthesis that his interpretation of the tradition seems highly integrated. While his predecessors also attempted to integrate the three streams that flowed into the Śrīvaiṣṇava tradition, Veṅkaṭanātha's effort to do so seems to be more explicit and obvious. This can be seen by analysing many of his works. For instance, in *Pāñcarātrarakṣā*, he demonstrates his commitment to the Pāñcarātra understanding of the daily rituals; in his summary work on Nammāḻvār's *Tiruvāymoḻi*, he demonstrates his profound affinity and oneness with the thought of the Āḻvārs; and in his commentaries on *Śrībhāṣya* and *Gītābhāṣya*, and also in his *Īśāvasyopaniṣad Bhāṣya*, he emerges as a true Vedāntist. It seems to me that this combination of the three streams, namely, the Pāñcarātra, the *Āḻvār* devotional and the Vedāntic is crucial to his understanding of the ultimate reality as *Īśatva* (both Nārāyaṇa and Lakṣmī), *cit,* and *acit* (sentient and nonsentient).

In this chapter, I shall try to explore the the influence of the Pāñcarātra and, in light of that, to examine Veṅkaṭanātha's conception of the ultimate reality as Lakṣmī-Nārāyaṇa.

Veṅkaṭanātha's Defense of the Pāñcarātra

Veṅkaṭanātha begins his defense of the Pāñcarātra by pointing out that both Yāmuna and Rāmānuja, having refuted the preliminary point of view (*pūrvapakṣa*), namely, "On account of impossibility of origination," "And there is no (origination) of the instrument from the agent" (*Brahma Sūtras*, 2 : 2 : 40, 41) affirmed the *siddhānta*, namely, "Or if they are of the nature of that which is knowledge and so on, there is no contradiction to that (i.e., the *Bhāgavata* doctrine)," "And on account of contradiction" (*Brahma Sūtras*, 2 : 2 : 42, 43).[11] In other words, Veṅkaṭanātha's defense of the Pāñcarātra system of ritual tradition presupposes the defense by his predecessors.

In the Pāñcarātra Āgamas, the ritual tradition is classified into three categories, namely, rituals for daily worship (*nitya*), occasional rituals (*naimittika*), and rituals related to specific wishes (*kāmya*). While the *nitya* rituals are considered *sāttvika*, or superior, the latter two are considered *rājasika* and *tāmasika*, respectively, in view of the fact that they are only for limited purposes. But every *Bhāgavata* must

---

11. Veṅkaṭanātha, *Śrīpāñcarātrarakṣā*, edited by Pt. M. Duraiswami Aiyyangar, & Pt. T. Venugopalacharya, (Madras: The Adyar Library & Research Center, 1967), p. 2.

perform the *nitya* rituals daily without any desire for fruit or material benefit. In the Śrīvaiṣṇava tradition also, the *nitya* rituals are seen as most important because a Śrīvaiṣṇava devotee must perform perpetual service (*nityakaiṅkarya*) to the Lord. Both Rāmānuja's writings and those of Yāmuna reflect this understanding. Veṅkaṭanātha also follows the same line of thought. It is precisely for the same reason that Veṅkaṭanātha defends the Pāñcarātra ritual tradition.[12] He firmly believes that the Pāñcarātra is self-revealed.[13] He points out that even in the *Mahābhārata*, etc., the worship of the Lord is ordained through the methods of Pāñcarātra.[14] Furthermore, referring to *Pādma Saṃhitā* and *Hayagrīva Saṃhitā*, he points out that the Pāñcarātra *siddhānta* is intended for the sake of liberation (*mokṣa*).[15]

The significance of the Pāñcarātra daily rituals is that, unlike the Vedic rituals, they are open to all classes through initiation (*dīkṣā*). Referring to Rāmānuja's *Vaikuṇṭhagadya* and *Nityagrantha*, he emphasizes the usefulness of following the daily rituals.[16] He says that just as the auspicious thread (that married women wear around their neck) and clothes, etc., protect the bride, the Lord's daily service (*nityakaiṅkarya*) will protect the one who has surrendered (*prapanna*).[17]

The entire defense of the Pāñcarātra daily rituals seems to rest on two important aspects, namely, the element of *prapatti* and the significance of *Arcāvatāra*. Expounding on the worship before noon (*ijyā*), Veṅkaṭanātha points out that according to the *Nityagrantha* of Rāmānuja, *ijyā* proper must be preceded by *śaraṇāgati* (*prapatti*). He refers to Rāmānuja's words— "Now I shall speak about the practice of the worship of the supreme absolute Lord"—with which the *Nityagrantha* begins, and tries to explain the meaning of the word "now" (*atha*). He says that the meaning of '*atha*' must be understood as presupposing *prapatti* (*prapatti pratipādanānantaram*). To substantiate his point he refers to Rāmānuja's words again—"(with words such as)...that alone must be restored to whole (*akhila*), etc."[18] and also—"I, the one who has no other help, take refuge at your lotus

---

12. In the *Pāñcarātrarakṣā* Veṅkaṭanātha defends the five daily rituals, namely, *abhigamana* (early morning ablutions), *upādhāna* (preparation for worship and gathering of materials to be offered during the morning rituals), *ijya* (main worship of the Lord before mid-day meal), *svādhyāya* (recitation and study of sacred scriptures during the afternoon), and *yoga* (meditation on the Lord before sleep).

13. *Pāñcarātrarakṣā*, p. 32.

14. Ibid., p. 21.

15. Ibid., pp. 7-8

16. Ibid., pp. 57-58.

17. Ibid., p. 78.

18. *Nityagrantha*, p. 182.

feet."[19] In his *Śaraṇāgatigadya,* Rāmānuja also elaborates on the same theme:

> Pray Thee, bless my sincere and real *śaraṇāgati* at the lotus feet of Bhagavān so that it may become well and truly performed with all its *aṅgas* (formalities) and be continued without interruption till the goal of *Puruṣārtha* is reached. This (*śaraṇāgati*) is with the object of securing myself the privilege of the occupation of eternal service (*nityakaiṅkarya*) to the Lord....[20]

Thus, following the line of Rāmānuja, Veṅkaṭanātha sees *śaraṇāgati* as a presupposition to the performance of daily rituals. This point becomes more evident toward the end of *Pāñcarātrarakṣā*, where he considers the entire daily ritual activity as eternal service to the Lord—"all these activities are of the form of service (to the Lord)."[21]

The second aspect, namely, the significance of *Arcāvatāra* needs to be seen in the context of Yoga (meditation), one of the daily rituals. While in the entire daily ritual activity the *Arcāvatāra* of the Lord becomes the central focus, it is more so in the process of meditation. He points out that Nāthamuni and others took refuge in the *Arcāvatāra,* which is the embodiment of six auspicious qualities. Its wholeness is established by such sentences as "The *mantra* image (*mantrabiṃba*) constitutes the six supreme auspicious qualities—(*sarvātisayaṣāḍguṇyaṃ samasthitaṃ mantrabiṃbayoḥ*)."[22] He further explains that there are three kinds of worship—mental worship (*mānasī*), external worship (*homa pūja*) and image worship (*berapūja*). Of the three, *berapūja* is considered higher because it produces devotion to the Lord easily and it is the very embodiment of Brahman (*Brahmarūpiṇi*). He mentions four activities that are related to the image worship—worship with adoration (*arcana*), worship with salutation (*praṇāma*), worship with sacrifices (*yāja*) and worship with meditation/reflection (*cintana*)—(*tam arcet taṃ praṇamet taṃ yajet taṃ vicintyet*).[23]

From the above summary of Veṅkaṭanātha's *Pāñcarātrarakṣā* it can be shown the extent to which he took Pāñcarātra seriously in his own interpretation of the Śrīvaiṣṇava tradition. Three basic concepts have emerged from the above survey, which points toward Veṅkaṭanātha's strong leanings to Pāñcarātra: 1) *pañcakālakriyas* (the five daily rituals); 2) *prapatti/śaraṇāgati* as the basic attitude to performing the daily rituals, since the rituals are considered to be *nityakaiṅkarya*; and 3) *Arcāvatāra* (image incarnation) to be the focus

---

19. *Śaraṇāgatigadya*, 12. (Translation mine)—quoted in Veṅkaṭanātha's *Pāñcarātrarakṣā*, pp. 138-39.

20. Ibid., trans. K. Bhashyam, (Madras: Viśiṣṭādvaita Pracāriṇi Sabha, 1970), p. 4, v. 2.

21. Veṅkaṭanātha, *Pāñcarātrarakṣā*, p. 167.

22. Ibid., p. 163.

23. Ibid., p. 163.

of all the daily rituals including meditation (*yoga*). While these three elements are basic to the Pāñcarātra ritual tradition, the Śrīvaiṣṇava tradition also appropriated these systematically, and Veṅkaṭanātha's work and that of his predecessors amply support them. This means that the Pāñcarātra ritual tradition was fundamental to Veṅkaṭanātha's theological interpretation of the tradition.

In his *Tattvamuktākalāpa*, he expounds the three *pramāṇas*, namely, *pratyakṣa, anumāna, āgama* (*śabda*), and *smṛti* in light of his defense of the Pāñcarātra Āgamas. In his defense of the Pāñcarātra Āgamas in *Tattvamuktākalāpa*, he follows the same outline and arguments as his predecessors did.[24] Then, having defended the Pāñcarātra on the basis of the assumption that the author of the Vedas and the Āgamas is the Lord (*Bhagavān* Viṣṇu), he sets out to argue that *smṛti* is a valid *pramāṇa*.[25] Furthermore, it is interesting to note that he uses the term "*Āgama*" to refer to "*Śabda*." He seems to take Āgama as being on a par with the Vedas. This way of treating the Āgamas further reinforces the point that he indeed took the Pāñcarātra tradition very seriously. Moreover, he normally has two sets of proof texts to establish his points: one is the Vedas and the other is what he calls the *śāstra* of the *Bhagavān*, referring to the Pāñcarātra Āgamas. He normally quotes from both of these traditions to make his point.

Veṅkaṭanātha's Conception of the Lord

Both in his philosophical and devotional writings Veṅkaṭanātha gives great significance to the pure and auspicious qualities of the Lord, and holds the tension between the transcendental and the accessible qualities. He begins his benedictory verse in his *Īśāvasyopaniṣad Bhāṣya* with—"We meditate on Vāsudeva possessed of a multitude of pure and excellent qualities. . . ."[26] While commenting on the first *śloka* of the above text he stresses that the Lord is entirely different from the soul (*jīva*)—(*jīvāt atyanta vilakṣaṇatayā*); that he is the support of everything (*sarvādhāra*); and that everything has the Lord as its Self (*atadātmakaṃ kiñcidapi nāsti*).[27] The transcendent nature of Brahman (Lord) is such that he is both inside of everything as well as outside of everything. Veṅkaṭanātha quotes the Upaniṣadic passage—"Whatever

---

24. Veṅkaṭanātha, *Tattvamuktākalāpa*, (*kārika*, 122, 123) with Hindi commentary by Sivaprasad Dvivedi (Śrīdharācārya), (Ayodhya: Tattvamuktākalāpa Prakāśan, 1984), pp. 324-27.

25. Note that the Advaita system does not accept smṛti as a valid *pramāṇa*. See *Tattvamuktākalāpa*, pp. 327-29; also see p. 330—"*smṛtiḥ pratyakṣam aitihyaṃ catuṣṭayam*" *iti vākye smṛtiḥ prathamam eva pramāṇatvena upadīyate*—"In view of the sentences such as '*smṛti*, *pratyakṣa*, *itihāsa*, *anumāna*, the four pramāṇas'—the foremost place of *smṛti* is supported." (Translation mine).

26. Veṅkaṭanātha, *Īśāvasyopaniṣad Bhāṣya* , p. 29 (of the text).

27. Ibid., pp. 2-3 (of the text).

is in the world, seen or even heard, pervading all that both inside and outside Nārāyaṇa stands." (Taittirīya Nārāyaṇa, 10:1).[28]

Veṅkaṭanātha affirms the oneness of reality that is characteristic of the Viśiṣṭādvaita system. At the same time, however, he does not compromise the transcendent nature of Brahman. Brahman is in everything as the "Inner Ruler," and also beyond everything. Interpreting the word "*ekatvam*" in the seventh *mantra* of *Īśāvasyopaniṣad Bhāṣya*, he points out that "*ekatvam*" does not refer to substance-identity (*svarūpaikya*) between mutually incompatible terms.[29] The oneness is achieved, rather, through the principle of co-ordination (*samānādhikaraṇa*), as in the analogy of *śarīra-śarīri bhāva*.

Thus, the relationship between the Lord and everything else is one of higher to lower, as illustrated in the case of Rāma and Sugrīva. (Rāmāyaṇa, *Sundarakāṇḍa*. 35 : 51).[30] In this way, Veṅkaṭanātha emphasizes the transcendent nature of the Lord and the lowliness and creatureliness of the devotee. In his *Rahasyatrayasāra*, he says:

> In relation to nonsentient things He is *Śeṣi*, because they exist for His purposes. In relation to sentient beings or *jīvas* endowed with intelligence, He is *Śeṣi* in the special sense of being *svāmi* (i.e., Master) whom it is their duty to serve, and this is the manner in which we should understand while uttering the *mantras*. Our being *śeṣa* to the Lord we share in common with non-sentient things but we are *śeṣas* in a special sense also being His servants (*dāsaḥ*).[31]

Again, he says that it is precisely in view of the lowliness and creatureliness of the devotees that the Lord makes himself accessible to the devotee. Thus, while the Lord's transcendence and rulership are emphasized, his accessibility is also emphasized. Many of Veṅkaṭanātha's descriptions of the Lord include both transcendent and accessible qualities in one and the same *śloka*, indicating a tension maintained between the two natures of the Lord. For instance, in his *Dramiḍopaniṣad Tātparya Ratnāvalī and Sāra*, he maintains this tension in almost every other *śloka*. On the one hand the Lord's worthiness to be praised is emphasized, while on the other his exceeding love for the devotee and accessible nature are also emphasized. Expounding on Nammāḻvār's thought he says:

> The Lord is worthy to be cherished and served; fit to be enjoyed; with a glorious form; exceeding by far all objects of pleasure; bestows the ends of life with causes therefor; easily accessible for refuge; removes all sorrow from his devotees;
>
> . . . .
>
> The Lord hath gracious qualities, boundless and beyond compare!

28. Ibid., p. 42 (of the text).
29. Ibid., p. 45.
30. Ibid., p. 46.
31. Veṅkaṭanātha, *Rahasyatrayasāra*, trans. M. R. Rajagopala Ayyangar, (Kumbakonam: Agnihotram Ramanujam Tatachariar, n.d.), p. 29.

The fount of infinite *rasa*-bliss supernal is He!
He hath countless worlds for his support!
See, He is the Director of all things sentient and otherwise!
Of infinite glory, He hath the universe for His form!

Then he goes on to add:

> He lets Himself be bound by His devotees; countless are His gracious qualities, and births of His own volition; He displays His love unto all—high and low; easily accessible to the worshippers; He lets Himself be known—this knowledge He confers;
>
> . . . .
>
> Of His own accord, He has placed His redemptive foot on all beings (while He strode the worlds, as Trivikrama); Therefore our Lord is accessible to everyone! Don't you see? saith Śaṭakopa.[32]

Elsewhere, he also notes that the Lord comes to his devotees because of his fullness (*pūrṇatvāt*).[33] This idea of the Lord's *paratva* and *saulabhya* is brought out in his *Dehalīśastuti*. He speaks of the Lord whose form transcends the three worlds in his *Vāmana avatāra*. Yet, that very Lord, he says, is willing to be squeezed between the three Āḷvārs who were taking shelter at the doorstep during a rainy night. Veṅkaṭanātha extols the Lord saying:

> There is nothing to wonder at these entire worlds being limited by Thy three expansive feet (steps). That this illimitable Form (Body) (of Thine) became so brief as to be cribbed, cabined, and confined in a portion of a particular house along with (Thy) devotees—that alone appears to be wonderful to us here.[34]

In maintaining the tension between the *paratva* and *saulabhya* of the Lord, Veṅkaṭanātha is certainly continuous with the thought of Rāmānuja.

In his *Rahasyatrayasāra,* Veṅkaṭanātha further discusses this dual nature of God in the context of explaining the meaning of *Caramaśloka* (Gītā. 18:66). He says that the words "*māṃ*" and "*ahaṃ*" in the *Caramaśloka* are used primarily to indicate God's accessibility and his absolute independence. He says that "*māṃ*" indicates that the Lord is the "Universal Savior," "Universal *Śeṣi.*" "Lord of Śrī," etc., all of which indicate his good nature (*sausīlya*) and

32. Veṅkaṭanātha, *Dramiḍopaniṣad Tātparya Ratnāvalī*, with commentaries in Tamil and English by Uttamūru Vīra Rāghavācārya (Madras: Ubhaya Vedānta Granthamālā, 1st edition, 1983), pp. 9, 11, and 13. (Although the translation is not literal, it seems to bring out the intent of Nammāḷvār as understood by Veṅkaṭanātha).

33. Ibid., p. 60, vv. 70—*pūrṇatvāt gopanagarījana sulabhatayālolanāḍaṃbu-rāśeḥ| mokṣasparsecchayā ca svayamabhisaratīty āha kṛṣṇaṃ śaṭhāriḥ||*

34. Veṅkaṭnātha, *Dehalīśastuti*, trans. D. Ramaswamy Ayyangar, (Madras: The Viśiṣṭādvait Pracāriṇi Sabha, 1973), p. 17. (v. 9).

accessibility (*saulabhya*).[35] And "*ahaṃ*" indicates "the power of accomplishing what is to others impossible."[36] He elaborates:

> *Īśvara* who thus waits for an occasion or opportunity as stated in the passage: "The Lord expects a prayer for protection" (*LT.* 17:79-80) is ever favorably inclined saying "when will these (*jīvas*) pray for my help?" This attitude of His is suggested by the word *māṃ* (me). The word *ahaṃ* (I) shows His attitude of readiness to confer, for His own glory, the desired fruit as quickly as possible saying "when shall I take back (and wear) (these *jīvas*) like jewels from which the dirt (*prakṛti*) has been removed."[37]

Obviously, the idea of God "waiting" for the devotee to approach him is in line with the same idea expressed in the *Lakṣmī Tantra.* The intention here is that even though the Lord is omniscient and compassionate, he lets the devotee approach him in order for the law and order of the world not to be disturbed.

Veṅkaṭanātha sees this dual nature in God as complementary. He says:

> Even if a person is independent and omnipotent, if he is not accessible, no one will seek him (for protection). Even if a person is sought (for protection) on account of his easy accessibility, he cannot award the desired fruit if he is dependent on others.[38]

While he stresses the *dual nature* in God, he also talks about the *puruṣakāratva* of Śrī-Lakṣmī (Śrī's role as the mediatrix). While commenting on different meanings of Śrī[39] he develops the *puruṣakāratva* aspect of Śrī-Lakṣmī. For him, Śṛī-Lakṣmī's *puruṣakāratva* does not necessarily deny the accessible nature of God. Even though the Lord is depicted as the Father who disciplines the sinner, Veṅkaṭanātha ultimately does not deny the compassionate dimension of God. While he distinguishes the two functions of the Lord and his consort, he does not distinguish their essential nature. Explaining the meaning of "*śrīyate*" and "*śrayate*" he says:

> Among them (i.e., among the six meanings of Śrī) when we take the word to mean that she (Lakṣmī) is resorted to by those who desire spiritual rebirth and that she resorts to the Supreme Ruler of all in order to give them spiritual rebirth, we may take the following *śloka* (for authority): "When Thy beloved Lord is displeased with a man who has committed serious offenses in order, like a father, to reform him, Thou O Mother sayest to Him, 'What is this? Is there any man in the world who has no faults?' and persuadest Him by suitable devices to accept the offender by making Him forget (*vismārya*) his offenses. Therefore art Thou our Mother." (*Śrīguṇaratnakośa*, 52). As

---

35. Veṅkaṭnātha, *Rahasyatrayasāra,* op.cit., p. 502.
36. Ibid., p. 529.
37. Ibid., p. 501.
38. Ibid., p. 501.
39. Ibid., p. 427. Veṅkaṭanātha refers to six different meanings of Śrī given in Pāñcarātra Āgamas.

> stated in the *śloka*, she helps to mitigate the anger of the Supreme Ruler who wields the rod of punishment for the sake of promoting the welfare of the offender. Thus she sees to it that the Lord's natural compassion becomes the cause of the man's (spiritual) rebirth.[40]

Notice that here Veṅkaṭanātha shows that Śrī-Lakṣmī intercedes between the offender and the Lord; and he also stresses that the Lord's "rod of punishment" is for the sake of the "welfare of the offender." Furthermore, what Śrī-Lakṣmī does is to bring out the "Lord's natural compassion" so that that compassion becomes the basis for the spiritual rebirth of the offending devotee. In other words, while affirming the compassionate, motherly nature of the divine consort, he does not compromise the Lord's compassion.

Veṅkaṭanātha's Conception of Śrī-Lakṣmī

Unlike his predecessor, Rāmānuja, Veṅkaṭanātha is quite clear in portraying his understanding of the divine consort. He states his position quite openly and clearly. His position on Śrī-Lakṣmī is in many ways opposite to the views of Piḷḷai Lokācārya. He presents Śrī-Lakṣmī as the Lord's attribute, who shares in not only his accessible nature but also in his transcendent nature. In other words, he does not conceive the Lord as *para* and his divine consort as *saulabhya,* but rather affirms that both of them share mutually in the same "substance." While there is no substance-identity between the Lord and his *śeṣa* (sentient and nonsentient beings), there is an ultimate substance-identity between the Lord and his consort. They belong to the same substance, which is constituted of the six attributes, namely, *jñāna, aiśvara, vīrya, śakti, bala*, and *tejas*.

In his *Śrīstuti*, Veṅkaṭanātha speaks of Śrī-Lakṣmī as an attribute and ornament of the Lord (v.1); as one through whose will the process of creation, maintenance, and dissolution continues (v.4); as one who is inseparably associated with Viṣṇu and who possesses innumerable attributes (v.5); as the ruler of the world (v.8); as the abode of compassion and "*kāmadhenu*" of all (v.24). He also speaks of her as the Mother and Viṣṇu as the Father (v.23); and he adds that both of them belong to the *Śeṣin* nature (v.16); and both together form the divinity (v.9).

The above position, reflected in *Śrīstuti*, is further discussed extensively in his *Rahasyatrayasāra*. Discussing the five most important things that a seeker after salvation should know,[41] Veṅkaṭanātha expounds the nature of Brahman which is the first and foremost thing to be known. The essential nature (*svarūpa*) of

---

40. Ibid., p. 427.

41. Ibid., p. 33. The five things that Veṅkaṭanātha refers to are the following: "Brahman, the nature of individual self who is the seeker of the attainment, the means of attainment (*upāya*), the fruit resulting from it, and also the hindrances to the attainment of Brahman. . . . "

Brahman is described in terms of *jñāna*, infinite bliss (*ānanda*) and inseparability from the divine consort, Śrī-Lakṣmī. He says:

> Among these, the essential nature of Brahman, which is the object of attainment, is revealed in the first letter *a* in *oṃ* [aum] and in the word '*Nārāyaṇa*' in *Tirumantra* and in the words '*Nārāyaṇa*' with the adjectives '*Śrīmān*' occurring in *Dvayam* and in the words 'me' and 'I' occuring in *Caramaśloka*. It is in this way that they should be considered. While doing so, one should think of His essential nature (*svarūpa*) as infinite bliss ever inseparable from His consort, Lakṣmī, who in every form and in all situations, participates in all His actions.[42]

Thus, the essential nature of Brahman is to be understood in relation to his inseparability from the divine consort. To substantiate his point, Veṅkaṭanātha quotes from Pāñcarātra Āgamas, Purāṇic and epic texts, and also from the works of the early *ācārya*-s, as well as from the hymns of the Āḻvārs.[43] With many of these texts, he supports the notion of inseparability of the Lord and his divine consort, thereby establishing his position on Śrī-Lakṣmī on the principle of "inseparability." The notion of inseparability, as shown in the second chapter of this study, is an integral concept of the Pāñcarātra Āgama tradition. For him, the Lord and his consort are inseparable in their essential nature (*svarūpa*), but are distinguished in their functions:

> In this context we have to understand a difference in their activities, a division of labor, as it were; for the Lord is concerned with the punishment (of the evildoer) and Lakṣmī with pleading to Him for mercy on behalf of the sinner; the *Mīmāṃsakas* have declared that the object which is stated by analogy to have attributes similar to those of another object actually described must be different by that very circumstance from that other object. So in this case, as it has been stated by analogy or *atideśa*, "Just as Viṣṇu is everywhere, so also in (sic) Lakṣmī, Bhagavān and Lakṣmī. This difference should be understood as referring (here) only to the difference in their functions or activities.[44]

Then he quotes from Parāśara Bhaṭṭar and Nammāḻvār to support his point.[45] This functional difference between the Lord and his divine consort is not like the difference between the Lord and other gods. Those gods, in his view, are created by Viṣṇu. He refers to the Āḻvārs and says:

> The Āḻvārs too have spoken of these differences between the Lord of all on one side and Brahmā, Rudra, and the other gods on the other, in passages such as the following: "The gods are only the food eaten by Bhagavān and vomited afterwards (eaten during the *pralaya* and vomited after creation); are there any (gods) who are not of the nature of this vomit?' (*Peria*

42. Ibid., p. 33; also see p. 41.
43. Ibid., p. 33-35.
44. Ibid., p. 68.
45. Parāśara Bhaṭṭar, *Guṇaratnakośa*, 34; and also see Nammāḻvār, *Tiruvāymoḻi*, 1:3:6.

Tirumoḻi. 11:6:2). "Nārāyaṇa created the god with four faces, and the god with four faces created Śaṅkara" (*Naṇmugan Tiruvaṇḍaḍi,* 1).[46]

While Veṅkaṭanātha refers to Brahmā, Śiva, and other gods in such mundane terms and sees them primarily as creatures of Lord Nārāyaṇa, he perceives Lord Nārāyaṇa and his consort as sharing essentially the same nature (*svarūpa*) in terms of *jñāna, aiśvarya,* etc. In other words, what he is trying to affirm is that the subject and the attribute have the same essential nature; and that only by understanding the attribute could one understand the subject. In this sense, there is no radical separation or distinction between the subject and the attribute. Defining the meaning of the term "*Śrīmān*" in the *Dvaya mantra,*[47] he says,

> The word *Śrīmat* in the first part (of *Dvaya*) is to show that, when Nārāyaṇa becomes the Redeemer, He is with His attribute (Lakṣmī). Aruḷapperumaḷ Emberumannār states: "Before understanding the substantive which has attributes, the attributes have to be understood. Therefore to understand Hari who has Lakṣmī for His attribute, the attribute 'Lakṣmī,' has (first) to be understood."[48]

This idea, that by understanding the attribute one understands the substantive, ties in with his position stated in his other philosophical works. It is precisely because of this integral connection between the substantive and the attribute that he takes the attributes such as '*Śrīnivāsa*' (Rāmānuja uses it in his auspicious *śloka* in his *Śrībhāṣya*) and '*Śrīmān*' (in *Dvaya mantra*) very seriously and discusses very extensively.

Discussing the meaning of the suffix '*matup*' in "*Śrīmān,*" Veṅkaṭanātha tries to show the special connection between the Lord and his divine consort. For him, it indicates an eternal connection between them. He says:

> This eternal connection between Bhagavān and Śrī is indeed such that even when He assumed the form of a *Brahmacārin* (in *Vāmanāvatāra*), He is said 'to have concealed, with the deer skin, His Spouse, abiding in His chest.' (*Dehalīśastuti,* 11).[49]

Furthermore, for Veṅkaṭanātha, this eternal connection between the Lord and his divine consort is a special connection, unlike his relationship with the *śeṣa*-s (*cit* and *acit*). By virtue of being the consort of the Lord, Śrī-Lakṣmī's relationship to him is not general but rather unique. He says:

---

46. Veṅkaṭanātha, *Rahasyatrayasāra*, op.cit., p. 83.

47. *śrīmannārāyaṇāya caraṇau śaraṇaṃ prapadye| śrīmate nārāyaṇāya namaḥ||*

48. Veṅkaṭanātha, *Rahasyatrayasāra*, op.cit., p. 426. I have not been able to trace the quotation that Veṅkaṭanātha uses for his support.

49. Ibid., p. 433.

> The relationship which appears to be general really means, on the strength of the Śruti, the specific relationship (of being the spouse). Since He is called the spouse of Her who is resorted to for protection and who is (also) the world's Mother, His being the Supreme Being and His easy accessibility are both indicated (thereby).[50]

Again, it is precisely because of this specific relationship that Veṅkaṭanātha speaks of the Lord and his consort as equal partners for the purpose of protecting the devotees. He uses the principle of "*sanniyogaśiṣṭanyāya*" (logic of the learned for a good usage) to affirm both the Lord and his consort as *upāya*. He explains this above principle as follows:

> If two things are enjoined as necessary, wherever one of them is mentioned, the other should also be considered as indicated.[51]

Applying this principle to Śrī-Lakṣmī, he says that "wherever Bhagavān is referred to, Lakṣmī should also be considered as referred to . . . ."[52] To support his position he further quotes from Bhaṭṭar's *Guṇaratnakośa*, 28: "Since Thou (Lakṣmī) art ever inseparably connected with Thy Lord, even the Vedas (*Śruti*) do not mention Thee separately." Thus, while meditating upon the Lord, maintains Veṅkaṭanātha, Śrī-Lakṣmī must also be meditated upon. This must be followed when meditating on the '*Tirumantra*' and on the "*Praṇava*" in the '*Tirumantra*.'[53]

Affirming the *śeṣitva* of both the Lord and his consort he says:

> When *Īśvara* is the *śeṣi* of all, He is always (to be thought of as) with his consort, for it has been said, "The two kinds of glory (*nityavibhūti* and *līlāvibhūti*) are *śeṣa* to me and to her, O Brahmā, and this is declared in the Vedānta and in my *śāstras* (*Pāñcarātra Āgamas*)" (*Viśvaksenasaṃhitā*). So also it is said "Being *śeṣi* is single and it rests with two (Bhagavān and Lakṣmī)." In the *Agniṣomīya* Sacrifice, the deity (to whom the *havis* or offering is made) is not *Agni* alone nor *Soma* alone: the deity of the sacrifice (which is single) is *Agni* and *Soma*. So also in this offering of the self, the deity to whom the offering is intended is both (Bhagavān and Lakṣmī). In order to reveal this, it was said "Being *śeṣi* is single and it rests with two."[54]

In the above passage and in several other passages, Veṅkaṭanātha clearly affirms the *śeṣitva* of both the Lord and his divine consort. This position is quite characteristic of the Pāñcarātra tradition. Veṅkaṭanātha, nevertheless, draws his support not only from the Pāñcarātra Āgamas such as *Sāttvata-*, *Viśvaksena-*, *Ahirbudhnya*

---

50. Ibid., p. 433.
51. Ibid., p. 355.
52. Ibid., p. 355.
53. Ibid., p. 356. (*Oṃ namo Nārāyaṇāya* is called the *Tirumantra* or *Aṣṭākṣara mantra*).
54. Ibid., p. 358.

Saṃhitās and the *Lakṣmī Tantra*, but also from his predecessors, namely Yāmuna (*Catuśślokī*, *Stotraratna*), Rāmānuja (*Śrībhāṣya*, *Śaraṇāgatigadya*) and Bhaṭṭar (*Śrīvacanabhūṣaṇa*, *Śrīguṇaratnakośa*). Moreover, he draws his support from the Āḷvārs. He points out that the Āḷvārs also understood the Supreme Deity as the Lord and his divine consort. He refers to *Tiruvaṇḍaḍi*: 100,[55] and also quotes from the hymns of Nammāḷvār. He says:

> And Nammāḷvār, who received the gift of knowledge free from all delusion and *bhakti* from Bhagavān and who occupies the highest place in the line of those who have performed *prapatti*, has stated the same truth (namely, that Lakṣmī should also be considered along with Bhagavān as our refuge and our goal): "You have enabled me to have a vision of Thyself and Thy consort (Lakṣmī) with the shining bracelets, standing together." (*Tiruvāymoḷi* 4:9:10).[56]

Thus, for Veṅkaṭanātha, both Lakṣmī and Nārāyaṇa are *upāya*,[57] as they together constitute the Supreme Deity, Brahman. Even though he quotes from the Āḷvārs, what is significant about Veṅkaṭanātha's understanding of Śrī-Lakṣmī, as pointed out earlier, is that he thinks of himself as following the line of interpretation that his predecessors, especially Rāmānuja, developed. Time and again he resorts to the support from his predecessor, Rāmānuja, and says:

> The author of *Śrībhāṣya*, too, has said Bhagavatī Śrī in the same way as He says Bhagavān Nārāyaṇa in that context; i.e., he calls Her *Bhagavatī* to show that she has the same distinction as Her spouse.[58]

It is in this sense that he sees the significance of the term '*Śrīnivāsa*' that Rāmānuja used in his auspicious *śloka* at the beginning of the *Śrībhāṣya*.

Significance of 'Śrīnivāsa' for Veṅkaṭanātha

Rāmānuja's use of the attribute '*Śrīnivāsa*' becomes paradigmatic for Veṅkaṭanātha. Responding to the Advaita contention that Brahman is eternally pure (*nityaśuddha*) and attributeless (*viśeṣasūnya/nirviśeṣa*), Veṅkaṭanātha affirms that Brahman is known through the attributes, and therefore, they form the subject matter of inquiry (*jijñāsā*). In other words, the universal is known through the particular (*viśeṣa*), and what is attributeless (*nirviśeṣa*) is not known through valid means (*pramāṇa*) of knowing. Thus, *viśeṣa* is the reason for the inquiry into Brahman. Otherwise, he says, there is no reason for the inquiry into

---

55. Ibid., p. 85.
56. Ibid., p. 86.
57. I have discussed this point subsequenty in this chapter by comparing the views of Lokācārya and Veṅkaṭanātha.
58. Veṅkaṭanātha, *Rahasyatrayasāra*, op.cit., p. 430; cf. *Śaraṇāgatigadya* 1 ("*bhagavatīṃ śriyaṃ devīm*")

Brahman.[59] Furthermore, he says that if the attributes are considered as fabrications, then there is also no reason for the inquiry.[60] This means the inquiry into Brahman is really an effort to know the attributes of Brahman. He holds the *sāmānya* (in this case of Brahman) and *viśeṣa* (Brahman's attributes) in mutual tension, since *viśeṣa* is the correlative (*pratisaṃbandhi*) of *sāmānya*: "Without the particularity (*viśeṣa*) the generality (*sāmānya*) is unaccomplished and without the generality the particularity is disconnected" (and therefore does not exist).[61]

Thus, in explicating the meaning of Brahman Veṅkaṭanātha takes the attributes of Brahman very seriously, since it is fundamental to the Viśiṣṭādvaita system developed by his predecessors. What this *viśeṣa* and *sāmānya* refer to is explained in his *Tattvaṭīkā* (commentary on the *Śrībhāṣya*). There he interprets *sāmānya* as referring to Brahman and *viśeṣa* as refering to '*Śrīnivāsa*.'[62] Besides, Veṅkaṭanātha points out that '*Śrīnivāsa*' is the most well known name of God (Brahman). Brahman's qualities, such as *satyatva*, etc., are, indeed, indicated by the term '*Śrīnivāsa*.' Since Brahman (Nārāyaṇa/Viṣṇu) is the eternal support of Śrī, he is known as '*Śrīvatsavakṣaḥ*'(one who bears Śrī in his chest) and '*Nityaśrī*' (one who is always accompanied by Śrī).[63] Veṅkaṭanātha further elaborates:

> Here, terms such as '*akhila*' (complete) indicate Brahman as the cause of everything; (similarly), *vinata* etc., indicate Brahman as the knowledge that leads to *mokṣa*; 'the one who is illumined by all the *Śrutis*, etc.,' (*śrutisirasi vidīpte*) indicates that Brahman is established by all the Upaniṣads; and Para Brahman indicates the Lord as the abode of Śrī (*Śrīnivāsatvam*).[64]

From the above discussion it becomes clear that Veṇkaṭnātha takes '*Śrīnivāsa*' as a very significant attribute of God. For him, terms such as '*sat*,' etc., refer to none other than Nārāyaṇa, who is the consort of Śrī-Lakṣmī.[65] He takes the crux of all the passages as indicating that the meaning of Brahman is *Śrīnivāsa* alone—(*Śrīnivāsaiva Brahma sabdārthaḥ*).[66] Rāmānuja, in his *Śrībhāṣya*, qualifies the term Brahman

59. Veṅkaṭanātha, *Adhikaraṇasārāvalī Śatadūṣaṇi ca*, edited by Śrī Kāñcī Prativādibhayaṅkara Annaṅgārācārya (Madras: A. Sampatkumara/Liberty Press, 1940), p. 51.

60. Ibid., p. 52. (*viśeṣasya tu kalpitatve tajjijñāsa vaikalpyam*).

61. Ibid., p. 52. (*nirviśeṣe sāmānyasiddheḥ nissāmānye ca viśeṣāyogāt*).

62. *Brahma iti sāmānyaśabdaḥ, śrīnivāsayiti viśeṣasabdaḥ*—Veṅkaṭanātha, *Tattvaṭīkā* (in *Vedānta Deśika Granthamālā*), edited by Śrī Kāñcī Prativādibhayaṅkara Annaṅgārācārya, (Kāñcīpuram: Granthamālā Office, 1941), p. 9.

63. Ibid., pp. 9-10.

64. Ibid., pp. 10-11 (Translation mine).

65. Ibid., p. 11 (*nārāyaṇasabdokta śrīpatir eva satādi śabdārthaḥ*) Translation mine.

66. Ibid., p. 11 (Translation mine).

with '*Śrīnivāsa*,'[67] thereby indicating the inseparable nature of the relationship between the Lord and his divine consort. This usage by Rāmānuja becomes paradigmatic for Veṅkaṭanātha's understanding of the ultimate reality in terms of Nārāyaṇa, who is always associated with Śrī-Lakṣmī. For him, this inseparable Lakṣmī-Nārāyaṇa is indicated by the term '*Śrīnivāsa,*' and that very *Śrīnivāsa* is Brahman. *Śrīnivāsa* is Brahman's natural correlative, just as *viśeṣa* is the natural correlative of *sāmānya*, and the two are never understood separately. Thus, the ultimate reality, in the view of Veṅkaṭanātha, includes both Lakṣmī and Nārāyaṇa as equal partners.

Veṅkaṭanātha's Critique of Lokācārya's Position

Having looked at the positions of both Lokācārya and Veṅkaṭanātha on Śrī-Lakṣmī it may be useful to place the two positions together and see how the two positions could be clarified further. In order to do that, I shall begin with the criticism of Lokācārya's position by Veṅkaṭanātha. At the outset, it is important to make two points clear. Firstly, from the available writings of both Lokācārya and Veṅkaṭanātha, it appears that the two scholars never had a face to face debate on any of the issues upon which they disagreed. This means the debate is rather indirect. Secondly, Lokācārya does not indulge in any argumentation in his writings, but rather, states his position in a direct way with extreme brevity. The structure of his writings follow the *sūtraic* form, which in turn required elaborate commentary by Manavālamāmuni. On the other hand, Veṅkaṭanātha does engage in an active confrontation with the views of Lokācārya. His writings do suggest that he was basically responding to the views of Lokācārya on several issues in the tradition. Thus, his *Rahasyatrayasāra*, in which he addresses himself to the issues already discussed by Lokācārya, was, perhaps, written after Lokācārya's *Śrīvacanabhūṣaṇa*.

What I propose to do in this section is to attempt to analyze Veṅkaṭanātha's critique of Lokācārya and try to construct the response of Lokācārya in so far as Veṅkaṭanātha responded to Lokācārya's position on Śrī-Lakṣmī. Before proceeding any further, one more point of clarification may be in order. Veṅkaṭanātha's response to the views of Lokācārya is very systematic. It is quite conceivable that his response might have evoked an ongoing conversation, if not a debate, among the members of the Śrīvaiṣṇava community both during the thirteenth century and afterward. We have, however, no indication from the writings of Lokācārya that he ever replied to the critique of Veṅkaṭanātha. As such, what we have at our disposal is the position stated by Lokācārya in his writings and the counter position of Veṅkaṭanātha on those very issues. Since it is

---

67. Rāmānuja, *Śrībhāṣya,* trans. George Thibaut, (SBE), (Delhi: Motilal Banarasidass, 2d edition, 1966), p. 3.

Veṅkaṭanātha who takes issue with Lokācārya's position, methodologically it may be useful to take Veṅkaṭanātha's critique as a starting point in constructing the "debate." It also helps to locate the issues that were crucial in understanding the position of the goddess. Here I use the term "debate" rather loosely, and in no sense imply that there was a direct debate between the two theologians of the tradition. In my presentation of this "debate," I shall attempt to take adequate care to avoid onesidedness, and describe the issues from both sides as adequately as the materials themselves present them.

Both Lokācārya and Veṅkaṭanātha affirm the reality of the divine consort; both affirm her role as mediatrix (*Puruṣakāra*) in the scheme of salvation of the *jīva*-s. Where they disagree radically is in their description of her essential nature (*svarūpa*). While Lokācārya perceives her basically as *Śeṣa*, who is subordinate and subservient to God, Veṅkaṭanātha, on the other hand, perceives her as *Śeṣin*, who shares essentially the same nature of God and who is a co-equal partner both in the creative process of the universe and also in the scheme of salvation of the *jīva*-s. In other words, for Lokācārya God alone is the means (*Upāya*) for the salvation of the *jīva*-s, whereas for Veṅkaṭanātha both God and his divine consort together constitute *Upāya* and, therefore, they both are objects of meditation. That is to say, the Lord together with his consort is considered as a single *Upāya*.

The point of disagreement on Śrī-Lakṣmī between the two scholars is located in their interpretation of the word "*Śrīmat*" in the *Dvayamantra* (*Śrīmannārayana caraṇau śaraṇaṃ prapadye*| *Śrīmate nārāyaṇāya namaḥ*||). Stating the position of Lokācārya, Veṅkaṭanātha says:

> There are some who hold that, in the former part of the *Dvaya*, the word *Śrīmat* is an *upalakṣaṇa* (an accidental sign by which the thing is distinguished and not a permanent attribute or *viśeṣaṇa*), whereas in the latter part, the same word means a permanent attribute of Nārāyaṇa. If this were true, it would follow that the words "I seek as my refuge," "*śaraṇaṃ prapadye*," would apply only to Nārāyaṇa and not to Śrī or Lakṣmī who, in that part, according to them, is not meant to be taken as an inseparable attribute (*viśeṣaṇa*). It would follow that the dative and the *namaḥ* would apply to the attribute and the substantive, *viz.*, Śrī and Bhagavān. (It would then mean that Lakṣmī is not to be sought as the *Upāya* but that adoration and service are due to her as well as to her spouse, Nārāyaṇa.[68]

Veṅkaṭanātha states the position of Lokācārya fairly accurately, even while sounding doubtful about the validity of that position. He then presents his own argument against Lokācārya's position. He argues:

> It may be asked whether, if we take *Śrīmat* as an inseparable attribute of Nārāyaṇa in the first part of the *Dvaya* also, it would not follow that there are two *Upāyas viz.*, Nārāyaṇa and Lakṣmī, and whether this would not be

68. Veṅkaṭanātha, *Śrīmad Rahasyatrayasāra*, trans. M. R. Rajagopala Ayyangar, (Kumbakonam: Agnihotram Rāmānuja Thathachariar, n.d.), p. 249.

> at variance with the texts which say that there is no other *Upāya* than Bhagavān. We counter this objection by asking whether, if we take Lakṣmī as the inseparable attribute, as you hold, in the second part of *Dvaya*, it would not follow that there are two objects of attainment, namely, Bhagavān and Lakṣmī and whether this would not be at variance with the text which says "There is no other interest or object of attainment than Bhagavān."[69]

Veṅkaṭanātha's point here is to show that Lokācārya, while trying to avoid the implication of two "means" (*Upāya*-s), falls into the trap of implying that there are two "objects of attainment" (*upeya*-s). While accepting the word "*Śrīmat*" as applicable to both Nārāyaṇa and Lakṣmī in the second part of the *Dvaya*, argues Veṅkaṭanātha, Lokācārya does not fully explain how he could avoid the implication of "two objects of attainment." At this point, Veṅkaṭanātha is not really explaining his position, but rather is trying to find gaps in the interpretation of Lokācārya. Nevertheless, he goes on to explain the reason why he could not accept "*Śrīmat*" as an accidental mark either in the first part or in the second part of the *Dvaya*. He says:

> Certain qualities, certain forms (*vigrahas*), and certain activities are necessary for *Īśvara* being the *Upāya*. Likewise certain other qualities, certain other forms, and certain activities are ever associated with *Īśvara* as the object of attainment. These necessary (things), also, would be at variance with *Īśvara* being the only *Upāya* and the only object of attainment respectively. So they, too, would have to be considered as accidental features and not inseparable attributes, but this would be against the view of these critics who hold that *Īśvara* is the Protector or Savior only in virtue of (such attributes as) His omnipotence and His compassion. So they cannot concede that these qualities are only accidental features (*upalakṣaṇa*).[70]

If the word "*Śrīmat*" is accepted as an accidental mark (in the first half of *Dvaya*), by the same logic, all other auspicious qualities of the Lord must also be taken as accidental features. But this, says Veṅkaṭanātha, is not acceptable to Lokācārya's position because he affirms the inseparable nature of the attributes such as "omnipotence" and "compassion." He continues to argue that, inasmuch as "omnipotence" and "compassion" are considered inseparable attributes (*viśeṣaṇa*) of God on the basis that they are "useful for the purpose of protection" of the *jīva*-s[71] ,the word "*Śrīmat*" must also be accepted as an inseparable attribute (*viśeṣaṇa*) of God for the same purpose of the protection of the *jīva*-s. He says, "The respective uses of particular things or beings are in accordance with their nature, and may be understood from the *pramāṇa*-s and from tradition."[72] By her very nature, Śrī-Lakṣmī is useful in the protection of the *jīva*-s. In order to support his argument, Veṅkaṭanātha quotes from Nammāḷvār,

69. Ibid., p. 250.
70. Ibid., pp. 250-51.
71. Ibid., p. 251.
72. Ibid.,

Yāmuna, Rāmānuja, and Parāśara Bhaṭṭar, as well as from the Rāmāyaṇa, *Sāttvata Saṃhitā* (Pāñcarātra Āgama), and other sources.[73] He says that attributes such as "omnipotence" and "compassion" are only nonsentient qualities. If such nonsentient qualities can be accepted as inseparable, he argues:

> Why do you object to the idea of Lakṣmī being the attribute (*viśeṣaṇa*) and Nārāyaṇa being the substantive (*viśeṣya*), when this divine couple have the same pleasure or relish in all actions and when there is the authority of the *śāstras* for it?[74]

Thus, Veṅkaṭanātha does not want to radically separate the substantive and the attribute (the Lord and his consort), but rather sees the two as a single entity. On the one hand, he affirms that, even when the Lord gains some excellence from his consort, it does not necessarily mean that he was wanting something previously. On the other hand, Veṅkaṭanātha also affirms that there is a mutual exchange of excellence between the Lord and his consort.[75]

The basic point of Veṅkaṭanātha, in contrast to that of Lokācārya, comes down to the following: for Veṅkaṭanātha, the attribute "*Śrīmat*" is as inseparable from the Lord (Substantive) as any other auspicious quality of the Lord. As a matter of fact, if there is any hierarchy at all among the various attributes based on sentient and nonsentient nature of attributes, "*Śrīmat*" should be higher than all the other attributes because Śrī is a sentient attribute as opposed to the other nonsentient attributes such as omnipotence and compassion. Thus, in his criticism, Veṅkaṭanātha gives special significance to the attribute "*Śrīmat*," fearing that Lokācārya has reduced the attribute "*Śrīmat*" to a secondary status (*upalakṣaṇa*). The point that he wants to affirm, however, is that Śrī-Lakṣmī, by virtue of her being inseparable from the Lord, is also part of the *Siddhopāya*. From this standpoint, he criticizes Lokācārya for being inconsistent in interpreting the attribute "*Śrīmat*" in both parts of the *Dvayamantra*.

I shall now explain the position of Lokācārya on this issue. He takes the attribute "*Śrīmat*" as an accidental feature (*upalakṣaṇa*) in the first part, and in the second, as an inseparable attribute (*viśeṣaṇa*). By taking the "*Śrīmat*" as an accidental feature in the first part of the *Dvaya*, he obviously avoids the suggestion that Śrī-Lakṣmī also is the "means" (*Upāya*) to salvation. At the same time, even when taking the same attribute as an inseparable attribute, he does not suggest that Śrī-Lakṣmī is the "object of attainment," as Veṅkaṭanātha seems to have misconstrued. All that Lokācārya does is to suggest that it is acceptable to render service to Śrī-Lakṣmī, in as much as she is a mediator (*Puruṣakāra*), though not the "means"(*Upāya*).

73. Ibid., pp. 251-53.
74. Ibid., pp. 253-54.
75. Ibid., pp. 254-55.

As explained earlier in Chapter Five, what is most important for Lokācārya is the affirmation of the independent nature of God's omnipotence and compassion. In other words, independent of both the *karma*-s of *jīva*-s as well as any other mediator, God showers his grace upon the *jīva*-s. When he rejects the divine consort as another alternative means (*Upāya*) what he is trying to do is to avoid any dilution of God's independent nature. Thus, in the ultimate analysis, in Lokācārya's scheme there can be only one "means" (*Upāya*) and only one "object of attainment" (*Upeya*). The main condition of *prapatti* is, "The Lord only is to be the object of *prapatti*."[76] But at a certain level, Lokācārya does affirm the divine consort as a "means." Her function as a mediator is merely to lead to the right means (*Upāya*), the Lord.

As to Veṅkaṭanātha's criticism that Lokācārya is inconsistent in his interpretation of "*Śrīmat,*" it must be pointed out that Veṅkaṭanātha seems to miss the point of Lokācārya because he sees it only from his standpoint. In fairness to both, it must be stated, however, that both of them are affirming that there is only one "means" (*Upāya*) and only one "object of attainment" (*Upeya*). Veṅkaṭanātha arrives at his position by affirming an ultimate oneness between the Lord and his consort, whereas Lokācārya arrives at his position by subordinating everything, including the divine consort, to the Lord. While Lokācārya finds it difficult to compromise the radical independence of God's omnipotence and compassion, Veṅkaṭanātha finds it difficult to radically separate the attribute and the substantive (Lakṣmī and Nārāyaṇa). In this affirmation, Veṅkaṭanātha seems closer to the *Lakṣmī Tantra*.

76 Lokācārya, *Śrīvacanabhūṣaṇa*, p. 20. (Lester's comment on v. 24).

CHAPTER EIGHT

TRADITION: CONTINUITY AND CHANGE
(Clarifying Issues in Understanding Śrī-Lakṣmī)

The Śrīvaiṣṇava tradition of South India traces its origin and development basically to two important traditions, namely the *bhakti* tradition of the Āḷvārs and the philosophical tradition of Vedānta. Not only Western scholars but also the traditional Śrīvaiṣṇavas themselves subscribe to the above view. Hence the claim for dual Vedānta (*Ubhaya Vedānta*). Neither of the two traditions, however, adequately explains the ritual tradition of the Śrīvaiṣṇavas. Among the many things remembered about Yāmuna and Rāmānuja, the two most prominent teachers of the community, their contribution to the establishment of a ritual tradition that is basically drawn from the Pāñcarātra is of great significance to later developments in the Śrīvaiṣṇava history. Earlier in this study, I have shown the significance of the Pāñcarātra ritual tradition for Yāmuna and Rāmānuja and even to the teachers that succeeded them. Moreover, the role of Śrī-Lakṣmī in the total salvific process of the *jīvas*, and her place in the ritual, can only be expounded in light of the Pāñcarātra ritual tradition. For it is the Pāñcarātra ritual tradition that provides a significant place to Śrī-Lakṣmī in the Śrīvaiṣṇava rituals. The Pāñcarātra tradition also tries to explain how Śrī-Lakṣmī fits into the ontological scheme that ultimately affirms the oneness of all reality (*ekāntikavāda*).

In the earlier chapters, I have tried to show how the understanding of Śrī-Lakṣmī is closely tied with the Pāñcarātra tradition. I have also tried to show that the Śrīvaiṣṇava tradition is continuous with the Pāñcarātra tradition. In order to do this, I have surveyed the Vedic materials and then presented the Pāñcarātra understanding of Śrī-Lakṣmī, basing my assessment primarily on the *Lakṣmī Tantra* and the *Ahirbudhnya Saṃhitā,* both of which consider the Goddess very significant in their ontological scheme. In light of the Pāñcarātra notion of Śrī-Lakṣmī, I have investigated the writings of the early *ācārya*-s, beginning with Yāmuna up through Veṅkaṭanātha (*alias* Vedānta Deśika). I have attempted to show that the later *ācārya*-s of the tradition were not only continuous with the teachings of the early *ācārya*-s, but that they actually brought new dimensions into the tradition. More specifically, the thirteenth century teachers reflect the sectarian views that eventually led to the division of the tradition into Northern culture (*Vaṭakaḷai*) and Southern culture (*Teṅkaḷai*) during the eighteenth century, C.E. I have also attempted to expound the differences between the understanding of the two thirteenth century teachers, namely, Lokācārya and Veṅkaṭanātha.

The Vedic and the epic materials present Śrī-Lakṣmī in association with prosperity, sovereignty, and beauty. As a minor deity she is characterized by her "inconstancy" although she finally settles down with Viṣṇu. In the Vedic materials her association with Viṣṇu presupposes his supremacy over all Īśvaras and Goddesses. As such, Śrī-Lakṣmī is seen as Viṣṇu's consort occupying a subordinate position, responsible mainly for the prosperity and well-being of kings and their subjects. She symbolizes auspiciousness and beauty.

There seems to be no single position within the Pāñcarātra tradition on the ontological status of Śrī-Lakṣmī. Different texts of the Pāñcarātra present varied dimensions of Śrī-Lakṣmī. The *Lakṣmī Tantra* obviously assumes an equal status for Śrī-Lakṣmī, whereas the *Ahirbudhnya Saṃhitā* presents Viṣṇu as the primary deity and Śrī-Lakṣmī as the consort of Viṣṇu, as in the husband-wife relationship of the Indian family structure. In other Pāñcarātra texts, Śrī-Lakṣmī appears as the consort of Viṣṇu and only a few verses are assigned to her in the context of the ritual (e.g., *Sāttvata-*, *Pauṣkara-*, and *Pādma Saṃhitā*-s). Some texts make no reference to Śrī-Lakṣmī except that she is seated at Viṣṇu's feet (e.g., *Parama Saṃhitā,* Ch.1, v.58). Although the Pāñcarātra texts present divergent notions of the status of Śrī-Lakṣmī in relation to Viṣṇu, in general the Pāñcarātra point of view, among other things, presents Śrī-Lakṣmī as being in charge of the creative process of the universe. She is constituted of the same attributes (*ṣadguṇa*-s), namely, *jñāna, aiśvarya, vīrya, bala, śakti*, and *tejas*, as Viṣṇu. When she distinguishes herself as Viṣṇu's *śakti,* Viṣṇu remains, as it were, in obscurity, and Śrī-Lakṣmī as Viṣṇu's *śakti* dominates the entire realm of creation, maintenance, and destruction. As pointed out earlier (vide Ch. 2), Śrī-Lakṣmī, as *jagannirmāṇaśakti* of the Lord, out of her own desire to create, pervades the entire universe. Therefore, her essential nature is characterized as "*sisṛkṣā.*"

Notice that in the Pāñcarātra tradition, it is not Viṣṇu who desires to create but Śrī-Lakṣmī herself. This point is important since Viṣṇu, both in his *Para* and *Vyūha* forms, remains in the realm of pure creation (*suddha sṛṣṭi*). Śrī-Lakṣmī, on the other hand, has contact with both pure creation and the nonpure creation, for she brings the material universe into being. Thus, the material universe, with all sentient and nonsentient beings, is in direct contact with Śrī-Lakṣmī, whereas it is only in indirect contact with Viṣṇu. Śrī-Lakṣmī, as Viṣṇu's *śakti,* operates as the connecting medium between Para Vāsudeva and the material universe. In other words, in the Pāñcarātra scheme, there seems to be some part of Īśvara that cannot simply come into direct contact with the material universe unless his other aspect, which is his *śakti*, functions as the medium. The *śakti* of Īśvara can absorb all the impurity of the material universe, since she seems to form the substance with which both pure creation and nonpure creation are made.

The *Lakṣmī Tantra* attributes the functions of creation, maintenance, and dissolution to Śrī-Lakṣmī. The Pāñcarātra conception of Para Vāsudeva as transcendent does not necessarily imply a hierarchy between Īśvara and his *śakti*, as higher and lower, because they are never separable. One has to be careful in assuming such a radical hierarchy between Īśvara and his *śakti*. Whereas the *Lakṣmī Tantra* places Śrī-Lakṣmī on a par with Viṣṇu, the language of the *Ahirbudhnya Saṃhiā* is not very clear. It does emphasize the inseparability of the Lord and his *śakti*, but at the same time does not commit itself to the equal status of both. Both in the *Lakṣmī Tantra* and in the *Ahirbudhnya Saṃhitā*, however, there seems to be an ostensible sequence of order in which Para Vāsudeva and his *śakti* manifest themselves in the course of the creative process. This order of manifestation seems to be only functional and no status ranking is attributed at the ontological level. Śrī-Lakṣmī's connection with the material universe (or nonpure creation—*śuddhetara sṛṣṭi*) and the order in which she appears at creation as Para Vāsudeva's *śakti*, might be misconstrued to suggest that there is a status difference between the two of them. We have already noted in an earlier chapter (Ch.2), that the *Lakṣmī Tantra* uses a *dvandva* (*trayornauḥ*) to refer to a joint initiative. The entire universe is said to have emerged out of the billionth particle of the Lakṣmī-Nārāyaṇa complex. There, the text undoubtedly speaks of a "dual divinity," and the universe forms part of that "dual divinity." Conceiving the reality in such *dvandva* terms is not unknown in Indian speculation. We only need to refer to the Vedic *dvandva* deities such as Indra-Agni, Indra-Varuṇa, and Mitra-Varuṇa.[1]

Even if we take the suggestion of Otto Schrader, which is based on the *Ahirbudhnya Saṃhiā*, and accept a certain hierarchy between Viṣṇu and his *śakti*, the hierarchy seems more of a functional nature than of an essential nature (*svabhāva*). Viṣṇu wills, and his *śakti* carries out the task of creation. The two seem to perform two distinct functions and yet they are inseparably one. They are not only connected inseparably by virtue of their mutually complementary functions but also by virtue of their essential nature being one. In this regard, while the *Lakṣmī Tantra* categorically affirms the essential oneness of the nature of Viṣṇu and his *śakti*, the *Ahirbudhnya Saṃhitā* affirms a close proximity of two equal principles. It says, "Owing to extreme closeness (*ati saṃśleṣāt*), the two all-pervading ones, Nārāyaṇa and His *śakti*, have become, as it were, a single principle (*ekaṃ tattvam iva*)."[2] Both Āgamas ascribe to Viṣṇu and his *śakti* the six auspicious qualities.

The Pāñcarātra Āgamas attribute greater significance to the six auspicious qualities that constitute the divine reality. These six

1. Indra-Agni: *The Ṛg Veda*, 3:12:1 ff; Indra-Varuṇa: ibid., 7:82:1 ff; 7:83:1 ff; 7:84:1 ff; Mitra-Varuṇa : ibid., 5:62:1 ff; 5:63:1 ff; 5:64:1 ff; 5:65:1 ff; 5:72:1.

2. Otto Schrader, *Introduction to the Pāñcarātra and the Ahirbudhnya Saṃhitā*, p. 118.

auspicious qualities are not simply descriptive adjectives but attributes that reveal the very nature of Īśvara, and are perceived as real "essences" that the divine reality is made up of. The divine reality is perceived as identical with knowledge (*jñāna*), and the other five attributes are an extension of that basic nature, namely, *jñāna*. The *Lakṣmī Tantra* makes it clear that *jñāna* is the essential nature of both Nārāyaṇa and Lakṣmī (*jñānātmakaṃ paraṃ rūpaṃ brahmano mama cobhayoḥ*).[3]

What the *Lakṣmī Tantra* and other Āgamas are trying to do is to provide a new answer to the old philosophical problem, namely, the problem of duality in the divine nature. The Āgamas have perceived Lakṣmī and Nārāyaṇa as two aspects of the same divine principle. This is accomplished by using the formula of six auspicious qualities (*ṣāḍguṇya*) and the principle of inseparable (*apṛthak*) relation. By visualizing Lakṣmī-Nārāyaṇa as sharing in the same *ṣaḍguṇa*-s and remaining always in an inseparable relation, the Āgamas attempt to overcome the ostensible duality between Īśvara and his *śakti*. Even the ostensible duality is explained as functional rather than essential.

In line with the Pāñcarātra understanding of Śrī-Lakṣmī, Yāmuna understands Īśvara basically in terms of the *ṣaḍguṇa*-s (*jñāna*, etc.). He does use the expression "*jñānādiṣāḍguṇyanidhi*"[4] to describe Īśvara, and at several other places he uses expressions such as "*jñānādi. . . .*" which recall the Pāñcarātra notion of Īśvara. Neevel, in his work on Yāmuna, has already shown this substantially. He points out that Yāmuna not only uses the six *guṇa*-s to describe Īśvara but presents the six *guṇa*-s in exactly the same order as in the Pāñcarātra Āgamas. He says:

> Since Yāmuna presents the six qualities in precisely this order it is clear that he was openly and self-consciously integrating this *Pāñcarātrika* view of the *Paramātma* or *Brahman* as one major aspect of his attempt to demonstrate the complete compatibility of Pāñcarātra and Vedānta.[5]

If Yāmuna is so rooted in the Pāñcarātra tradition and integrated it into the Vedāntic system, it is unlikely that he would have ignored the aspect of Śrī-Lakṣmī which is undoubtedly a dominant theme in the Pāñcarātra Āgamas. The fact that he wrote a separate hymn called *Catuśślokī*, and also added several verses in his *Stotraratna* on Śrī-Lakṣmī, shows that he, indeed, took the aspect of the divine consort very seriously. She does fit into the overall ontological scheme of Yāmuna perfectly. By perceiving her as an inseparable match of the Lord's, and further comprehending her in the Lord's cosmic form (*viśvarūpa*), he accords to her a position that is uniquely befitting her role as mediatrix. She mediates between Īśvara and his souls as an

3. *LT*. 2:25.
4. Vide chap. 3.
5. Neevel, op.cit., p. 171.

equal partner of Īśvara, standing in inseparable relation to him. Yāmuna's expressions, such as "inseparable match" and "comprehending in Thine (the Lord's) form," are loaded with Pāñcarātra notions of Śrī-Lakṣmī. Furthermore, she is described as "sole ruler of the world" (*lokaikeśvarī*) and as the one who creates, maintains, and dissolves the three worlds. These expressions fit very well the Pāñcarātra notions of Śrī-Lakṣmī. It is unlikely that Yāmuna would have used these expressions totally without regard to their implications in the Pāñcarātra Āgamas. In the process of integrating the Pāñcarātra tradition with the Vedāntic tradition, he obviously appropriated the Pāñcarātra notion of Śrī-Lakṣmī. Comprehending Śrī-Lakṣmī within the cosmic form of Īśvara rather than outside of Īśvara as an independent entity is more logical within the scheme of Yāmuna. In his conception, therefore, the Lord and his divine consort fit together in a holistic scheme as two sides of the same reality.

Turning now to Rāmānuja, we have seen that he adopts the same arguments that Yāmuna offered in support of the Pāñcarātra Āgamas. Unlike Yāmuna, however, Rāmānuja did not compose any independent hymn in praise of Śrī-Lakṣmī. Therefore, the only way to go about understanding Rāmānuja's notion of Śrī-Lakṣmī is to take his commentarial materials and devotional materials together, and also to see how the tradition remembers him in the biographical materials, even though most of those materials come from a much later period (i.e., the fifteenth and sixteenth centuries or perhaps even later).

As far as his writings are concerned, there is no doubt that Rāmānuja remains relatively silent as to how exactly he understood the divine consort in relation to the total scheme of his metaphysics. In this regard Carman's observations are well-founded.[6] Rāmānuja, however, breaks his silence occasionally and makes some very valid and significant statements about the divine consort. As I have attempted to show in Chapter 3, these occasional statements appear to be more than passing remarks. They seem to make sense only when seen from the standpoint of the total scheme of Rāmānuja's thought. What makes these statements more significant is their appearance in the *maṅgala śloka*-s, which are considered vital to the theology of Rāmānuja.

The basic structure and thesis of Rāmānuja's system does not differ in any way from that of Yāmuna. What Rāmānuja does is to take the system deeper into the Vedānta and provide it a stronger Vedāntic foundation. In so doing, he uses a language that is uniquely Vedāntic. Since the major inquiry in the Upaniṣads concerns the ultimate reality, Brahman, understandably a discussion of the divine consort did not call for his attention. Nevertheless, in so far as he expressly addresses her as the Mother of the universe and describes her with such qualities as are appropriate to the Lord (Viṣṇu) and seeks her protection, it is important to see how Śrī-Lakṣmī fits into his scheme rather than simply disregarding that dimension, a dimension which has been a

6. J. B. Carman, *Theology of Rāmānuja*, p. 238 f.

very significant part of the Śrīvaiṣṇava ritual tradition to the present day.

From the standpoint of the Viśiṣṭādvaita system there can be only two possible positions in order to accommodate the divine consort: 1) First, to reduce the divine consort to the status of an ornament like any other of the ornaments of Īśvara, such as his weapons, the *Śeṣa* on which he sleeps, the attendants, etc., that accompany him always. This possibility is suggested by Carman in his *Theology of Rāmānuja.* In this suggestion, Śrī-Lakṣmī is considered an attribute like any other attribute of Īśvara. The problem with this suggestion is that it does not explain adequately all those statements that Rāmānuja makes about the divine consort. It certainly helps preserve the unity in the divine nature, but it does not account for the place of Śrī-Lakṣmī in the total scheme of the salvation of the *jīva*-s. In other words, no matter how special a kind of *śeṣa* she is, the question of how Śrī-Lakṣmī, as *śeṣa* of Īśvara, is ontologically inseparable from Īśvara and is part of the salvific process of the *jīva*-s, is not fully explained.[7] If Śrī-Lakṣmī has a significant role in the salvific process of the *jīva*-s, she must have an ontological status in relation to Viṣṇu, and her intervention as mediatrix cannot be the same as that of anyone who has some special favor in the sight of Īśvara, as is the case of an *ācārya*. In other words, Śrī-Lakṣmī's place cannot be simply the same as that of an *ācārya* in so far as an *ācārya* can also perform the role of the mediator between Īśvara and his devotees. In Rāmānuja's own thought, the mediatorial role of Śrī-Lakṣmī seems to be much more significant than that of the *ācārya*. This is clearly reflected in his *Śaraṇāgatigadya.*

2) The alternative is to see the divine consort as that aspect of the total reality of Īśvara that symbolizes Īśvara's compassion and mercy for the *jīva*-s. In this alternative, there is no radical separation between the two natures of Īśvara (*paratva* and *saulabhya*). It seeks only to make the divine consort more integral to the complete nature of Īśvara. Further, this view takes seriously into account why Rāmānuja makes such parallel statements as "Viṣṇu is all-pervading—she (Śrī-Lakṣmī) is all-pervading."[8] In his prayer to the divine consort in *Śaraṇāgatigadya*, Rāmānuja uses a language that certainly elevates the divine consort to a position that ranks her on a par with the Lord. If Rāmānuja perceived the divine consort only as someone a little above the attendants and other deities and goddesses, it would have been unnecessary for him to have used words such as "Mother of the whole world," and to have attributed to her all the auspicious qualities

---

7. Although we do not find any direct explanation in the writings of Lokācārya, the later theologians point out that, according to Lokācārya, all the *nityamuktas* are participants in the creative process. In that sense, Śrī-Lakṣmī can be seen as participating in the creative process of God. But the question, then, is whether Śrī-Lakṣmī is considered by Lokācārya as a *nityamuktā*. Cf. Tirumalīśa Aṇṇāvappaṅgār Svāmi, et al. *Pūrvācārya Saṃpradāya Dvayābhimatā Aṣṭādaśabheda Saṃgrahaḥ* (Cennapuri: Liberty Press, 1978), p. 13, v. 22.

8. Vide chap. 3.

such as "Greatness" and "Rulership," etc. And it would have also been unnecessary to use systematically the same qualities with exactly the same compounds and to speak of her as being worthy of Īśvara's natural form (*svabhāva*) and qualities. If Rāmānuja thought of the divine consort as lower than the Lord, the passage in the Bhagavad Gītā 10:34, in which Viṣṇu and his consort are identified as one, should have needed some explanation. In the Gītā passage, it is Kṛṣṇa (Viṣṇu) who says "I am Śrī, etc." Rāmānuja simply restates the same thing in his commentary and adds no explanation. In paraphrasing the statement, however, he does make some significant changes in the sentences. Notice that the Gītā passage 10:34 reads as follows:

> *kīrtiś śrīr vāk ca nārīṇāṃ smṛtir megha dhṛtiḥ kṣamā*
> (Among women I (Viṣṇu) am Kīrti, Śrī, Vāk, Smṛti, Medhā, Dhṛti, and Kṣamā).

Now, compare this with Rāmānuja's rephrasing of the same verse:

> *śrīrahaṃ| nārīṇāṃ kīrtiś cāhaṃ vāk cāhaṃ smṛtiś cāhaṃ megha cāhaṃ dhṛtiś cāhaṃ kṣamā cāham||*
> (I am Śrī; Among women I am also Kīrti, I am Vāk too. And I am Smṛti. I am also Meghā. And I am Dhṛti. And I am Kṣamā).[9]

While the Gītā passage includes Śrī along with other names, Rāmānuja separates Śrī from the list of other names and gives it an independent place in the verse. This can be noticed in the restructuring of the syntax to bring "*nārīṇām. . . .*" after the mention of Śrī. Thus he goes on to add that among women he (Viṣṇu) is also Kīrti, Vāk, etc. Although Rāmānuja does not provide any explanation for this change in the reading, it seems to have a structural relation to the way he relates Śrī-Lakṣmī to Viṣṇu elsewhere, in a passage that I referred to earlier.[10] This identification of Viṣṇu and Śrī-Lakṣmī in the Gītā passage (according to Rāmānuja's own reading in his comment) fits well with his parallel statement—"Viṣṇu is all-pervading— Śrī is all-pervading"; it also fits with his affirmation that Śrī-Lakṣmī is the "Mother of the whole world;" and finally, it fits with the way he attributes the same auspicious qualities to Viṣṇu and Śrī-Lakṣmī.

Even if we were to suppose that some later commentator interpolated this change in Rāmānuja's reading of the Gītā passage 10:34 in order to have the philosopher affirm an equal status for Śrī-Lakṣmī, such a commentator surely would have made it unambiguous as to what Rāmānuja's position is. And furthermore, he would have made similar changes in other places as well.

One ontological problem with placing Śrī-Lakṣmī on the *śeṣa* side of the equation is that it would mean Śrī-Lakṣmī belongs to the

---

9. *Gītābhāṣya*, trans. Sampatkumaran, p. 301.
10. See chap. 3.

material creation. According to the Pāñcarātra metaphysics, the Lord and his *śakti* belong to the pure substance (*śuddha sattvam*). When the Lord's *śakti* is distinguished from him, she becomes engaged in the process of creation, and from her emerge the pure creation, the nonpure creation, as well as the impure creation (i.e., the lower creation—the material world). Thus, in this sense the Pāñcarātra Āgamas affirm both ontological as well as functional oneness. Because of her inseparable relation to Para Vāsudeva, she is one with him and hence on a par with him. (This position is clearly found in the *Lakṣmī Tantra,* although the *Ahirbudhnya Saṃhitā* places more emphasis on Viṣṇu by showing that Śrī, as Īśvara's *śakti*, functions at the will of the Lord). It is because of her connection with both Para Vāsudeva and the material world that she stands in a unique relationship to the Lord on the one hand, and to the world and the *jīva*-s on the other. She belongs to the *śeṣin* side of Īśvara and yet occupies a unique position of being the mediator between the Lord and his devotees.

By affirming that Śrī-Lakṣmī is the Mother of the universe, Rāmānuja implicitly accepts the Pāñcarātra point of view of ultimate reality. It is difficult to point out which particular Āgama text/s Rāmānuja was following in order to affirm Śrī-Lakṣmī as the Mother of the universe unless we know more about the Pāñcarātra Āgamas, either written or oral, that were in vogue during his time. Rāmānuja may not necessarily be following the point of view of the *Lakṣmī Tantra,* but it is certainly fair to say that his point of view could be interpreted as being closer to the *Lakṣmī Tantra* than other Pāñcarātra Āgamas.[11] It is unnecessary in this study to attempt to establish whether Rāmānuja was following the *Lakṣmī Tantra* or the other way around. My concern is only to show that there is the possibility for a theological position in which both the Lord and his divine consort are seen as equal, and that the positions of Yāmuna and Rāmānuja as well as that of the *Lakṣmī Tantra* could be interpreted as presenting this perspective. As I have shown earlier in the chapter on Veṅkaṭanātha, and as we shall see later, this position is articulated most vigorously by Veṅkaṭanātha, who draws his support both from Rāmānuja and the *Lakṣmī Tantra*, among other sources.

In Rāmānuja's own description of the Lord and the divine consort, we see a Pāñcarātra conception of the divine reality. The closeness of "doctrine and fundamental point of view" between disputed works (*Gadya*-s and the *Nityagrantha*) and the undisputed

11. From the writings of Rāmānuja we have evidence to show that he was familiar with three *Saṃhitās*, namely, the *Sāttvata-*, *Pauṣkara-* and *Jayākhya Saṃhitā*-s. But we have no evidence of his familiarity with the *Lakṣmī Tantra.* I have noted elsewhere that the *Lakṣmī Tantra* was first referred to by Nādādūr Ammāl, the teacher of Veṅkaṭanātha. With regard to the idea of Śrī-Lakṣmī as the 'Mother of the universe,' it is possible that Rāmānuja may have found that idea in the Purāṇic material, where it also appears. Nevertheless, it is still interesting that it fits in well with the idea of Śrī-Lakṣmī in the *Lakṣmī Tantra.*

works has been soundly demonstrated by Carman.[12] Once we accept the oneness of the teachings of Rāmānuja in both commentaries and devotional works, we will notice that Rāmānuja, indeed, did integrate the Pāñcarātra notions into his Vedāntic framework as much as Yāmuna did. Brahman, which Rāmānuja speaks of in his philosophical works, is also identified with the Pāñcarātra attributes such as *jñāna*, etc. Notice the way he lists the attributes of Īśvara in his *Śaraṇāgatigadya:*

> *svābhāvikānavadhikātiśaya jñānabalavīryaśaktitejaḥ.*
> (You are the ocean into which flow the rivers of natural, limitless, excellent qualities such as *jñāna, bala,* (*aiśvarya*), *vīrya, śakti,* and *tejas*).[13]

Evidently the description of Īśvara with attributes such as *jñāna*, etc., is consonant with the Pāñcarātra notion of the ultimate reality. Again, both in the *Vedārthasaṃgraha* and in the *Śaraṇāgatigadya*, he describes the divine consort as the "Mother of the universe."[14] When we place the description of the Lord and the divine consort together, what we find is the affirmation of the Pāñcarātra notion of Para Vāsudeva and his indistinguishable *śakti*, who constitute the ultimate reality. If Para Vāsudeva and his *śakti* are indistinguishable at the ontological level, then logically she must be on the *śeṣin* side of the equation and not on the *śeṣa* side. If she is only a little above the rest of the created beings, it is difficult to account for her role before and after the process of creation. Moreover, she would then be a creature of Īśvara. We will then have to explain how not only the three realities (*tattvatraya - Īśvara, cit,* and *acit*), but also a fourth reality,[15] namely, the divine consort (Īśvara's *śakti*), form one reality. Not only is there no possibility of a fourth reality in the scheme of Rāmānuja, but we find neither in the Pāñcarātra nor in the writings of Rāmānuja the idea that Śrī-Lakṣmī is created by Īśvara. In fact, Śrī-Lakṣmī as *śakti* of Īśvara, forming the material substance for the creation, makes sense only when viewed from the total complex of Īśvara's reality. One of the basic affirmations of the Viśiṣṭādvaita philosophy, according to Rāmānuja, is that Īśvara is both material cause (*pradhānakāraṇa*) and the instrumental cause (*nimittakāraṇa*). When Pāñcarātra speaks of the *śakti* of Īśvara as the material cause (*bhūti śakti*) and instrumental cause (*kriyā śakti*), it must be understood against the background of

---

12. Carman, op.cit., p. 218.
13. Rāmānuja, *Śaraṇāgatigadya,* p. 10, v. 4.
14. Rāmānuja, *Vedārthasaṃgraha,* pp. 170-71, v. 217.
15. This is because Śrī-Lakṣmī would fit neither the category of *Īśvara* nor of *cit* or *acit*. She cannot be *acit* because she is a conscious being; she cannot be in the category of *cit* because it becomes meaningless to think of Śrī-Lakṣmī involved in the process of creation if she is merely *cit*. She could not be *cit* and at the same time be creator of *cit*. And if she does not fit the category of *Īśvara*, then there must be a fourth category in which she fits. But neither the Pāñcarātra nor the Viśiṣṭādvaita systems provide for a fourth reality.

its basic affirmation that, in the ultimate analysis, Īśvara and his *śakti* are not two separable entities but that they form one single entity. Otherwise, its (Pāñcarātra) basic philosophical premise as *ekāntikavāda* would be meaningless. At the functional level, Para Vāsudeva remains in obscurity and his indistinguishable *śakti* performs the role as the creator. In this sense, there is no contradiction between Rāmānuja's affirmation that Īśvara is both the material cause and the instrumental cause, and the Pāñcarātra notion that Īśvara's *śakti* is the material cause (*bhūti śakti*) and the instrumental cause (*kriyā śakti*). Thus, Rāmānuja's basic philosophy is continuous with the Pāñcarātra philosophy and his understanding of Śrī-Lakṣmī is also continuous with the Pāñcarātra understanding.

Having made an attempt to clarify Rāmānuja's understanding of Śrī-Lakṣmī, it must be admitted, however, that whether or not one accords a lower status to Śrī-Lakṣmī or elevates her to the status of Viṣṇu, one really does not have adequate evidence to interpret Rāmānuja's writings. In view of this, what I have done in my study is to bring together the sporadic statements that Rāmānuja makes on Śrī-Lakṣmī and try to make sense out of them in light of his total scheme. In dealing with Śrī-Lakṣmī both Yāmuna and Rāmānuja seem to be continuous with the Pāñcarātra tradition, at least as far as the inseparability of the Lord and his consort is concerned.

The diversification of the tradition after Rāmānuja may be seen from Bhaṭṭar onward. In the case of Kuruttāḷvān and Piḷḷān[16] there is, in general, a great deal of continuity, especially in the case of Piḷḷān. John Carman and Vasudha Narayanan in their work do show that Piḷḷān was continuous with Rāmānuja's thought and that he even uses many of his expressions. Even though Bhaṭṭar is also largely continuous with his predecessors' thought, he brings new elements into the tradition. His choice of sources from Purāṇic and epic materials is certainly a significant move from the highly systematic work of Rāmānuja toward more fluid and popular forms of expression. His commentary on *Śrīviṣṇusahasranāma* is a significant move from the serene meditative type of the *upāsana bhakti* in which recitation of Īśvara's thousand names takes precedence over rigid ritual activities. In this sense, the Āḷvār emotional *bhakti* reappears in the thought of Bhaṭṭar. Furthermore, his *Guṇaratnakośa,* which is devoted to the praise of the divine consort, is much more elaborate than the *Śrīstava* of Kuruttāḷvān. What is characteristic of his theology is that his exposition of Śrī-Lakṣmī is more elaborate than that of his predecessors. He integrates the divine consort into the total scheme of

---

16. Since I have limited myself to the treatment of the major teachers of the tradition, I have not dealt with the writings of Kuruttāḷvān and Piḷḷān. Kuruttāḷvān is also known as Kureśa and Śrīvatśaṅkamiśra. Carman and Narayanan have provided some insight into Piḷḷān's understanding of Śrī-Lakṣmī in their recent joint work, *The Tamil Veda: Piḷḷān's Interpretation of the Tiruvāymoḷi* (Chicago: The University of Chicago Press, 1989).

the Śrīvaiṣṇava tradition much more explicitly than his predecessors did. His exposition on the Lord and his consort is equally balanced. As Carman and Narayanan point out, Yāmuna's *Catuśślokī* certainly served as a paradigm for Bhaṭṭar's *Guṇaratnakośa.*[17]

The continuity of Bhaṭṭar's thought with his predecessors, especially in understanding Śrī-Lakṣmī, may be demonstrated, first of all, in his language. In his exposition of Śrī-Lakṣmī, Bhaṭṭar uses categories of interpretation that are coherent with the Pāñcarātra tradition. He gives evidence to the fact that he understands Īśvara in categories that are loaded with Pāñcarātra conceptions of the Lord. He interprets the epithets of Viṣṇu—"*Caturātma*" (of four arms), "*Caturvyūha*" (of four forms), and "*Caturdamṣṭraḥ*" (of four teeth) in terms of four emanations of Para Vāsudeva—Vāsudeva, Saṃkarṣaṇa, Pradyumna, and Aniruddha.[18] Like his predecessors, he also understands Īśvara in terms of the other Pāñcarātra categories, namely, *jñāna, aiśvarya, vīrya, śakti, bala*, and *tejas*. He quotes from the Pāñcarātra texts to show that the six auspicious qualities basically affirm Īśvara's accessibility and love and other qualities, and at the same time to show that the evil qualities are denied:

> *jñānaśaktibalaiśvaryavīryatejāṃsyaśeṣataḥ.*
> *bhagavaccabda vācyāni vina heyaiḥ guṇādibhiḥ*||
> (The term *Bhagavān* expresses *jñāna, śakti, bala, aiśvarya, vīrya, tejas*, etc., infinite qualities except the evil qualities.)[19]

In Rāmānuja's exposition, this theme of auspicious qualities is of great significance. He repeatedly affirms that the Lord has no evil qualities (*heyaguṇa*-s) and is full of auspicious qualities (*kalyāṇaguṇa*-s). Bhaṭṭar follows the same idea and traces it to the Pāñcarātra tradition.

When they speak of *kalyāṇaguṇa*-s, both Bhaṭṭar and his predecessors certainly have in mind the basic and fundamental qualities of Īśvara, namely, the six auspicious qualities mentioned in the Pāñcarātra Āgamas. Rāmānuja, however, in his effort to develop the Vedāntic connections to the tradition, brings in categories from the Upaniṣads, etc., and describes Īśvara in terms of *satya, jñāna, ananta, ānanda*, etc. Bhaṭṭar, on the other hand, makes the Pāñcarātra connections more obvious. It is in his conception of the divine couple that the Pāñcarātra connections are made clearer. In the chapter dealing with Bhaṭṭar, I have tried to show that he continues the thought of Rāmānuja and provides sufficient evidence for his Āgamic basis in developing the notion of divine couple as the divine reality.[20] Bhaṭṭar also understands the essential relationship between the Lord and his divine consort as being characterized by inseparability. Although he makes a distinction between the Lord and his consort at the level of

17. Ibid., p. 52.
18. Bhaṭṭar, *Viṣṇusahasranāmābhāṣya*, trans. A. S. Raghavan, p. 263-65.
19. Ibid., p. 189 (Translation mine).
20. Ibid., p. 9-10 f.

ritual, at the ontological level, however, he perceives them as a single reality.

As the tradition develops further, the nature of the theological reflection becomes more prominently sectarian. The thirteenth century theological developments within the Śrīvaiṣṇava tradition have sown the seeds for the future division of the tradition into Northern and Southern schools.

Lokācārya, whom the Southern school follows, places a great deal of emphasis on *the independent nature of Īśvara*. However, at the same time, he also emphasizes that Īśvara willingly places himself at the disposal of the devotee. In the *Arcāvatāra*, Īśvara is totally at the behest of the devotee, as it were, and allows himself to be accessible. In other words, the Lord's accessibility does not depend on the devotee's initiative. On the other hand, the *jīva* is fully dependent on Īśvara. Furthermore, the Lord's accessibility goes as far as to ignore the defects of the devotee and the very defects of the devotee are taken as an occasion for the Lord's unconditional mercy.

Seen in light of Īśvara's unconditional love for the devotee, the role of Śrī-Lakṣmī seems out of place. Lokācārya's conception of the jīva's salvation does not require the mediatory role of the divine consort. Even though Lokācārya perceives Īśvara in both transcendent and accessible terms, he also sees Īśvara allowing himself to be influenced by his consort. In his conception, however, Śrī-Lakṣmī does mediate between the Lord and his devotees. The question remaining to be asked, however, is whether Lokācārya has a dual conception of Īśvara, i.e., as gracious and accessible to the devotees in spite of their defects; as a just and righteous father who demands that justice is maintained. Although the two notions, namely, the accessible and the transcendent natures, are not mutually exclusive (as shown in Rāmānuja's theology), Lokācārya genuinely struggles to maintain both natures simultaneously while affirming the role of the Goddess. Thus, when he speaks of Īśvara as an absolute reality, he affirms the two natures of Īśvara simultaneously. But when he moves to the functional level to bring in the role of the Goddess, he simply transfers the accessible nature to the divine consort and thus tries to integrate the role of the Goddess into his theological scheme.

The logical gap in Lokācārya's conception of the Goddess perhaps needs to be seen not only from a sociological standpoint but also in light of his attempt to reconcile the scriptural statements that provide for such a conception. Both the Āgamic materials and the epic materials present the Goddess as significant in the process of the devotee's salvation. Lokācārya seems to be rather hard-pressed to make sense of the scriptural references to Śrī-Lakṣmī and construct an ontology that is coherent with his conception of Īśvara. Lokācārya does affirm the Pāñcarātra view of inseparability of the Lord and his consort; he also affirms the role that Śrī-Lakṣmī plays both at the ontological level and at the functional level. For him, Śrī-Lakṣmī is involved both in the creative process of the universe and in the salvific process of the *jīva*-s. But she is ontologically inferior and functionally essential. By making Śrī-Lakṣmī ontologically inferior he brings her closer to the realm of humans and thus makes her more accessible to them. In constructing his ontology, he seems to rely on Āgamic materials that give more prominence to Viṣṇu than to Śrī-Lakṣmī (e.g., *Ahirbudhnya Saṃhitā*).

Moreover, his view makes sense from the sociological standpoint, given the Indian family structure. The sociological perception of woman seems to be reflected in his ontology. His conception of the Goddess's role in influencing the Lord on the one hand, while correcting the ignorance of the devotee on the other, is quite analogous to the role of the mother in an Indian social context. The father is normally perceived as the one who disciplines the child while the mother takes the role of pleading on behalf of the child. We find some clue to Lokācārya's scheme in that kind of traditional Indian familial relationship.

It is precisely from this sociological dimension that Lokācārya's scheme becomes clear. Manavālamāmuni, in his commentaries on Lokācārya's works, brings out this sociological dimension more clearly. In fact, Lokācārya himself makes the comment that Śrī-Lakṣmī's relationship to the Lord and his devotees is like "a mother who refuses to leave either her husband's bed or her child's crib."[21] Manavālamāmuni elaborates on this statement:

> As befitting her subservient nature, in order to give him pleasure, a wife does not leave her husband's bed. As appropriate to her protective nature, in order to watch over him, a mother stays by her child's crib. In the same way, Śrī also clings to her delighting and protecting roles as appropriate to her relationship with her husband and children.[22]

Lokācārya thus perceives Śrī-Lakṣmī in dual natures—she is the "Mother" of the universe and "wife" of the Lord.[23] She is *Śeṣin* in relation to the devotees and *Śeṣa* in relation to the Lord. In the ontological sense, the Lord is both the means and the end (*Upāya* and *Upeya*), but functionally Śrī-Lakṣmī is both the mediator and the goal (*Puruṣakāra* and *Prāpya*).[24]

Again, to underline the servant-master relationship, not only between the devotee and the Lord but also between the devotee and Śrī-Lakṣmī, Lokācārya uses a mundane analogy. He says:

> When a man takes a servant, even though the service contract does not specify the wife, service is certainly done for his wife. Like that we are servants of the Goddess.[25]

---

21. Lokācārya, *Mumukṣuppaḍi*, p. 59.
22. Ibid., pp. 59-60.
23. Ibid., p. 116.
24. Ibid., p. 115.
25. Ibid., p. 60.

Lokācārya's understanding of the divine consort becomes clearer from this sociological standpoint. Nevertheless, it does have an Āgamic basis inasmuch as some Āgamas (e.g., *Ahirbudhnya Saṃhiā*) depict Śrī-Lakṣmī as lower than Viṣṇu in terms of her ontological status.

On the other hand, Lokācārya's counterpart, Veṇkaṭanatha, maintains the tension between the two natures of Īśvara, namely, transcendence (*paratva*) and accessibility (*saulabhya*). This tension between Īśvara's two natures is expressed in the communicability between Īśvara and his devotees. It is in Īśvara's "squeezing" himself between the three Āḷvārs[26] that Veṅkaṭanātha finds that profound expression of the communicability between Īśvara and his devotees. In this we can certainly see continuity with Rāmānuja's thought.

In spite of holding the tension between Īśvara's two natures, Veṅkaṭanātha sees the possibility of Īśvara waiting for the devotee's initiative. The initiative on the side of the devotee is not to imply that Īśvara is somehow not capable of taking the first step, but rather emphasizes Īśvara's patience in waiting for an occasion to shower his grace on the devotee. In that waiting for an occasion, however, there may be some distance or lack of communicability between Īśvara and his devotee. In Veṅkaṭanātha's thought, this distance or lack of communicability is removed by the initiative of the divine consort.

I emphasized earlier that the intervention by the divine consort does not necessarily deny Īśvara's accessible nature. Veṅkaṭanātha holds the two natures in tension by placing no difference in the essential nature (*svabhāva*) of Īśvara and his consort. For him, the divine consort shares in both transcendent and accessible natures. This essential oneness (*svarūpa ekatva*) in the nature of Īśvara and his consort is because of the six auspicious qualities that both of them share. When he makes a functional difference between the Lord and his consort, it is perceived primarily from the standpoint of ritual and not ontology.

Unlike Lokācārya's conception of the divine consort, Veṅkaṭanātha's conception of her must be seen not from a sociological point of view but rather from the standpoint of the internal consistency of his overall metaphysical scheme. By affirming the equal status of Īśvara and his consort, Veṅkaṭanātha finds it easier to perceive them as a single reality. It is in that sense that Śrī-lakṣmī is integrated into his total scheme.

As an advocate of Viśiṣṭādvaita philosophy Veṅkaṭanātha tries to maintain logical consistency in his metaphysics. In order to maintain the ontological oneness of the ultimate reality he had to overcome the ostensible duality present in the divine reality. He maintains the oneness of the ultimate reality by perceiving Īśvara and his consort as substance and attribute. He makes the distinction between attributes

---

26. See Veṅkaṭanātha's *Dehalīśastuti*.

of Īśvara that are *sādhāraṇa* and *asādhāraṇa*. The *sādhāraṇa viśeṣaṇa*-s are Īśvara's auspicious qualities such as *vātsalya, kṛpā*, his ornaments, and so on. Śrī-Lakṣmī is not seen as a *sādhāraṇa* attribute but as an *asādhāraṇa* attribute who is inseparable from Īśvara in every condition. For instance, in his *avatāra*-s, Īśvara is separated from the *ādiśeṣa* on whom he reclines in his *vaikuṇṭha*. In Veṅkaṭanātha's perception, an *asādhāraṇa* attribute is characterized as "*svarūpa nirūpaka dharma*"—that which establishes or reveals the essential nature, whereas the *sādhāraṇa* attribute is characterized as "*nirūpita svarūpa viśeṣaṇa*"—having the quality of a revealed form. It does not reveal the essential nature of Īśvara fully. In Veṅkaṭanātha's view, it is not possible to understand the substance apart from its essential and inseparable attribute. For instance, in the example of cow and horse—by virtue of some common features both cow and horse may be said to belong to the category of animal. But there are essential features (e.g., dewlap) characteristic of a cow which distinguish it from a horse. Those essential attributes are inseparable from cowness. In the same way, Īśvara is known only in relation to his consort. Veṅkaṭanātha shows how Śrī-Lakṣmī is inseparably one with the Lord in his analysis of the term "*Śrīnivāsa*," which Rāmānuja himself uses in his *Śrībhāṣya* to qualify Brahman.[27] Thus, Veṅkaṭanātha's conception of Śrī-Lakṣmī is based primarily on 1) the inseparable nature of Īśvara and his consort; 2) the notion that substance and the attribute fundamentally share in the same essential nature (*svabhāva*); and 3) the principle that one is not understood without the other. All of these notions are fundamental to the conception of Īśvara and his *śakti* in the Pāñcarātra tradition according to the *Lakṣmī Tantra*. In so far as Rāmānuja does not make any clear distinction between the Lord and his consort, Veṅkaṭanātha seems to follow the line of Rāmānuja. He also vigorously supports his arguments by constantly referring to Rāmānuja. Furthermore, his view is closer to the *Lakṣmī Tantra*.

Among the eighteen theological differences between the two schools (the Northern and the Southern), certainly the question of Śrī-Lakṣmī is a subordinate one. In other words, it did not constitute the major difference on which the two schools were divided, although both schools strongly differ on this issue. But an understanding of the Śrivaiṣṇava tradition would be incomplete without an exposition of the understanding of Śrī-Lakṣmī. In so far as the position of Śrī-Lakṣmī is directly related to the understanding of faith and divine grace, the question of her status in relation to the Lord is crucial in its overall discussion. The Northern School (*Vaṭakaḷai*) insists on some measure of human response to divine grace. The Southern School (*Teṅkaḷai*), on the other hand, insists on total surrender (*prapatti*) to Īśvara. Both schools, however, do affirm the role of the divine consort in the process of the salvation of the *jīva*-s. In so far as the Northern School is concerned, the divine consort intervenes between Īśvara and his

27. Vide chap. 6.

devotees because divine justice requires punishment of the sinful. The Southern School also affirms the mediatorial role of the divine consort. Both schools affirm 1)the inseparability of Īśvara and his consort; 2) the role of the divine consort in the creation, maintenance, and dissolution of the world; 3) the role of the divine consort in the process of the salvation of the *jīva*-s. Their basic difference in regard to the divine consort, however, is on the question of her ontological status in relation to Viṣṇu.

The Southern School makes a distinction between the ontological level and the functional level. Thus, for them Śrī-Lakṣmī is ontologically inferior but functionally essential to the Lord. By being ontologically inferior, Śrī-Lakṣmī is seen as being closer to the *jīva*-s than is the transcendent Lord. The divine grace is mediated to the devotees through the divine consort who is closer to them. She stands uniquely close both to the Lord and his devotees simultaneously. The Southern School's position is summed up in a nutshell by Lokācārya's statement that Śrī-Lakṣmī neither leaves her husband's bed nor her child's crib. The Northern School favors the position of equal status of both the Lord and his consort by affirming that the Lord and his consort are essentially and functionally one in their ontological status. While the Southern School seems more concerned about bringing the divine consort closer to the devotees, the Northern School seems more concerned about bringing the divine consort closer to the Lord while still attributing to her the role of mediator. What the Northern School seems to be avoiding is the ambiguity involved in placing Śrī-Lakṣmī neither fully on the side of *Śeṣin* nor fully on the side of *Śeṣa*. By placing her fully on the side of *Śeṣin*, they attempt to achieve coherence to the overall philosophical scheme as per the Viśiṣṭādvaita system.

CHAPTER NINE

AFTERWORD

Interpretive Process of the Śrīvaiṣṇava Tradition

In almost every religious tradition, there are clearly identifiable phases that mark the various developments in the process of its interpretation. The history of the Śrīvaiṣṇava tradition is a clear case that illustrates such identifiable phases in its interpretive process. Although I do not intend to divide its history into rigidly defined phases, for the sake of a general understanding, I shall identify loosely five formative phases.

The first and the foremost phase is the period of the Āḻvārs, which I shall refer to as the period of fluidity. It is during this period that the hymns of the Āḻvārs evoked the unformulated and seminal forms, which would solidify into the concrete ideas of the subsequent Śrīvaiṣṇava theology. The hymns of the Āḻvārs were largely sung in the context of intense devotion for the deity Vāsudeva/Nārāyaṇa, identified as Viṣṇu of the Vedic pantheon. It is quite conceivable that the hymns of the Āḻvārs did not have the meaning that the later Śrīvaiṣṇava theologians have attributed to them. In other words, the ideas of Īśvara and his consort in those hymns were in flux and did not have any fixed theological agenda. They were ideas of Īśvara without boundaries. Those hymns were spontaneous, unrestrained, and unbounded responses of human consciousness to the majesty and mystery of Īśvara. Nevertheless, what became important to the later tradition were two things, namely, those very fluid notions of Īśvara and the context in which the hymns were sung—that context being the temple. Although the Āḻvārs were freelance singers, they associated themselves with the Vaiṣṇava temples in South India. By the time of the Āḻvārs, the temple worship with its Arcā form was already becoming a common factor in the Hindu worship. Certainly, for the Āḻvārs, the Arcā form became paradigmatic for their conceptions of Īśvara and his consort. Many of their hymns vividly describe the Arcā forms in various Viṣṇu temples. As I mentioned in the first chapter, Gonda points out that the pantheon represented in the iconography of the Gupta period is a simple one, namely Viṣṇu accompanied by his consort Lakṣmī either seated on his vehicle, Garuḍa, or sleeping on the cosmic serpent.[1] The Āḻvārs were perhaps familiar with this simple notion of Īśvara and his consort, coupled with some Purāṇic images. According to Gonda and other scholars, the

1. J. Gonda, *Die Religionen Indiens*, vol. 1. p. 115.

Pāñcarātra tradition was already in vogue in the South by the time of the Āḷvārs. Interestingly, the Āḷvārs were also known as the Bhāgavata-s, similar to the Pāñcarātrins. Nevertheless, the available scholarship does not fully establish whether the Āḷvārs and the Pāñcarātrins belong to the same group.[2] One thing common to both is that they both associated themselves with the Vaiṣṇava temples, and worshiped the Arcā form.

The next phase in the Śrīvaiṣṇava history is the period in which Nāthamuni collected the Āḷvār hymns. I shall refer to this period as the period of contextualization, since the hymns are now beginning to be placed in the context of the not yet fully formulated and articulated Śrīvaiṣṇava tradition. Obviously, the Āḷvār hymns might have survived in the popular memory. People, regardless of their theological views and caste barriers, might have been singing those hymns because they evoked a profound devotional fervor. For the first time, however, the hymns began taking a shape and organization in the hands of an orthodox brāhmin. By the very fact of collection, Nāthamuni not only provided orthodoxy to the theological content of the hymns, but also provided a systematic approach to the understanding of the hymns by the way he arranged them and set them to music. Since Nāthamuni did not write any commentary on the hymns, we do not know first hand exactly how he defined their meaning. Thus, the tradition had to depend largely on what Yāmuna and Rāmānuja said in their writings. Nevertheless, the later biographers of the early teachers[3] want the community to remember that Yāmuna's writings reflect the understanding of Nāthamuni. But neither Yāmuna nor Rāmānuja wrote any commentaries on the hymns of the Āḷvārs. It is quite possible that their views were conveyed by Piḷḷān in his commentary on the *Tiruvāymoḷi*. In other words, by the time we get to the commentary of Piḷḷān it is evident that those views have already passed through three major thinkers of the tradition. Thus, what survives in Piḷḷān's commentary on the *Tiruvāymoḷi* are the views of the first three major teachers of the tradition. It is only fair to admit that we do not know, and perhaps will never know, the original intent and meaning of the Āḷvār hymns. To go a step further, as far as the Śrīvaiṣṇavas are concerned, it is unnecessary to know or speculate as to what might have been the original intent and meaning of the hymns.[4] For the historian of religion it might be of some value to know, if at all we can, the original meaning of the hymns. But at this stage, all that we know is the meaning that Nāthamuni, Yāmuna, and Rāmānuja, in a long

---

2. Dennis Hudson's research on the Kāñcīvaram temple might tell us something in this regard. His work was in progress at the time of writing this book.

3. I refer to the *Divyasūricaritam*, among others.

4. The fact that the Āḷvār hymns, left to themselves, could be interpreted in other ways is illustrated by the way F. Hardy interprets them in his *Viraha Bhakti*, in which he tries to show that the *Āḷvār bhakti* is part of the *Kṛṣṇa bhakti*.

chain of succession, communicated to Piḷḷān. The hymns come to us through the hands of the Śrīvaiṣṇavas. My observations in this context are not meant to cast doubt on the authenticity of the Śrīvaiṣṇava interpretation of the hymns of the Āḷvārs, but rather to point out that in the process of interpretation of a given tradition the attribution and fixation of meaning takes place only later. For all the subsequent teachers, the views of the founding teachers become canonical.

The third phase in the Śrīvaiṣṇava history is what I call the period of systematization. This is the most significant phase, since the views of the tradition are carefully thought out and set once for all on the basis of the accepted orthodox *pramāṇas*. During this period two important things happen: 1) fixation of the meaning of the tradition; and 2) ritualization of the tradition.

Firstly, while Yāmuna in his *Siddhitraya* systematically spelled out the Viśiṣṭādvaita philosophy, Rāmānuja in his *Śrībhāṣya, Gītābhāṣya*, and *Vedārthasaṃgraha* elaborately developed the philo-sophical tenets of the tradition. If a given tradition has to make sense to the orthodox Hindus, such a tradition has to be based on the *Prasthānatraya*, namely, the Upaniṣads, the *Brahma Sūtra*-s and the *Bhagavad Gītā*, all of which are accepted as normative to the Vedāntic tradition.[5] Rāmānuja, making extensive use of the Upaniṣadic texts, writes commentaries on the *Brahma Sūtra*-s and the *Bhagavad Gītā*. It is quite possible that since Rāmānuja was seeking Vedic orthodoxy for the Śrīvaiṣṇava tradition, he did not go beyond the *Prasthānatraya* to comment on the hymns of the Āḷvārs. Instead, he commissioned Piḷḷān to write a commentary on the *Tiruvāymoḷi* of Nammāḷvār. The fact that he commissioned Piḷḷān to write a commentary on the *Tiruvāymoḷi* shows that Rāmānuja surely accepted Nammāḷvār[6] as an authority for the Śrīvaiṣṇava tradition. In other words, by com-missioning Piḷḷān to write a commentary on the *Tiruvāymoḷi,* he establishes the norm that apart from the Vedic sources there is another source that is comparable and on a par with the Vedas. What is interesting here is that the Tamil Āḷvār tradition is not simply incorporated into the Vedic tradition, but rather is given an independent status on a par with the Vedas. The Vedic and the Āḷvār traditions are seen as two authentically distinct traditions coming together in the Śrīvaiṣṇava tradition. In order to signify the equality of status, the *Tiruvāymoḷi* is called, quite appropriately, the *Tamil Veda*. Thus, the Śrīvaiṣṇavas arrive at the tradition of the dual Vedānta (*Ubhaya Vedānta*).

In defining the tradition, both Yāmuna and Rāmānuja dealt with issues that are primary in relation to the other orthodox Hindu traditions. Thus, their discussions are limited to the *pramāṇa-s*, the understanding of Brahman, etc., among other issues. Issues such as

---

5. Śaṅkara has already set this norm for the Vedāntic tradition.

6. Among all the Āḷvārs, it is in the hymns of Nammāḷvār, especially in the *Tiruvāymoḷi*, that we find a systematic and coherent articulation of the Viśiṣṭādvaita philosophical ideas.

divine grace and the role of human beings in the process of salvation, the question of Śrī-Lakṣmī as the mediatrix, etc., did not call for their attention. The apologetics in which both Yāmuna and Rāmānuja were engaged were meant for outsiders and not insiders. The chief concern of the two was to define the tradition and provide a strong Vedāntic foundation to it so that the tradition was respected as equal with the other orthodox traditions of the Hindus. It is in this interpretive process that much of the meaning of the tradition is fixed within a set structure for the subsequent generations. Any modifications of the interpretation by subsequent teachers is possible only within those parameters. The later interpreters are forced to return constantly to the founding teachers to support their interpretations. In that sense, the writings of both Yāmuna and Rāmānuja become paradigmatic to the subsequent teachers. This is evident from the way Bhaṭṭar, Piḷḷai Lokācārya, and Veṅkaṭanātha constantly attempt to find support for their views in the writings of the early teachers. This clearly establishes the role and significance of the *Ācārya* in the process of the interpretation of the tradition. The idea behind the ceremony called *dīkṣā*, in which one is initiated into the tradition, presupposes the authoritative status of the *Ācārya*. The disciple receives the teachings from his *Ācārya* without questioning. Disagreement with the teacher means the disciple either finds another teacher or he himself becomes a teacher of a new tradition. This dynamic is seen clearly in the very life of Rāmānuja. He begins his study with his teacher Yādava Prakāśa. However, he leaves Yādava Prakāśa and accepts Tirukacci Naṃbi, a non-brāhmin disciple of Yāmuna, as his teacher.

For an interpretation to be authoritative, subsequent teachers—apart from quoting from the works of the founding teachers—have to trace their lineage to those founding teachers. The biographers make this very clear with regard to all the subsequent teachers. In this process of reification and fixation of meaning, it is also important for the tradition to have a structure that sustains the interpretation. This brings us to the second element that shaped the Śrīvaiṣṇava tradition's interpretive process.

Simultaneous with their attempts to provide a strong Vedāntic foundation to the tradition, both Yāmuna and Rāmānuja provided it with a ritual basis. However metaphysically profound a religious tradition is, in order for it to be sustained it must have a ritual basis because it is in the context of the ritual that the abstract philosophical ideas take concrete shape and expression. In the case of the Śrīvaiṣṇava tradition, this ritual basis is provided by the Pāñcarātra Āgama tradition. Yāmuna defends the Pāñcarātra Āgama tradition in his *Āgamaprāmāṇya*. Rāmānuja incorporates a defense of the Pāñcarātra Āgama tradition in his *Śrībhāṣya*. In addition to this, the biographers (e.g., *Divyasūricaritam*) report that Rāmānuja went from temple to temple establishing the rituals along the lines of the Pāñcarātra Āgama tradition, although much of his success is said to be limited to the South Indian temples.[7] By establishing the rituals on the lines of the Pāñcarātra Āgama tradition both Yāmuna and Rāmānuja provide a ritual basis for the worship of the divine consort. Similar to the representations in the iconography of the Gupta period, Viṣṇu and his consort are always worshiped together in the Śrīvaiṣṇava temples. There is very clear evidence of worship of Viṣṇu together with his divine consort not only in the *Lakṣmī Tantra* and the *Ahirbudhnya Saṃhitā* but also in the other Pāñcarātra Āgamas such as the *Sāttvata-*, *Pauṣkara-*, *Jayākhya-*, and *Pādma Saṃhitā*-s. Furthermore, the two teachers provide some basis for the divine consort as the mediatrix in their devotional writings, which are used basically in the ritual context. Although their theological treatises do not make clear the mediatorial role of the divine consort, by providing a ritual basis for it in their devotional hymns and by defending the Pāñcarātra Āgamas in general, both Yāmuna and Rāmānuja provide some basis for the later interpreters to advocate this point of view. In other words, the ongoing interpretive process of the Śrīvaiṣṇava tradition is sustained not only by the theological treatises of the early teachers, but also on the basis of the ritual tradition that the early teachers had established. The doctrine and the ritual practice are to be seen as two significant columns on which the Śrīvaiṣṇava tradition stands. Even though the pundits in the tradition can follow the intricate doctrinal points, what matters for an ordinary devotee is the ritual tradition that he participates in. It is primarily in the ritual that he finds his faith being sustained. Though the teachers of the community interpret the teachings through their commentaries, it is in ritual action that the teaching is effectively communicated.

The period of systematization is followed by a phase I refer to as the period of popularization. Although in my study I covered only Bhaṭṭar's writings as a sample of this period, I should mention that, in

---

7. The Vedic rituals do not provide for temple rituals wherein the deity is worshiped in the *Arcā* form. It is the Āgama ritual texts that provide the procedures for the temple rituals. Both the Vaikhānasa and the Pāñcarātra Āgamas provide for the ritual procedures in the Vaiṣṇava temples. Nevertheless, the Śrīvaiṣṇavas follow only the Pāñcarātra manuals (with the exception of Tirupati temple in South India, where the Vaikhānasa Āgamas are followed). We do not yet have any conclusive evidence that the Āḷvārs were part of the Pāñcarātra tradition. Our first awareness of the connection between the Śrīvaiṣṇavas and the Pāñcarātra Āgamas, as far as I know, comes from the *Āgamaprāmāṇya* of Yāmuna. The question as to why Yāmuṇa chose to defend the Pāñcarātra Āgamas and not the Vaikhānasa Āgamas still remains unanswered. As I pointed out in chapter three, there is a claim that Yāmuna wrote *Kāṣmīrāgamaprāmāṇya*, in which he is said to have defended the Vaikhānasa Āgamas. But we do not have any conclusive evidence as to the authorship of *Kāṣmīrāgamaprāmāṇya*. In the absence of any clear evidence either way, it is possible to speculate that Yāmuna's defense of the Pāñcarātra Āgamas perhaps has to do with some connection between the Āḷvārs and the Pāñcarātra ritual tradition. Future scholarship will have to provide us with more information on this before any conclusions can be drawn.

fact, both Piḷḷān and Śrīvatśaṅkamiśra (Bhaṭṭar's father) also belong to this phase. What is most noticeable during this period is that the interpretive process draws material largely from the epic and Purāṇic sources. The *Mahābhārata* and the *Rāmāyaṇa* play a significant role in the process of the interpretation of the tradition during this period. As I pointed out in the chapter on Bhaṭṭar, most of the theological points are supported and authenticated by these texts. The doctrinal points are illustrated by examples drawn from these texts. In fact, everything from these texts becomes paradigmatic for the interpretive process. Thus, the characterizations of Sītā in the *Rāmāyaṇa* and Draupadī in the *Mahābhārata* become paradigmatic for the understanding of the role and the significance of the divine consort. The epic texts were not only popular at that time, but they also provided greater scope for developing and understanding of the mediatorial role of the divine consort. It is also during this period that hymn writing takes precedence over rigorous commentarial writing. The teachers of the Śrīvaiṣṇavas during this time write hymns on almost every aspect of the tradition. Śrīvatśaṅkamiśra writes hymns on Varadarāja (Viṣṇu), Lakṣmī, Śrīraṅgam, etc., and Bhaṭṭar writes, in addition to his commentary on the *Thousand Names of Viṣṇu*, a hymn on Śrī-Lakṣmī and *The Eight Śloka*-s on the three *mantra*-s (namely, *Aṣṭākṣara, Dvaya*, and *Carama Śloka*). The hymns become the most important vehicles of communication for the teachings of the *Ācārya*-s. By this time Śrī-Lakṣmī, undoubtedly, becomes an important theme in the writings of the teachers. In other words, what remained latent in the writings of the early teachers now becomes much more clearly articulated, although the intricate doctrinal points associated with the divine consort are still not clearly spelled out. Nevertheless, the role of the divine consort as the mediatrix is now accepted in the tradition beyond doubt. With the acceptance of the role of the Goddess as the mediatrix, the stage is set for further clarification of intricate doctrinal points, such as the role that human beings can play in the process of their salvation, the nature of the grace of Īśvara, and, connected to these, the question of the role and status of the Goddess in mediating between Īśvara and his devotees.

As the differences of opinion begin to be felt, the Śrīvaiṣṇavas enter a very crucial and volatile period and yet one of the most productive period in their history. This is the period normally known as the period of schism, but I shall refer to it as the period of diversification. The division had not yet taken place, but the tradition was clearly moving in the direction of divergent views. This period also coincides with the Muslim invasion of the South. Thus, the tradition was not only threatened by internal conflicts but also by the external invasion. The external threat, however, did not seem to help soften the internal disagreements.[8] During this time, the Śrīvaiṣṇavas

8. It is interesting to note that when the temple of Śrīraṅgam was invaded by the Muslims, Piḷḷai Lokācārya is said to have protected the son of Veṅkaṭanātha.

are witness to two major thinkers, namely, Piḷḷai Lokācārya and his younger contemporary Veṅkaṭanātha. Among their many differences, the question of the divine consort, undoubtedly, becomes a point of disagreement between the two. While both of them try to draw their support from their preceding teachers, they also draw from two distinct sources. On the one hand, Piḷḷai Lokācārya relies mostly on the hymns of the Āḻvārs; on the other hand, Veṅkaṭanātha relies mostly on the Pāñcarātra Āgama Texts, one of which is the *Lakṣmī Tantra*. As the divergent views come to surface, the tradition becomes more and more reified along the lines of the doctrinal differences. It is during this process of internal reification that we witness a genre of literature that is called *Secret Texts* (*Rahasya Granthas*). While Piḷḷai Lokācārya's works in general are called *Aṣṭādaśa Rahasya*-s (*Eighteen Secrets*), Veṅkaṭanātha writes a *Defense of the Secrets* (*Rahasyarakṣā*). The purpose and the nature of the *Secret Texts* are such that only the properly initiated can approach them through a qualified *Ācārya*. Thus, the tradition now becomes more and more closed. Considering the more open socioreligious context in which the Āḻvārs sang their hymns, this later development in the history of the Śrīvaiṣṇavas is certainly very significant in the process of the interpretation of their tradition. The terminology and the meaning of the terminology is clearly defined and fixed for the understanding of the later interpreters. For instance, the term *Puruṣakāra*[9] takes the specific meaning of "mediatrix," referring to the divine consort.

Thus, while the nature of the interpretive process becomes more and more reified from within, the teachings of the tradition are more and more scrutinized and thereby protected from the distortions of noninitiates. Meanwhile, however, the process of ritualization continues in intensity. In order to sustain the Pāñcarātra order of worship, Veṅkaṭanātha writes a defense of the Pāñcarātra (*Pāñcarātrarakṣā*) in which he clearly defends and describes the five daily rituals that a Śrīvaiṣṇava should follow. From now on, even the singing of the Āḻvār hymns takes a very clear ritualistic form. Not only the order in which they are sung, but also the occasion and the place of the singing of the hymns is gradually defined.

Furthermore, the notion of *bhakti* and *prapatti* take on very clear ritual overtones. *Śaraṇāgati* in the Pāñcarātra tradition is an extremely complex ritual act and not just surrendering to the Lord. As I spelled out elsewhere in this study, *śaraṇāgati* has six elaborate components with their *aṅga*-s and *nyāsa*-s.[10] The same ritual details are incorporated into the Śrīvaiṣṇava tradition. The notion of *nitya-kaiṅkarya* (eternal service) clearly comes to mean performing daily rituals in the presence of the Lord and his divine consort. Rāmānuja's *Nityagrantha* had already established this very notion; Veṅkaṭanātha's commentary on Rāmānuja's *Nityagrantha* further clarified this and

9. The term literally means "maker of person."
10. *LT*. 17:60-73.

established the ritualistic notion of *nityakaiṅkarya*. The fluid tradition of devotion begun with the Āḷvārs is now highly ritualistic in its orientation.

It is against this background of the process of ritualization that one has to understand the role and the significance of the divine consort. For both Yāmuna and Rāmānuja, *śaraṇāgati* to the Lord is incomplete without their *śaraṇāgati* to the divine consort. For the later interpreters, as seen in the writings of Bhaṭṭar, divine grace is clearly mediated through the divine consort. For Piḷḷai Lokācārya, the divine consort is one among other mediators (e.g., *Ācarya*), but she is the best mediator. The devotees, in their attempt to become the *nityamukta*-s (eternal *mukta*-s), must emulate the divine consort. She must also be approached with *prapatti* because she is the highest of the *Śeṣa*-s. Veṅkaṭanātha accepts the mediatorship of the divine consort but he also sees her as the equal partner of the Lord (as *Śeṣin*).

Whatever status is accorded to the divine consort, all the teachers see her role in the context of the ritual. She is worshiped along with the Lord, and the presence of the divine consort is sustained in the daily rituals. Yāmuna's *Four Verses* (*Catuśślokī*) is composed in the context of ritual; Rāmānuja sings his *Śaraṇāgatigadya* in the context of ritual, where he is said to have had the vision of the divine couple; Bhaṭṭar, in his *Śrīguṇaratnakośa*, speaks about Śrī-Lakṣmī basically in the context of the temple of Śrīraṅgam;[11] and furthermore, both Piḷḷai Lokācārya and Veṅkaṭanātha discuss the question of the divine consort in the context of the *Dvaya mantra*. All this not only signifies the role and significance of the divine consort, but also emphasizes that her role and significance is sustained largely through the ritual context. Outside the ritual context her presence is veiled.

The presence and the significance of the divine consort needs to be seen in the unfolding of the ritual basis of the Śrīvaiṣṇava tradition. This ritual basis, as noted earlier, is provided by the Pāñcarātra Āgama tradition. The elements that are unseen or unnoticed in the purely metaphysical speculations become obvious in the ritual context. The presence of the divine consort, hardly noticed in the metaphysical writings of Yāmuna and Rāmānuja, becomes an inescapable reality in the context of the ritual. She is so real in the ritual context that the two *Ācārya*-s were forced to acknowledge her presence in their devotional writings. This, I believe is primarily due to the influence of the Pāñcarātra Āgamas. Both Yāmuna and Rāmānuja had exposure to the older Pāñcarātra Āgamas, including the *Ahirbudhnya Saṃhitā*, for it was available, if we accept Schrader's argument, by the eighth century C.E. This means, even if one were to debate the status

11. Bhaṭṭar describes Śrī-Lakṣmī as "the Queen of Śrīraṅgam" (*Śrīraṅgeśvarī*), "Beloved of the Lord of Śrīraṅgam," "Lakṣmī of the house of the Lord of Śrīraṅgam" and so on in his *Śrīguṇaratnakośa*.

accorded to Śrī-Lakṣmī by these two early teachers, the presence of the goddess in the ritual context is evidently admitted by them, and for that they had the authority of at least *Jayākhya-* and the *Ahirbudhnya Saṃhitā*-s. My analysis has shown that there is definite correspondence between the position of these two early teachers and that of the *Lakṣmī Tantra* on the question of the status of the goddess.

The doctrinal teachings can remain vague and unclear without the help of the ritual tradition. The ritual presents the reality as it is, while the doctrinal formulations inadequately fumble to articulate the various dimensions of the tradition. For this very reason, the ritual preserves the various dimensions of the tradition untainted and without any bias.

Ritual elements and the structure of the ritual can be separable. In other words, one has to make a distinction between the elements of the ritual and the structure of the ritual. Once the structure of the scheme is laid out, it is only a matter of incorporating the various elements in accordance with the total scheme. The structure is relative to the theological scheme of the tradition, but the elements of the ritual can free themselves from the structure and transcend the meaning. The ritual elements take specific meaning only within the structure of the ritual. It is for the theologians of the tradition to speculate and clarify from time to time those dimensions through their doctrinal formulations and expositions. Yet the ritual elements, with all their complexities, can transcend the meanings and interpretations attributed to them. Guidelines for interpretation are, however, provided by the process of the fixation and systematization of meaning. The teachers of the tradition have the "keys" to the interpretation of those ritual elements. But the people, who accept those interpretations, do so in relation to their loyalties to the teachers and the tradition. There is always the possibility of another interpretation from another dimension. The ritual elements are the same, but they are restructured in accordance with the meaning and the interpretation given to them.

The presence of Śrī-Lakṣmī in the ritual context is an important aspect. She survives in the ritual in consonance with the meaning and the interpretation attributed to her. The way she is interpreted and understood is specific and relative to the scope given to her in the theological scheme of the teachers. Undoubtedly, Śrī-Lakṣmī is an important dimension in the theological scheme of both Piḷḷai Lokācārya and Veṅkaṭanātha. The meaning and the interpretation accorded to her by them is relative to the scope given to her in their respective theological schemes. Outside of that theological scheme, the divine consort transcends the interpretation and meaning accorded to her. For this reason, a fuller understanding of the Goddess in the Śrī-vaiṣṇava tradition must be sought not only in the theological speculations of the tradition, but also in the context of the ritual tradition that occasions such theological speculations. Until that ritual tradition is explored, the theological speculations of the teachers will remain obscure.

Limit of the Historian of Religion

For the insider, the theological scheme must make sense in order for his faith and practice to be sustained. For the historian of religion, the question of right or wrong with regard to a given interpretation is unimportant and perhaps irrelevant. He sees the elements and their interpretation as the insider sees it, both in the context of the theological speculations as well as in the context of the ritual. The historian of religion digs into the tradition to see what possibilities and scopes there are on which the insiders can base their theological views. He brings them out as faithfully and coherently as possible in order to make sense of the tradition. The purpose of his exposition of the tradition is not to provide an alternative interpretation to the existing inside interpretations, but to explain to the outsiders, and to a certain extent to the insiders also, the intricacies of the theological views as they are understood within the tradition. Thus, the value of his exposition lies not so much in attempting to answer which interpretation is right as in the attempt to enable the outsiders to understand the insiders' point of view. In such an endeavor, there is always the possibility that the insiders also might find the exposition useful for their self-understanding. The questions of 'right' or 'wrong' are suspended for one's own private reflection, because once we ask such questions we are taking on the role of the insider. Such an enterprise is the privilege of the insider because he must be clear in his mind which one to follow for his own faith to be sustained. The outsider does not necessarily have such concerns. He remains content with understanding the interpretation of the insiders. As W. B. Kristensen says, "Every religion ought to be understood from its own standpoint, for that is how it is understood by its own adherents."[12] Nevertheless, the historian of religion plays a crucial role in clarifying issues that are often missed both by the insider and the outsider. In the end, perhaps a fuller understanding can emerge only in a mutual dialogue between scholars from inside and outside.

Some Unexplored Questions in Understanding Śrī-Lakṣmī

At this point, perhaps it is important and useful to mention some significant areas that have not been covered in this study and may be pursued in a subsequent study. Although I have presented the Pāñcarātra viewpoints, obviously I have not been able to fully study all the available Pāñcarātra texts and therefore, my conclusions on the Pāñcarātra perspectives are rather tentative. Only an exhaustive study of all the major texts of the Pāñcarātra corpus will eventually provide us with a fuller understanding of, among other important aspects, Śrī-Lakṣmī and how much of that understanding has survived in the Śrī-

12. W. B. Kristensen, *The Meaning of Religion*, trans. J. B. Carman, (The Hague: Martinus Nijhoff, 1960), p. 6.

vaiṣṇava tradition. A comprehensive study of the Pāñcarātra texts, though it would have provided us with a deeper insight into the Śrīvaiṣṇava ritual tradition and its possible connections with the Tantric traditions,[13] was beyond the scope of this work. At the present stage of scholarship in this field, we still have to clarify the connections between the Pāñcarātra and the Tantric traditions on the one hand, and the connections between the Pāñcarātra and the Āḷvārs and the Bhagavatas on the other. There is a growing sense among scholars in this field that the Pāñcarātra and the Āḷvār traditions are linked in many ways.[14]

The other significant area that has not been covered in this study is the whole spectrum of the Āḷvār tradition. A comprehensive study of the understanding of Śrī-Lakṣmī in the hymns of the Āḷvārs in itself would constitute a major project. Given my present limitations, I could not undertake such a comprehensive study in this work. Furthermore, without fully exploring the Pāñcarātra texts, it would be difficult to gain an insight into the Āḷvār conceptions of the divine consort. Exploring those conceptions will certainly provide us with significant insights into the understanding of the Goddess.

Since I have limited myself to the commentaries and hymns of the major *Ācārya*-s of the tradition during its formative period, I have not dealt with the representation of Śrī-Lakṣmī in the rituals, both daily and occasional (e.g., festivals, etc.). This will hopefully reinforce further the idea that the presence of the Goddess in Śrīvaiṣṇava theology is intrinsically related to the ritual tradition. Related to this is her representation in various local myths as well as in temple architecture, another area that will be extremely significant in clarifying the understanding of the Goddess. A whole range of symbolism connected to Śrī-Lakṣmī can be explored through those myths and architectural images inside the Vaiṣṇava temples. Thus an understanding of the symbolism related to Śrī-Lakṣmī is bound up with exploring the Pāñcarātra manuals.

---

13. Pāñcarātra is also referred to as Tantra/Yogatantra, e.g., *Parama Saṃhitā*, chap. 1, vv. 33, 36-47.

14. Dennis Hudson is one such scholar who is working on exploring the Pāñcarātra and Āḷvār connections in his current study of the Vaikuṇṭhaperumāḷ temple in Kāñcīpuram of South India. J. B. Carman, Vasudha Narayanan, and Francis X. Clooney are currently working together on the translation of *Tiruvāymoḷi* of Nammāḷvār. These studies would certainly provide us with more materials in which we could explore the understanding of the Goddess, Śrī-Lakṣmī.

APPENDIX ONE

TEXT OF CATUŚŚLOKĪ OF YĀMUNA[1]

kāntas te puruṣottamaḥ phaṇipatiḥ śayyāsanaṃ vāhanaṃ
vedātmāvihageśvaro yavanikāmāyājaganmohinī|
brahmeśādisuravrajas sadayitas tvaddāsadāsīgaṇaḥ
śrīr ityeva ca nāma te bhagavati brūmaḥ kathaṃ tvāṃ vayam|| (1)

yasyās te mahimānam ātmana iva tvadvallabho 'pi prabhur
nālaṃ mātum iyattayā niravadhiṃ nityānukūlaṃ svataḥ|
tāṃ[2] tvāṃ dāseti prapanneti ca stoṣyāmyahaṃ nirbhayo
lokaikeśvari lokanāthadayite dānte dayāṃ te vidan|| (2)

īṣattvatkaruṇānirīkṣaṇa sudhāsaṃdhukṣaṇād rakṣyate
naṣṭaṃprāk tadalābhatas tribhuvanaṃ saṃpratyanantodayaṃ|
śreyo na hy aravindalocanamanaḥ kāntāprasādādṛte
saṃsṛtyakṣara vaiṣṇavādhvasu nṛṇāṃ saṃbhāvyate karhicit|| (3)

śāntānantamahāvibhūtiparamaṃ yadbrahmarūpaṃ harer
mūrtaṃ brahma tato'pi yatpriyataraṃrūpaṃ yadatyadbhutaṃ|
yānyanyāni yathāsukhaṃ viharato rūpāṇisarvāṇi tā-
nyāhuḥ svair anurūparūpa vibhavair gāḍhopagūḍāni te|| (4)

---

1. The text is taken from *Catuśślokībhāṣyam, Stotraratnabhāṣyam, and Gadyatrayabhāṣyam: With Commentary by Vedānta Deśika* (Madras: Śrī Vedānta Deśika Seventh Centenary Trust, n.d.). Translations are mine. Since I have incorporated the translation in the main text, I have not included it here. See chapter 3 for translation.

2. *tvām*—a variant reading found in the text, *Catuśślokīvyākhyānam*. ed. Veṅkaṭācārya and Puduppattu Tiruveṅkaṭācārya (Kāñcīpuram: Śrīnivāsa Press, 1913. Telugu Script).

APPENDIX TWO

SELECTED VERSES FROM THE TEXT OF STOTRARATNA OF YĀMUNA[1]

kaśśrīḥ śriyaḥ paramasattva samāśrayaḥ kaḥ
kaḥ puṇḍarīkanayanaḥ puruṣottamaḥ kaḥ|
kasyāyutāyutāśataikakalāṃśakāṃśe
viśvaṃ vicitra cidacit pravibhāgavṛttam|| (12)

cakartha yasyā bhavanaṃ bhujāntaraṃ
tava priyaṃdhāma yadīyajanmabūḥ|
jagatsamastaṃ yadapāṅgasaṃśrayaṃ
yadarthaṃ aṃbhodhiramanthyabandhi ca|| (37)

svavaiśvarūpyeṇa sadānubhūtayā
'py apūrvavad vismayamādadhānayā|
guṇena rūpeṇa vilāsaceṣṭitais
sadā tavaivocitayā tava śriyā|| (38)

tayā sahāsīnam anantabhogini
prakṛṣṭavijñānabalaikadhāmani|
phaṇāmaṇivrātamayūkhamaṇḍala
prakāśamānodara divyadhāmani|| (39)

apūrvanānārasabhāvanirbhara-
prabaddhayā mugdhavidagdhalīlayā|
kṣaṇāṇuvatkṣiptaparādikālayā
praharṣayantaṃ mahiṣīṃ mahābhujaṃ|| (44)

acintyadivyādbhutanityayauvana-
svabhāvalāvaṇyamayāmṛtodadhiṃ|
śriyaḥ śriyaṃ bhaktajanaikajīvitaṃ
samarthamāpatsakham arthikalpaṃ|| (45)

1. The text is compared with the one produced by the Granthamālā publishers (1958), edited by P. B. Aṇṇaṅgārācārya, and the one produced by Śrī Rāmakrishna Math (1979) by Svāmi Ādidevānanda. Only those verses that were used for the discussion in this book are incorporated here. For a complete translation refer to Svāmi Ādidevānanda. The translations of these verses are mine. See chapter 3 for translation.

BIBLIOGRAPHY

Primary Sources—Texts and Translations

Aiyyangar, Krishnaswami S., ed. & trans. *Parama Saṃhitā*. Baroda: Oriental Institute, 1940.

Āṇḍavan, Tirukkuṇḍaṇḍai. *Śarīrakasārābodhini: A Commentary on Śrī Bhāṣya of Śrī Rāmānuja*. Bangalore: Śrīrām Press, 1975.

Aṇṇaṅgarācārya, Śrī Kāñcī Prativādi Bhayaṅkara, ed. *Śrī Bhagavad Rāmānuja Granthamālā*. Kāñcīpuram: Granthamālā Office, 1956.

———. *Śrī Bhagavad Rāmānuja Granthamālā*. Telugu script. Madras: A. Sampatkumar, 1939.

———. *Stotramālā*. Kāñcīpuram: Granthamālā Office, 1958.

Ayyangar, Narasiṃha, M. B. *Vedāntasāra of Bhagavad Rāmānuja*. Text with translation, edited by V. Krishnamacharya. Madras: Adyar Library, 1953.

Ayyangar, Rajagopala, M. R. *Śrīmad Rahasyatrayasāra of Vedānta Deśika*. Translation with introduction. Kuṃbakoṇam: Agnihotram Rāmānuja Tātācāriar, 1956.

———. *The Stotraratna of Yāmuna*. Text and translation. Madras: Published by the translator, n.d.

Bhaṭṭar, Śrī Parāśara. *Aṣṭaślokī*. Commentary in Hindi by T. Bheemacharya, and English by S. N. Shastri. Bombay: Śrīnivās Udyog Pratiṣṭhān, 1971.

———. *Śrī Guṇaratnakośa*. Commentary by Kaṇḍāḍa Vīrarāghavācārya. Cennanagar (Madras): Śrīniketana Press, 1895.

———. *Śrī Viṣṇusahasranāma Bhāṣya (Bhagavadguṇadarpaṇākhyam)* Sanskrit text. Kāñcīpuram: P. B. Annaṅgarācāriar, 1964.

———. *Śrī Viṣṇusahasranāma Bhāṣya*. Translation by A. Śrīnivāsarāghavan. Madras: Śrī Viśiṣṭādvaita Pracāriṇī Sabha, 1983.

———. *Śrī Viṣṇusahasranāma Bhāṣya*. Translation by L. Venkataratnam Naidu. Tirupati: Tirumala Tirupati Devasthanams, 1965.

———. *Śrī Viṣṇusahasranāma with Nirukti Ślokas*. Text and translation of the Introduction by K. Bhashyam, edited by Uttamūru Vīrarāghavācārya. Madras: Viśiṣṭādvaita Pracāriṇī Sabha, 1960.

———. *Śrīraṅgarājastava*. Commentary of Śrī Veṅkaṭācārya; Telugu script. Chennapuri: Śrīniketana Press, 1879.

———. *Commentary on the Śrī Viṣṇusahasranāmam*. With Śaṅkara's commentary, trans. K. E. Parthasarathy. Madras: Ganesh & Co., n.d.

———. *Kriyādīpam*. Seventy Two stanzas in a collection of Śrīvaiṣṇava manuals of worship. Title page missing.

Bhāṣyam, K., trans. *Śrī Bhagavad Rāmānuja's Śaraṇāgatigadya*. In Ubhaya Vedānta Granthamālā Series. Madras: Liberty Press. n.d.

Dāsa, Śrīnivāsa. *Yatīndramatadīpika*. Sanskrit text with English translation and notes by Svāmi Ādidevānanda. Madras: Śrī Rāmakṛṣṇa Maṭh, 1949.

Govinda (Embār). *Hari Āradhana Krama* [Forty stanzas in a collection of Śrīvaiṣṇava manuals of worship] Title page missing.

Govindacārya, Śrī. *Śrī Parameśvara Saṃhitā*. Śrīraṅgam: S. R. Vijayaraghava Ayyangar, 1953.

Gupta, Sanjukta., trans. *Lakṣmī Tantra: a Pāñcarātra Text*. Leiden: E. J. Brill, 1972.

Jīyar, Pinbaḷahiya Perumāḷ. *Ārāyirappaḍi Guruparaṃparaprabhāvam* (Tamil in Tamil script). Trichi: S. Krishnasvāmi Ayyangar, 1968. [An edition in Telugu script has been published in Kāñcīpuram by the Śrīvaiṣṇavagrantha Mudrāpaka Sabhai, n.d.]

Josyer, G. R., ed. *Śeṣa Saṃhitā: a Pāñcarātra Āgama*. Mysore: Coronation Press, 1981.

Kūrattālvan (Kūreśa). *Yamakaratnākaram* [With commentary] Madras: Śrīvaiṣṇavagrantha Mudrāpaka Sabhai, n.d.

Krishnamacharya, Embar., ed. *Jayākhya Saṃhitā*. Baroda: Oriental Institute, 1931.

Krishnamacharya, V., ed. *Ahirbudhnya Saṃhitā*, vols 1 & 2, revised editions. Madras: The Adyar Library and Research Center, 1966.

———. *Lakṣmī Tantra: A Pāñcarātra Āgama*. Madras: The Adyar Library and Research Center, 1975.

———. *Viṣṇusmṛti*. Commentary by Keśava Vaijayanti of Nanda Paṇḍita. Madras: The Adyar Library and Research Center, 1964.

Lokācārya, Piḷḷai. *Artha Pañcakam*. Hindi and English translations by T. Bheemachary and S. N. Shastri. Indore: Bharati Publications, 1972.

———. *Śrīvacanabhūṣaṇamu*. Sanskrit text and translation by P. B. Annaṅgarācārya. Kāñcīpuram: Granthamālā Office, 1943 (Telugu script).

———. *Śrīvacanabhūṣaṇa*, trans. Robert C. Lester. Madras: The Kuppuswami Sastry Research Institute, 1979.

———. *Śrīvaiṣṇavasamācāra Niṣkarṣam*. Cennapatnam: Ananda Press, 1909 (Telugu script).

———. *Tattvatraya: A Manual of Viśiṣṭādvaita*, trans. M. B. Narasimha Iyengar. Madras: M. C. Krishnan, 1974.

Mumme, Patricia Y., trans. *Mumukṣuppaṭi of Piḷḷai Lokācārya with Manavālamāmuni's Commentary*. Bombay: Ananthacharya Indological Research Institute, 1987.

Naṃbi, Vaṅgi Puraṭṭu. *Nityagrantha or Kārikāḥ* [526 Stanzas in a Collection of Śrīvaiṣṇava Manuals of Worship] Title page missing.

Nāyanār, Aḷakiyamanavāḷa Perumāḷ. *Ācāryahṛdayam*. Edited by P. B. Annaṅgarācārya. Padippikkappattadu: Gītācārya Press, 1939.

Padmanābhan, Seetha., ed. *Śrīpraśna Saṃhitā*. Tirupati: Kendriya Sanskrit Vidyapeetha, 1969.

Padmanābhan, Seetha. & V. Varadachari., eds. *Pādma Saṃhitā*. Madras: Pāñcarātra Pariśodhana Pariṣad, 1982.

Pādma Saṃhitā. Published by Tridaṇḍi Śrīmannārāyaṇa Rāmānuja Jīyar, (Place of publication and date not mentioned).

Paṇḍita, Garuḍavāhana. *Śrī Divyasūricarita*. Kāñcī: P. B. Annaṅgarācārya, 1953.

Piḷḷai, Vādukku Tiruvīdi. *Muppattārāyirappaḍi* [Thirty-six Thousand—known as *Īḍu*—A Commentary on Nammāḷvār's *Tiruvāymoḷi*; S. Krishnamāchārya's edition] Madras: Noble Press, 1925-30 (Tamil script).

Puduppaṭṭu, TiruVeṅkaṭācārya. *Jitantā Stotram*. With the Commentary of Peria Āccana Piḷḷai. Padippikkapattana: Śrīniketana Press, 1919 (Telugu script).

Raghavacharya., ed. *Parāśara Saṃhitā*. Bangalore: Vāgīśvari Press, 1898 (Telugu script).

Rāmānuja. *Śrībhāṣya*. Text, English rendering of Sūtras, comments, and index by Svāmi Vireśvarānanda, & Svāmi Ādidevānanda. Calcutta: Advaita Āśrama, 1978.

———. *Śrībhāṣya,* Pt. 2, edited by R. D. Karmarkar. Poona: University of Poona, 1962.

———. *Śrībhāṣya*, Pt. 3, edited by R. D. Karmarkar. Poona: University of Poona, 1964.

———. *Śrīmadgītābhāṣyam*. Śrīraṅgam (Nellur Branch): Sarasvati Nilaya Press, 1897.

———. *Gadyatrayam*. With Commentaries of Śrutaprakāśikācārya in Sanskrit, Periya Vāccan Piḷḷai in Maṇipravāla, Vedāntācārya (Deśika) in Sanskrit. Kāñcīpuram: Śrīnivāsa Press, n.d. (Telugu script).

———. *Gadyatrayam*. With commentaries of Sudarśana Sūri, Peria Āccana Piḷḷai and Vedānta Deśika—Sanskrit and Tamil texts. Kāñcīpuram: Śrīnivāsagrantha Mudrāpaka Sabhai, 1916. (Telugu script).

———. *Gītābhāṣya*, trans. M. R. Sampatkumaran. Madras: Prof. M. Ragavacharya Memorial Trust, 1969.

———. *Gītābhāṣya*, edited by Abhinava Deśika T. Vīrarāghavācārya. Madras: Ubhaya Vedānta Granthamālā, 1972.

———. *Vedāntadīpa* (Bonner Orientalistische Studien). Bonn: Selbtverlag des Orientalischen Seminars der Universität, 1964.

———. *Vedārthasaṃgraha* [Introduction and annotated translation by J. A. B. van Buitenen] Poona: Deccan College, Postgraduate Research Institute, 1956.

———. *Vedārthasaṃgraha*, trans. S. S. Raghavachar. Mysore: Śrī Rāmakṛṣna Āśrama, 1968.

Rāmānujamuni, Yadugiri Yatirāja Sampatkumar., ed. *Śrī Pauṣkara Saṃhitā*. Madras: Jñānapaṇḍitar Press, 1934.

———. *Pādma Saṃhitā*. Cennapattana: G. R. Press, 1846 (Telugu script).

Sampatkumaran, A., ed. *Śrī Bhagavad Rāmānuja Granthamāla* [Includes all the nine works of Rāmānuja] Kāñcīpuram: Granthamālā Office: 1956.
Śāstri, Mahadeva, A., ed. *The Vaiṣṇava Upaniṣads: With Commentary on Śrī Upaniṣad.* Madras: The Adyar Library and Research Center, 1953.
Śrīnivāsācārya. *Yatīndramatadīpikā,* edited by P. B. Annaṅgarācārya. Kāñcīpuram: Granthamālā Office, 1945.
Śrītattvaprakāśikāyām. Tippul: Venkatacharya, 1890 (Tamil work in Telugu script).
Sūri, Sudarśana. *Śrutaprakāśikā.* Sanskrit commentary on Rāmānuja's *Śrībhāṣya,* 2 volumes. New Delhi: Government of India, 1967.
———. *Tātparyadīpikā.* Commentary in Sanskrit on Rāmānuja's *Vedārthasaṃgraha.* Vṛndāvana: no name of publisher, 1900.
Svāmi, Brahmatantrasvatantra. *Guruparaṃpara Prabhāvam* [Including *Yatirājavaibhavam* and Vedānta Deśika's *Vaibhava Prakāśika Stotram,* edited by Śrīnivasa Raghavacharya] Padippikkappattana: Śrīnivāsa Press, 1911 (Telugu script).
Thibaut, George., trans. *The Vedānta Sūtras.* With the commentary of Rāmānuja. S. B. E., vol. XLVIII. Delhi, Patna, Varanasi: Motilal Banarsidass, 1966.
Tiruveṇkaṭācāriar, Citrakūṭam Kaṇḍāḍai., ed. *Vārttāmālai* [Tamil utterances of "Śrīvaiṣṇavas beginning with Nāthamuni," printed in Telugu script with the title page spelled as *Vārtāmala*] Tiruvellikkeṇi: Śrī Śarasvati Bhaṇḍāra Mudrākṣaraśālai, 1887.
van Buitenen, J. A. B. *Rāmānuja on the Bhagavad Gītā: A Condensed Rendering of His Gītābhāṣya.* With copious notes and an introduction. Delhi: Motilal Banarsidass, 1968.
Veṅkaṭanātha (Śrī Vedānata Deśika). *Stotras-1.* Śrīraṅgam: Śrī Vāṇī Vilās Press, 1976.
———. *Adhikaraṇasārāvalī & Śatadūṣaṇī,* edited by Śrī Kāñcī Prativādi Bhayaṅkara Annaṅgarācārya. Kāñcīpuram: A. Sampatkumaran (Granthamālā Office), 1940.
———. *Śatadūṣaṇī,* Pt. 1. With a commentary by Ācārya Śiva Prasād Dvivedi. Ayodya: Tattvamuktākalāpa Saṅgh, 1984.
———. *Śatadūṣaṇī,* Pt. 2. With a commentary by Ācārya Śiva Prasād Dvivedi. Ayodya: Tattvamuktākalāpa Sangh, 1985.
———. *Śatadūṣaṇī,* Pt. 3. With a commentary by Ācārya Śiva Prasād Dvivedi Ayodya: Tattvamuktākalāpa Sangh, 1986.
———. *Śatadūṣaṇī,* Pt. 4. With Hindi translation by Ācārya Śiva Prasād Dvivedi Ayodya: Tattvamuktākalāpa Sangh, 1987.
———. *Śrī Pāñcarātrarakṣā,* edited by Pt. M. Duraiswami Aiyangar & Pt. T. Venugopalacharya. Madras: The Adyar Library and Research Center, 1967.
———. *Śrīmad Vedānta Deśika Granthamālā* [Includes *Īśāvasyopaniṣad Bhāṣya, Catuśślokī Bhāṣya, Stotraratna Bhāṣya,* and *Gadya Bhāṣya,* edited by Śrī Kāñcī Prativādi Bhayaṅkara

Annaṅgarācārya] Kāñcīpuram: A. Sampatkumaran [Granthamālā Office), 1940.

———. *Śrīstuti*. With translation and commentary in Tamil by V. Anantācāriar. Place name and name of publisher not mentioned, 1978.

———. *Śubhāṣitānivi*, trans. K. S. Nāgarājan. Madras: Vedānta Deśika Research Society, 1972.

———. *Catuśślokībhāṣyam, Stotraratnabhāṣyam, Gadyatrayabhāṣyam*, edited by V. Śrīvatśaṅkācāriar. Madras: Śrī Vedānta Deśika Seventh Centenary Trust, n.d.

———. *Dayā Śatakam*. Translation and commentary by D. Ramaswamy Ayyangar. Tirupati: Tirumala Tirupati Devasthanams, 1961.

———. *Devanāyaka Pañcasat*. With meaning and commentary in English by D. Ramaswamy Ayyangar. Mylapore (Madras): A. T. M. Press, 1978.

———. *Dramiḍopaniṣad Tārparyaratnāvalī*. With commentaries in Tamil and English by Uttamūru Vīra Rāghavācārya. Madras: Ubhaya Vedānta Granthamālā, 1st edition, 1983.

———. *Dramiḍopaniṣad Tārparyaratnāvalī and Sāra*. With Sanskrit text and translation by R. Raṅgācāri. Madras: Vedānta Deśika Research Society, 1974.

———. *Īśāvasyopaniṣad Bhāṣya*. With introduction, translation, and notes by K. C. Varadācāri and D. T. Tātācārya. Madras: Vedānta Deśika Research Society, 1975.

———. *Haṃsa Sandeśa*. With commentary of Śvetāraṇyam Nārāyaṇa Śāstri, translation and notes by S. Nārāyaṇa Iyengar. Madras: V. Rāmasvāmi Śāstrulu & Sons, 1955.

———. *Haṃsa Saṃdeśa*. With Sanskrit commentary by Rangācāriar, translation and notes by N. V. Deśikācāriar & Kastūri Raṅga Ayengar. Madras: Vedānta Deśika Research Society, 1973.

———. *Nyāyapariśuddhi*. With a new commentary by Abhinava Deśika Vātsya Vīra Rāghavācārya. Madras: Ubhaya Vedānta Granthamālā, 1978.

———. *Paramata Bhaṅgam*, Pt. 1. With commentary by Villivalam Vātsya Nārāyaṇācārya Svāmi in Maṇipravāla. Cennai: Kiṭaikkumiṭaṅkaḷ Śrīnṛu Siṃhapriyā, 1979.

———. *Saṃkalpasūrodayam*, trans. M. R. Rajagopala Iyengar. Madras: Vedānta Deśika Research Society, 1977.

———. *Stotrāṇī*, vol. 2. Śrīraṅgam: Śrī Vāṇī Vilās Press, 1975.

———. *Stotrāṇī*, vol. 3. Śrīraṅgam: Śrī Vāṇī Vilās Press, 1976.

———. *Stotrāvalī Vibhāga*, edited by Śrī Kāñcī Prativādi Bhayaṅkara Annaṅgarācārya. Kāñcīpuram: Granthamālā Office, 1958.

———. *Tattvamuktākalāpa*. With *Sarvārthasiddhi*—Commentary of Veṅkaṭanātha, translation into Hindi by Ācārya Viśva Prasād Dvivedi, Śrīdharācārya. Ayodya: Tattvamuktākalāpa Prakāsan, 1984.

———. *Varadarāja Pañcasat*. Translation and commentary by D. Ramaswamy Ayyangar. Madras: Viśiṣṭādvaita Pracāriṇī Sabha, 1972.

———. *Yatirājasaptati*, trans. D. Ramaswami Ayyangar. Tirupati: Tirumala Tirupati Devasthanams, 1965.

———. *Yādavābhyudayam*. Text and translation by K. S. Kṛṣṇa Tātācāriar. Madras: Vedānta Deśika Research Society, 1976.

Veṅkatācārya, Vidvān. & Puduppaṭṭu Tiru Veṅkaṭācārya, eds. *Catuśślokī Vyākhyānam*. With the commentaries of Nārāyaṇa Āccana Piḷḷai and Peria Āccana Piḷḷai. Kāñcīpuram: Śrīnivāsa Press, 1913 (Telugu script).

Yāmuna. *Gītārthasaṃgraha*. With Veṅkaṭanātha's commentary and English translation by K. Bhāṣyam, Tamil translation by Uttamūru Vīrarāghavācārya. Madras: Ubhaya Vedānta Granthamālā, 1960.

———. *Gītārthasaṃgraha*. With English translation and explanatory notes by V. K. Rāmānujacāri. Kuṃbakoṇam: Published by the translator, 1931.

———. *Catuśślokī*. With Kureśa's Śrīstavam and Maṇipravāla commentary by P. B. Annaṅgarācārya. Padippikkappaṭṭana: Śrī Gītācārya Press, 1940 (Telugu script).

———. *Catuśślokī*. With commentary by Nāyanār Āccan Piḷḷai. Kāñcīpuram: Śrīnivāsa Press, 1913.

———. *Āgamaprāmāṇya*, trans. J. A. B. van Buitenen. Madras: Rāmānuja Research Society, 1971.

———. *Āgamaprāmāṇya*, edited by M. Narasiṃhācāri. Baroda: Oriental Institute, 1976.

———. *Ālvanḍar Stotraratna*. With translation and commentary in Hindi. Bombay: Śrīnivāsa Udyog Pratiṣṭān, 1972.

———. *Gītārthasaṃgraha*. With the commentary of Vedānta Deśika (*Gītārthasaṃgraharakṣa*), edited by P. B. Anantācāriar. Kāñcīpuram: Śrī Sudarśana Press, 1901.

———. *Siddhitraya*. Madras: Ubhaya Vedānta Granthamālā Book Trust, 1972.

———. *Stotraratna*, trans. Svāmi Ādidevānanda. Madras: Ramakrishna Maṭh, 1979.

———. *Stotraratna*. With commentary of Peria Āccan Piḷḷai, edited by Venkatacharya and Puduppaṭṭu TiruVeṅkaṭācārya. Kāñcīpuram: Śrīnivāsa Press, 1914 (Telugu script).

———. *Stotraratna*. With commentary of Peria Āccan Piḷḷai. Madras: Śrīniketana Press, 1879.

Secondary Sources

Aiyangar, Krishnaswami S. "The Yatirājavaibhavam of Āndrapūrṇa (Life of Rāmānuja)," in *The Indian Antiquary* 38, May 1909. pp. 129 ff.

Anantharangachar, N. S. *The Philosophy of Sādhana in Viśiṣṭādvaita.* Mysore: University of Mysore, 1967.

Andronov, M. *A Standard Grammar of Modern and Classical Tamil.* Madras: New Century Book House, Pvt. Ltd., 1969.

Apte, V. S. *The Practical Sanskrit-English Dictionary.* Delhi, Varanasi, Patna: Motilal Banarsidass, 1965.

Arden, A. H. *A Progressive Grammar of the Tamil Language.* Madras: The Christian Literature Society, 1969 (reprint).

Beane, Wendell Charles. *Myth, Cult, and Symbols in Śākta Hinduism.* Leiden: E. J. Brill, 1977.

Begley, Wayne E. *Viṣṇu's Flaming Wheel: The Iconography of the Sudarśanacakra.* New York: New York University Press for the College of Art Association of America, 1973.

Bhatt, S. R. *Studies in Rāmānuja Vedānta.* New Delhi: Heritage Publishers, 1975.

Bhattacharya, Narendranath. *History of the Śākta Religion.* New Delhi: Munshiram Manoharlal, 1974.

Carman, J. B. *The Theology of Rāmānuja: An Essay in Interreligious Understanding.* New Haven & London: Yale University Press, 1974.

Carman, J. B. & Vasudha Narayanan. *The Tamil Veda: Piḷḷān's Interpretation of the Tiruvāymoḷi.* Chicago: The University of Chicago Press, 1989.

Carpenter, J. Estlin. *Theism in Medieval India* [Hibbert Lectures, 2d. Series, 1919] London: William & Norgate, 1921.

Chakravarti, S. C. *Philosophical Foundation of Bengal Vaiṣṇavism—A Critical Exposition.* Calcutta: Academic Publishers, 1969.

Chandra, Ramprasad. *Archeology and Vaiṣṇava Tradition.* New Delhi: Indological Book Corp., 1977.

Das, Veena. *Structure and Cognition: Aspects of Hindu Caste and Ritual.* Delhi: Oxford University Press, 1982.

De, Sushil Kumar. *Early History of the Vaiṣṇava Faith and Movement in Bengal, from Sanskrit and Bengali Sources.* Calcutta: Firma K. L. Mukhopadyaya, 1961.

Dumont, Louis. *Affinity as a Value.* Chicago, London: The University of Chicago Press, 1983.

———. *Homo Hierarchicus: The Caste System and its Implications.* Chicago, London: The University of Chicago Press, 1980.

Dyszkowski, Mark S. G. *The Canon of the Śaivāgama and the Kubjikā Tantra of the Western Kaula Tradition.* Albany: State University of New York Press, 1988.

Eck, Diana L. *Darśan, Seeing the Divine Image in India.* Chambersberg, Pa.: Anima Books, 1981.

Esnoul, Anne Marie. *Rāmānuja et la Mystique Viṣṇouite*. Paris: Editions du Sevil, 1964.

Geldner, Karl F. *Der Ṛg Veda*, vols. 1-3 [Harvard Oriental Series, vols. 33-35] Cambridge: Harvard: University Press, 1951.

Ghate, V. S. *The Vedānta: A Study of the Brahma Sūtras with the Bhāṣyas of Śaṅkara, Rāmānuja, Niṃbārka, Madhva and Vallabha.* The Bhandarakar Oriental Research Institute, 1960.

Gonda, Jan. *Aspects of Early Viṣṇuism.* Utrecht: Oostoek, 1954.

———. *Die Religionen Indiens*, vols. 1 & 2. Stuttgart: W. Kohlhammer Verlag, 1960.

———. *Die Religionen Der Menschheit*, vols. 11 & 12. Stuttgart: W. Kohlhammer Verlag, 1963.

———. *Medieval Religious Literature in Sanskrit* [*A History of Indian Literature*, vol. 2., edited by J. Gonda] Weisbaden: Otto Harrassowitz, 1977.

Gopal, B. R. *Śrī Rāmānuja in Karnataka: An Epigraphical Study.* Delhi: Sundeep Prakashan, 1983.

Gopinatharao, T. A. *Śrī Subrahmanya Ayyar Lectures on the History of Śrīvaiṣṇavas.* Madras: University of Madras, Government Press, 1923.

Goswami, Bhagabat Kumar. *The Bhakti Cult in Ancient India.* Varanasi: Chowkamba Sanskrit Series Office, 1965.

Goudriaan, T. & Sanjukta Gupta. *Hindu Tantric and Śakta Literature* [*A History of Indian Literature,* edited by J. Gonda, vol. 1] Weisbaden: Otto Harrassowitz, 1977.

Govindacharya, Alakondavalli. "A Note on Yatirāja Vaibhavam," *The Indian Antiquary,* 40 (May 1911): 152.

———. "The Aṣṭādaśa-Bhedas," in *Journal of the Royal Asiatic Society,* (October 1910): 1103-12.

———. *The Divine Wisdom of the Dravida Saints.* Madras: C. N. Press, 1902.

Gupta, Sanjukta. "The Pāñcarātra Attitude to Mantra," in *Mantra*, edited by Harvey P. Alper. Albany: State University of New York Press, 1989, pp. 224-48.

Hardy, Friedhelm. *Viraha-Bhakti: the Early History of Kṛṣṇa Devotion in South India.* Delhi: Oxford University Press, 1983.

Hari Rao, V. N., ed. & trans. *Kōil Oḷugu: The Chronicle of the Śrīraṅgam Temple with Historical Notes.* Madras: Rochouse & Sons., 1961.

Harrison, Mark Hunter. *Hindu Monism and Pluralism.* London: Humphrey Milford, Oxford University Press, 1932.

Hawley, J. S. & Donna Marie Wulff, eds. *The Divine Consort: Rādha and the Goddess of India.* Boston: Beacon Press, 1986.

Hooper, J. S. M. *Hymns of the Āḷvārs* [The Heritage of India Series] Calcutta: Association Press, London: Oxford University Press, 1929.

Jagadeesan, N. "A History of Śrī Vaiṣṇavism in Tamil Country (Post Rāmānuja)" Ph. D Thesis in History, University of Madras, January 1967.

———. *History of Śrīvaiṣṇavism in the Tamil Country: Post Rāmānuja.* Madurai: Kodal Publishers, 1977.

Jaiswal, Suvira. *The Origin and Development of Vaiṣṇavism: Vaiṣṇavism from 200 BC-AD 500.* Delhi: Munshiram Manoharlal, 1967.

Kielhorn, F. *A Grammar of the Sanskrit Language.* Varanasi: The Chowkamba Sanskrit Series Office, 1970.

Kinsley, David. *Hindu Goddesses: Visions of the Divine Feminine in the Hindu Religious Tradition.* Berkeley, Los Angeles, London: University of California Press, 1988.

Klostermaier, Klaus K. *Mythologies and Philosophies of Salvation in the Theistic Traditions of India.* Waterloo, Ontario, Canada: Published for the Canadian Corporation for Studies in Religion, by Wilfred Laurier University Press, 1984.

Krishna, Nandita. *The Art and Iconography of Viṣṇu-Nārāyaṇa.* Bombay: D. B. Taraporevala, 1980.

Kumar, Pushpendra. *Śakti Cult in Ancient India* (with special reference to Purāṇic literature) Varanasi: Bharatiya Publishing House, 1974.

Kumarappan, Bharatan. *The Hindu Conception of the Deity as Culminating in Rāmānuja.* London: Luzac, 1934.

Lacombe, Oliver. *La Doctrine Morale et Métaphysique de Rāmānuja* [text and French translation and notes on *Śrībhāṣya,* 1.1.1). Paris: Adrien Maisonneuve, 1938.

Lele, Jayant. [ed). *Tradition and Modernity in Bhakti Movements.* Leiden: E. J. Brill, 1981.

Lester, Robert. "Rāmānuja and Śrī Vaiṣṇavism," Paper read at The American Association of Asian Studies, 1965.

———. "Rāmānuja and Śrī Vaiṣṇavism: The Concept of Prapatti or Śaraṇāgati," in *History of Religions,* [University of Chicago), 5 [Winter 1966): 266-82.

———. "The Nature and Function of Patañjalian-Type Yoga as the Means to Release [*Mokṣopāya*) According to Rāmānuja." Ph. D Dissertation, Yale University, 1962.

Lipner, Julius. *The Face of Truth: A Study of Meaning and Metaphysics in the Vedāntic Theology of Rāmānuja.* Hampshire: Macmillan, 1986.

Lott, Eric J. *God and the Universe in the Vedāntic Theology of Rāmānuja: A Study in His Use of the Self-Body Analogy.* Madras: Ṛāmānuja Research Society, 1976.

———. *Vedāntic Appraoches to God.* London: Macmillan, 1980.

Macnicol, Nicol. *Indian Theism from the Vedic to the Muhammadan Period* [Religious Quest of India Series, 1915). Delhi: Munshiram Manoharlal, 1968.

Manalapuzhvila, Antony. *Nature and Origin of the World According to Rāmānuja.* Alwaye [India): St. Joseph's Pontifical Seminary, 1966.

Mesquita, von Roque. "Yāmunamuni: Leben, Datierung und Werke" in *Wienner Zeitschrift für die Kunde Südasiens* (Wien). Sonderabdruck aus band 17 (1973): 177-93.

———. "Yāmunācāryas Lehre von der Grösse des Ātman" in *Wienner Zeitschrift für die Kunde Südasiens* (Wien). Sonderabdruck aus band 33 (1989): 129-50.

———. "Rāmānujas Quellen im Mahāpūrvapakṣa und Mahāsiddhānta des Śrībhāṣya" in *Wienner Zeitschrift für die Kunde Südasiens* (Wien). Sonderabdruck aus band 28 (1984): 179-222.

———. "Recent research on Yāmuna" in Wienner Zeitschrift für die Kunde Südasiens (Wien). Sonderabdruck aus band 17 (1973): 183-208.

———. "Zur Vedānta und Pāñcarātra-Tradition Nāthamunis" in *Wienner Zeitschrift für die Kunde Südasiens* (Wien). Sonderabdruck aus band 23 (1979): 163-93.

———. "Yāmuna's Vedānta and Pāñcarātra: A Review" in *Wienner Zeitschrift für die Kunde Südasiens* (Wien). Sonderabdruck aus band 24 (1980): 199-224.

Monier-Williams, M. *A Sanskrit-English Dictionary.* Delhi, Patna, Varanasi: Motilal Banarsidass, 1974.

Mukherjee, Prabhat. *The History of Medieval Vaiṣṇavism in Orissa.* Calcutta: R. Chatterjee, 1940.

Murthy, Srinivasa, H.V. *Vaiṣṇavism of Śaṅkaradeva and Rāmānuja—A Comparative Study.* Delhi, Varanasi, Patna: Motilal Banarsidass, 1973.

Narayanan, Vasudha. *The Way and the Goal: Expressions of Devotion in the Early Śrī Vaiṣṇava Tradition.* Washington, D. C.: Institute for Vaiṣṇava Studies & Center for the Study of World Religions, Harvard University, 1987.

Nayagar, Venugopala N. "Sītā as 'Pirāṭṭi'," in *Śrī Rāmānuja Vāṇi,* vol. 4, No. 4 (July 1981): 30-41.

Neevel, Walter G. Jr. *Yāmuna's Vedānta and Pāñcarātra: Integrating the Classical and the Popular.* Missoula, Montana: Scholars Press, 1977.

Nilakanta Sastri, K. A. A. *Development of Religion in South India.* Bombay: Orient Longmans, 1963.

———. *History of South India from Pre Historic Times to the Fall of Vijayanagar.* Madras: Oxford University Press, 1966.

North, Patricia Ann. *Mysticism and Prophetism in Hildegard of Bingen and in Rāmānuja: An Essay in History and Hermeneutics.* Ph. D Thesis, U.C.L.A., 1977.

Norton, James. "The Mahāsiddhānta of Rāmānuja's Śrībhāṣya," Unpublished Article.

Otto, Rudolph. *Siddhānta des Rāmānuja.* (German translation of Śrībhāṣya 1.1.1) Jena: Eugen Diederichs, 1917.

Parthasarathi, J. "Maṅgalāśāsana—A Special form of God-Realization," in *Śrī Rāmānuja Vāṇi*, vol. 4, No. 2, (Jan. 1981): 5-24.

Radhakrishnan, S. *The Vedānta According to Śaṅkara and Rāmānuja.* London: Allen & Unwin, 1928.

Raghavachar, S. S. "The Pāñcarātra," in *Śrī Rāmānuja Vāṇi*, vol. 3, No. 2, (Jan. 1980): 13-21.

———. *Introduction to the Vedārthasaṃgraha of Śrī Rāmānujācārya.* Mangalore: Sharada Press, 1973.

Raghavan, V. K. S. N. Raghavan. *History of Viśiṣṭādvaita Literature.* Delhi: Ajanta Publications, 1979.

Rajam, S. *An Intensive Course in Tamil.* Mysore: Central Institute of Indian Languages, 1979.

Ramanujam, B. V. *History of Vaiṣṇavism in South India up to Rāmānuja.* Annamalainagar: Annamalai University, 1973.

Ramanujan, A. K. *Hymns for the Drowning-Poems for Viṣṇu by Nammāḷvār.* New Jersey: Princeton University Press, 1981.

Rangachari, K. *The Śrīvaiṣṇava Brāhmans* (Bulletin of the Madras Government Museum) Madras: Printed by the Superintendent Government Press, 1931.

———. *The Śrīvaiṣṇava Brāhmans.* Madras: Government of India Series, General Section, Vol. 2, No. 2., 1931.

Raychaudhuri, H. *Materials for the Study of the Early History of the Vaiṣṇava Sect.* New Delhi: Oriental Books, 1975 (Reprint).

Rukmani, T. S. *A Critical Study of Bhagavata Purāṇa, with Special Reference to Bhakti.* Varanasi: Chowkamba Sanskrit Series Office, 1970.

Rāmānujam, B. V. "Divyasūri Caritam," *Journal of Indian History,* 13: 181-99.

Schrader, F. Otto. *Introduction to the Pāñcarātra and the Ahirbudhnya Saṃhitā.* Madras: The Adyar Library and Research Center, 1916.

Sengupta, Anima. *A Critical Study of the Philosophy of Rāmānuja.* Varanasi: Chowkamba Sanskrit Series Office, 1967.

Sharma, Arvind. *Viśiṣṭādvaita: A Study.* New Delhi: Heritage, 1978.

Shulman, David Dean. *Tamil Temple Myths: Sacrifice and Divine Marriage in the South Indian Śaiva Tradition.* Princeton, N.J.: Princeton University Press, 1980.

Singh, Satyavrata. *Vedānta Deśika: His Life, Works, and Philosophy—A Study.* Varanasi: Chowkamba Series, 1958.

Smith, H. D. "A Report on Some Unpublished Manuscripts of the Pāñcarātrāgama Canons with Special Reference to Works with Homonymous Titles," in *South Asia 3,* edited by Garciela de la Lama, El Colegio de Mexico, 1976.

———. "A Typological Survey of Definitions: The name 'Pāñcarātra'," in *Oriental Research* (Vols. 34-35 (1964-65, 1965-66) edited by V. Raghavan. Madras: Kuppuswami Sastri Research Institute, 1973.

———. "Vāhanas in the Cultic Art of South Indian Temples," *Proceedings of the Seminar on Temple Art and Architecture held in March 1980*, edited by K. K. A. Venkatachari. Bombay: Ananthacharya Indological Research Institute, 1981.

———. *A Descriptive Bibliography of the Printed Texts of the Pāñcarātrāgamas*, vol. 2. Baroda: Oriental Institute, 1980.

———. *A Source Book of Vaiṣṇava Iconography According to Pāñcarātra Texts* (Sanskrit texts compiled and arranged with commentary in English). Madras: Pāñcarātra Pariśodana Pariṣad, 1969.

Srinivasachari, P. N. *The Philosophy of Viśiṣṭādvaita.* Madras: The Adyar Library and Research Center, 1943.

Srinivasachari, S. M. *Fundamentals of Viśiṣṭādvaita: A Study Based on Vedānta Deśika's Tattvamuktākalāpa.* Delhi: Motilal Banarsidass, 1988.

Srinivasan, L. "Śrī Viṣṇusahasranāma Stotra" in *Śrī Rāmānuja Vāṇi,* Vol. 4, No. 3 (April 1981): 15-37.

Stein, Burton, ed. *South Indian Temples—An Analytical Reconsideration.* New Delhi, Bombay: Vikas Publishing House Pvt. Ltd., 1978.

Subrahmanian, N. "The Brāhmin in the Tamil Country (in Ancient and Medieval Times)" Unpublished Article.

Tattvananda, Swami. *Vaiṣṇava Sects, Śaiva Sects, Mother Worship.* Calcutta: Nirmalendra Bikash Sen Gupta, n.d.

Varadachari, K. C. *Āḻvārs of South India* (Bhavan's Book University, Vol. 143). Bombay: Bharatiya Vidyabhavan, 1966.

Varadachari, V. "Āgamas," in *Śrī Rāmānuja Vāṇi,* Vol. 5, No. 4 (July 1982): 30-39.

———. *Āgamas of South Indian Vaiṣṇavism.* Madras: Prof. M. Rangacharya Memorial Trust, 1982.

Vasu, Srisa Chandra, Rai Bahadur. *The Daily Practice of the Hindus, Containing the Morning and Midday Duties.* New York: A. M. S. Press, 1974.

Venkatakrishnan, M. A. "Kureśa's Five Hymns," in *Śrī Rāmānuja Vāṇi*, Vol. 3, No. 4 (July 1980): 35-44.

Whitney, W. D. *Sanskrit Grammar.* Cambridge: Harvard University Press, 1973.

———. *The Roots, Verb-Forms, and Primary Derivatives of the Sanskrit Language* (Supplement). Leipzig: Beitkopf and Härtel, 1885.

INDEX

Abhītistava 113
abhigamana 22
abhāva 35
ācārya 51, 72, 75, 76, 78, 95, 101, 105, 107, 108, 111, 113, 122, 133, 138, 152, 154, 155, 156, 159
Ācāryahṛdayam 95
accessibility 82, 89, 93, 99, 118, 119, 120, 124, 143, 144, 146
Acintyabhedābheda 36, 40
Acit 60, 96, 114, 124, 141
Acyuta 83
Acyutāṣṭaka 113
Adhikaraṇa 88
Adhikaraṇadarpaṇa 112
Adhikaraṇasārāvali 112
Ādhyātmakhaṇḍadvaya 78
Ādiśeṣa 92, 147
Āditya 17
Advaita 25, 35, 36, 39, 40
Advaitic 79
Advaitins 59, 61, 64
advitīya 62
æsthetic 12, 13, 14, 15, 47, 49
Āgama 42, 52, 60, 65, 75, 96, 97
Āgamaprāmāṇya 51, 55, 59, 60, 65, 152
Āgamic 52, 60, 73, 74, 84, 96
Agastya 86
Agni 18, 27, 124, 135
Agniṣomīya Sacrifice 124
ahaṃkāra 22, 24, 25, 35, 97, 99, 102
ahaṃtā 29, 31, 37, 38, 39, 41
Āhāraniyama 113
Ahirbudhnya Saṃhitā 5, 23, 25, 26, 27, 30, 37, 38, 42, 52, 96, 125, 133, 134, 135, 140, 145, 146, 153
aikaśāstravāda 112
aiśvara 121
aiśvarya 23, 24, 26, 29, 32, 33, 36, 41, 42, 57, 60, 66, 83, 123, 134, 143, 141
aiśvaryam 14
Aitareya Āraṇyaka 13
ajñāna 22
akhila 115, 126
akṣara 47
akṣaram 34
Alagīya Manavāla Perumaḷ Nayanar 95
alakṣmī 17
Āḷvār 4, 6, 51, 82, 96, 97, 101, 113, 114, 119, 122, 125, 133, 143, 146, 149, 150, 151, 155, 156, 159
aṃbā 82
ambrosia 83, 87, 92
anākāraḥ 98
ānanda 122, 144
ananta 144
Ananta Sūri 111
ananyārhatvam 103
anapāyinī 75, 93
Āṇḍān 101
aṅga-s 102, 116, 155
Aniruddha 24, 25, 28, 29, 30, 33, 34, 44, 46, 47, 98, 143
Āṇṭāl 96
antaryāmin 22, 24, 27, 28, 45, 69, 90, 98
antaryāmitva 98
anugraha 24
anumāna 117
anuṣṭāna 77
apāya 43
Appular 111
ārādhana 60
Araṇya Parva 86
Āraṇyakas 66
arcā 22, 24, 27, 28, 60, 90, 98, 149, 150
arcana 116
arcāvatāra 98, 99, 115, 116, 117, 144
ardhanārīśvara 41
ārdra 16
artha 48
Arthapañcakam 98
Āśa 16
asādhāraṇa 147
Aśokavana 105
āśraya 58
asta 38
Aṣṭādaśarahasya 96, 155
Aṣṭākṣara 154
Aṣṭākṣara Mantra 78
Aṣṭaślokī 77, 78, 93
āstika 112

asuras 62
Atharvaveda 13
aṭiyan 99
Ātma Siddhi 55, 59, 61
ātmanikṣepa 43
Ātreya Rāmānuja 111
auspiciousness 134
avākī 98
avatāra 24, 28, 47, 86, 89, 90, 98, 119, 147
Avesta 12
avyakta 22, 25
avyakta pradhāna 34
avyakta prakṛti 25
Avyaya 88
Ayodhya 81

bala 23, 24, 26, 29, 31, 32, 33, 41, 42, 57, 60, 66, 121, 134, 141, 143
Baladeva 30
Balarāma 30
Bali 18
baliṣṭha 13
beauty 12, 14, 16, 19, 20, 31, 47, 48, 57, 59, 61, 89, 91, 104, 134
berapūja 116
Bhagavad Gītā 16, 19, 74, 96, 139, 151
Bhagavadgītābhāṣya 67
Bhagavadguṇadarpaṇa 77
Bhagavatī 56, 125
Bhagavān 69, 82, 83, 86, 87, 88, 90, 93, 116, 117, 122, 123, 124, 125, 128, 129
Bhāgavata 107, 114
Bhāgavata Purāṇa 97, 107
Bhāgavata-s 150
bhajati 87
bhakti 2, 22, 86, 87, 125, 133, 143, 155
Bhārata 102
Bhārhut Stūpa 16
Bhāsā 34
Bhaṭṭar 2, 4, 5, 6, 8, 51, 77, 78, 79, 80, 82, 83, 84, 85, 86, 87, 88, 89, 90, 91, 92, 93, 96, 142, 143, 144, 152, 153, 154, 156
bhāva 35, 37, 38, 41
bhāvāsana 46
bhavat 38, 41
Bhaviṣyat Purāṇa 79
Bhedābheda 36
Bhedābhedavādins 74
Bhīṣma 65
bhoga 35
bhoktā 35
Bhūdevī 14, 15, 17, 70
Bhūmi 17
bhūtaśuddhi 44
bhūti 13, 18, 26, 30
bhūti śakti 23, 24, 29, 31, 39, 142
bound souls 61
Brahmā 25, 34, 56, 57, 58, 59, 62, 69, 73, 80, 86, 88, 89, 93, 122, 123, 124
Brahma Purāṇa 82, 83
Brahma Sūtras 65, 67, 88, 114, 151
brahmacārin 95, 123
brahmacarya 95
Brahman 6, 30, 32, 33, 36, 37, 38, 39, 42, 43, 44, 47, 49, 52, 58, 61, 62, 63, 65, 66, 69, 70, 73, 74, 75, 87, 116, 117, 118, 121, 122, 125, 126, 127, 136, 138, 141, 147
brahmasthāna 45
Brāhmin 64, 79, 83
buddhi 22, 25, 26, 34
buddhīndriya-s 25, 35

Caitanya 40
cakra 16
cañcalā 18
candra 17
Carama Śloka 78, 96, 119, 122, 154
cārusarvāṅgī 47
caryā 23
Caturātma 143
caturvyūha 28, 33, 143
Catuśślokī 9, 55, 56, 57, 58, 59, 61, 113, 125, 136, 143, 156
cetana 35
cetya 35
Chodana 87
Christianity 2
cintana 116
cintāmaṇi 31
Cit 60, 96, 114, 124, 141
Coḷa 62, 63, 64
compassion 58, 75, 80, 83, 84, 85, 87, 89, 90, 97, 99, 106, 121, 129, 130, 131
compassionate glances 58
Cosmic Day 25
Cosmic Egg 25, 34, 62
Cosmic Night 25
cosmic form 57, 58, 59, 63
creation 20, 24, 25, 26, 27, 28, 30, 32, 33, 37, 47, 74, 80, 81, 88, 90, 134, 135, 140, 141, 142, 148
creative principle 74

dāsa 58
Daśadīpaka Nighanṭu 113
dāsaḥ 118
Daśāvatāra Stotra 113
Dayāśatakam 113, 114
Dehalīśastuti 113, 114, 119, 123
deva 62, 68, 69
Devanāyakapañcasat 113
devī 84
devotion 79, 81, 82, 86, 87, 89, 114, 116
Dharma 18, 38, 48
Dharma Śāstras 83
Dhṛtī 67
dīkṣā 60, 115, 152
dissolution 20, 24, 25, 26, 32, 33, 74, 121
divine consort 1, 2, 3, 6, 7, 8, 9, 11, 51, 59, 61, 62, 63, 66, 69, 70, 71, 72, 73, 74, 78, 80, 82, 84, 85, 89, 90, 91, 92, 93, 102, 103, 104, 105, 106, 107, 108, 109, 121, 122, 123, 125, 127, 128, 131, 137, 138, 139, 140, 141, 143, 144, 145, 146, 147, 148, 153, 154, 155, 156, 157, 159
Divyaprabandham 51
Divyasūricaritam 55, 56, 64, 152
Dramiḍopaniṣad Tātparyaratnāvalī 113
Draupadī 14, 101, 108, 154
duḥkha 35
Duryodana 101
Duśśāsana 101
dvaita 53
Dvaya 84, 154
Dvaya Mantra 78, 96, 105, 123, 128, 130, 156

early Vedic 12
ekāntika 23, 30, 32, 35, 39
ekāntikavāda 133, 142
epic 4, 8, 11, 13, 14, 15, 17, 19, 20, 30, 31, 79, 80, 82, 96, 97, 101, 105, 134, 142, 145, 154
esoteric 22

five nights 22
five prakara-s 28
five-day sacrifice 22

gada 16
Gadya 75
Gadyatraya 64, 113
gandhadvāra 16
gandharva-s 35
Garuḍa 19, 56, 92, 149
Gauri 34
Gāyatrī 111
generosity 85
Gītābhāṣya 63, 67, 112, 114, 151
Gītārthasaṃgraha 55, 112
Gītārthasaṃgraharakṣā 112
glory 58, 67, 80
Godāstuti 113
goptṛtvavaraṇam 43
gotra 111
grace 12, 43, 47, 49, 81, 85, 100, 102, 104, 105, 106, 107, 108, 146, 148
Guha 102
guṇa-s 22, 23, 25, 26, 29, 30, 41
Guṇaratnakośa 77, 78, 80, 81, 85, 91, 92, 124, 143
Gupta period 149, 153
guru 77

Haṃsasandeśa 113
Hanumān 105
Hari 37, 42, 65, 85, 93
Haviṣka 16
Hayagrīva Saṃhitā 115
Hayagrīva Stotra 113
heyaguṇa-s 143
Highest Puruṣa 57
hiṃsa 43
Hiraṇyagarbha 34
homa pūja 116
Hṛī 16, 82
Hṛṣīkeśa 34

icchā 32
ijyā 22, 115
incarnation 111, 117
inconstancy 134
inconstant 18, 20, 47
Individual Soul 24, 39
Indra 14, 18, 30, 47, 83, 88, 135
Indrarātra Saṃhitā 23
inseparability 20, 42, 68, 75, 90, 92, 122, 135, 142, 144, 145, 148
Īśa 39, 56
Īśatva 114
Īśāvasyopaniṣad Bhāṣya 112, 113, 114, 117, 118
Īśitavya 39
Īśvara 57, 60, 61, 96, 98, 120, 124, 129, 134, 135, 136, 137, 138, 139, 140, 141, 142, 143, 144, 145, 146, 147, 148, 149, 154

Īśvara Saṃhitā 23, 52
Īśvara Siddhi 55
Īśvarī 58
Itihāsa 28, 79, 80, 96, 97

Jain 63
Janaka 91
Jananī 80, 82
Jātavedas 18
Jayā 37
Jayākhya 4, 6, 7, 23, 153
Jayākhya Saṃhitā 23, 30
jijñāsā 126
Jīva 24, 25, 26, 42, 47, 59, 62, 63, 65, 69, 72, 84, 89, 92, 96, 97, 98, 99, 100, 101, 102, 103, 104, 105, 106, 107, 108, 109, 117, 118, 120, 128, 129, 130, 131, 133, 138, 140, 144, 145, 148
jīvātmas 84
jñāna 23, 24, 26, 28, 29, 32, 33, 36, 41, 42, 57, 60, 62, 63, 66, 77, 83, 121, 122, 123, 134, 136, 141, 143, 144
jñānabalavīryaśakti 141
Junāgarh inscription 19
jvālantī 17
jyeṣṭha 13
Jyotiṣkuḍi 96

Kadaṃba record 19
kāla 19, 24, 25, 47
Kālidāsa 113
kalyāṇaguṇa-s 143
kāma 48
kāmadhenu 121
kāmya 115
kanaka 36
karīṣin 16
karma 24, 25, 62, 104
karman 43, 103
karmendriya-s 25
karmic 103, 104, 108
karta 35
Kaṭhā Upaniṣad 96
Kausītakī Brāhmaṇa 83
Kavitārkikasiṃha 111
Keśava 34
Kīrtī 67
kleśas 62
koṇa-s 46
kriyā 23, 26, 30, 35
kriyā śakti 23, 24, 29, 31, 35, 142
kṛpā 103, 147
Kṛṣṇa 16, 19, 30, 97, 98, 101, 104, 105, 106, 107
Kṣamā 67
kṣatra 13
Kubera 18
kuṇḍala 36
Kureśa 8, 9
Kuruttāḷvān 142, 143
Kuṣāṇa 16
kūṭastha puruṣa 24

Lakṣmaṇa 91, 97
Lakṣmī Tantra 5, 6, 7, 8, 21, 23, 25, 26, 27, 28, 29, 30, 31, 36, 37, 38, 39, 40, 41, 42, 43, 44, 45, 52, 74, 83, 84, 92, 96, 120, 125, 131, 133, 134, 135, 136, 140, 141, 147, 148, 153, 155
Lakṣmīkalyāṇa 78
Lakṣmīvān 84, 92
laya 88
līlāvibhūti 124
Liṅga 87
loka 86
Lokācārya 2, 4, 5, 7, 8, 95, 96, 97, 98, 99, 100, 101, 102, 103, 104, 105, 106, 107, 108, 109, 111, 121, 127, 128, 129, 130, 131, 134, 144, 145, 146, 147, 148, 155, 156, 157
Lokāyata 112
lolā 18
luster 12

Mādhava 65, 82, 90
Madhva 74
Madhvācārya 53
Mādhyamika 112
mahā āgasaḥ 85
Mahābhārata 11, 13, 14, 16, 17, 18, 22, 30, 79, 96, 97, 101, 105, 106, 115, 154
mahābhūta-s 22, 25
Mahālakṣmī 34
Mahāmāyā 34
mahāpralaya 57, 88
Mahāśrī 34
mahat 25, 26, 34, 35
Mahāvidyā 34
Mahāyāna Buddhism 2
Maheśvara 88
mahimā 62
mahiṣī 85
maintenance 14, 20, 24, 26, 32, 33, 74, 121, 134, 135, 148

Maithilī 81
Manas 24, 25
Manavālamāmuni 127, 145
maṇḍala 45, 46
maṇḍapa 45
maṅgalaśloka-s 2, 61, 66
Maṇipravāḷa 78, 82, 96
mantra 22, 40, 43, 44, 46, 47, 48, 49, 78, 83, 84, 90, 96, 116, 118, 154
mantrabiṃba 116
Marīcī 25
Mārkaṇḍeya Purāṇa 14, 79, 87
mātā 82
mātṛkā 37, 44
Matsya Purāṇa 79
māyā śakti 24
Medhā 67
Medhā Sūktam 83
mediator 89, 97, 98, 102, 103, 104, 105, 106, 107, 108
mediatrix 59, 63, 69, 70, 72, 75, 78, 82, 85, 89, 90, 93, 106, 120, 128, 137, 138, 152, 153, 154, 155
meditation 22, 23, 47, 86
Meghasandeśa 113
Mīmāṃsaka 55, 59, 60, 122
Mitra 135
mokṣa 48, 97, 115, 126
Mother of the universe 68, 69, 73, 83, 90
mudra 44
mukta 160, 156
mūlaprakṛti 24, 25
Mumukṣuppaḍi 96

Nācciar 96
nāga-s 35
Nāgendrālaya 64
nāma 22
naimittika 115
naivedya 60
Nāḷāyira Divyaprabandham 4
Nammāḷvār 63, 78, 95, 96, 113, 114, 118, 122, 125, 130, 151
Nampiḷḷai 95
Nāradīya Pāñcarātra 22
Nārāyaṇa 15, 16, 18, 23, 29, 31, 32, 37, 38, 39, 40, 41, 42, 43, 44, 47, 49, 52, 63, 66, 67, 69, 73, 86, 88, 114, 118, 122, 123, 125, 126, 127, 128, 129, 130, 131, 149
Nārāyaṇapuri 64
Nārāyaṇī 37
nāstika 112
nāṭaka-s 112
Nāthādūr Ammāḷ 5
Nāthamuni 4, 51, 55, 116, 150
Nāyikā 83
Netā 80
nīlā 35, 70
nimeṣa 32
Nimitta 88
Nimittakāraṇa 88, 142
nirhetuka kṛpa 85
nirmalya 60
nirviśeṣa 125, 126
Nitya 77, 114, 115
Nityagrantha 64, 70, 113, 115, 141, 156
nityakaiṅkarya 115, 116, 117, 156
nityamukta-s 24, 156
nityapuṣṭa 16
Nityaśrī 126
nityaśuddha 125
nityasūri-s 24
nityavibhūti 124
niyati 24, 25
Nyaiyāyika 55, 59
nyāsa 44, 155
Nyāsatilaka 113
Nyāya 55
Nyāyapariśuddhi 112
Nyāyasiddhāñjanam 112
Nyāyatattva 51, 55

Padmā 34
Pādma 4
Pādma Saṃhitā 23, 115, 134, 153
Pādma Tantra 22
Padmodbhava Saṃhitā 23
Pādukāsahasra 113
pañcakālika 60
Pāñcāla king 16
pañcamahābhūta-s 22
Pāñcarātra 114, 115, 116, 117, 125
Pāñcarātra Āgama 1, 4, 26, 31, 32, 42, 51, 52, 53, 59, 60, 61, 65, 70, 71, 72, 74, 75, 80, 83, 84, 90, 96, 97, 102, 113, 114, 117, 122, 124, 125, 130, 136, 137, 140, 144, 152, 153, 155, 156
Pāñcarātra rite 23
Pāñcarātra sacrifice 15
Pāñcarātrarakṣā 113, 114, 116, 155
Pāñcarātrika 55
pañcarūpa-s 28
Pāṇḍavas 14
pāpmān 13
para 22, 27, 28, 71, 90, 98, 134

Para Vāsudeva 98, 134, 135, 140, 141, 142, 143
Parakālāditya 19
param 40
Parama 23
Parama Saṃhitā 4, 22, 23, 30, 134
Parama Vyoma 24
paramapuruṣārtha 43
pāramārtha 44
pāramārthika 36, 40
Paramatabhaṅga 112, 113
Paramātma 136
parameśvaram 28
Parāśara Bhaṭṭar 122, 130
pāratantryam 103
parātītam 40
paratva 2, 71, 73, 98, 119, 138, 146
Pauṣkara 4, 6, 7, 23, 134, 153,
Pauṣkara Saṃhitā 52
perfect souls 61
Peria Tirumoḷi 96, 123
Piḷḷai Lokācārya 95
Piḷḷān 2, 4, 8, 63, 75, 78, 82, 142, 150, 151, 154
pīta 35
prabhāśa 17
pradhāna 34, 74
pradhānakāraṇa 142
Pradyumna 24, 28, 29, 30, 33, 34, 44, 46, 47, 98, 143
Prahlāda 14
Prajāpati 15, 18, 25
Prakāśa Saṃhitā 38
Prakṛti 19, 25, 26, 27, 53, 61, 74, 84, 92, 120
pralaya 38, 39, 123
pramāṇa 62, 117, 126, 130, 151
prāṇa 34
praṇāma 116
Praṇava 124
praṇayinī 85
prapanna 58, 75, 115
Prapannapārijāta 5
prapatti 45, 97, 101, 102, 115, 116, 125, 131, 148, 155, 156
Prāpya 146
Prasthānatraya 151
pratyakṣa 117
pravacana 77
prāyaścitta 43
prīti 43
priyā 85
prosperity 12, 13, 14, 15, 16, 17, 18, 19, 20, 31, 43, 83, 91, 134
pūja 60
Puṇḍarīkākṣa 37, 87, 111
puṇḍra 22
Purāṇas 27, 28, 79, 80, 86, 97
Purāṇic 11, 18, 20, 79, 96, 122, 142
puraścaraṇa 40
Pure Activity 36, 37
Pure Bliss 23
Pure Consciousness 6, 35, 36, 37, 47
Pure Creation 24, 26, 29, 32, 33, 35, 46, 52, 134, 135, 140
Puruṣa 15, 16, 18, 19, 22, 23, 25, 26, 27, 61, 108
Puruṣakāra 63, 72, 75, 78, 82, 97, 98, 101, 102, 104, 105, 107, 108, 128, 131, 146, 155
puruṣakāratva 120
Puruṣamedha (sacrifice) 15
Puruṣanirṇaya 55
Puruṣārtha 116
Pūrvamīmāṃsā 55, 112

radiance 12
Rāghava 91
Rahasya Granthas 155
Rahasyarakṣā 112, 155
Rahasyatrayasāra 56, 113, 118, 119, 121, 127
rajas 26, 33, 34, 69
rājasika 115
rajo guṇa 24, 25
rākṣasis 101
Rāma 19, 80, 81, 85, 91, 92, 98, 101, 102, 103, 107, 108, 118
Rāmānuja 2, 4, 5, 6, 7, 8, 21, 23, 51, 52, 53, 63, 64, 65, 66, 67, 68, 69, 70, 71, 72, 73, 74, 75, 76, 77, 78, 79, 84, 86, 95, 96, 97, 111, 112, 113, 114, 115, 116, 119, 121, 123, 125, 127, 130, 133, 137, 138, 139, 140, 141, 142, 143, 144, 146, 147, 148, 150, 151, 152, 153, 156
Rāmāyaṇa 17, 18, 79, 80, 81, 83, 91, 92, 96, 97, 102, 105, 106, 118, 130, 154
Raṅga 63, 64, 66, 70, 71, 77, 81, 82
Raṅganāyakī 81
rātri 22, 23
Rāvaṇa 80
released souls 61
Ṛg Veda 15, 16, 86
Ṛg Veda Saṃhitā 19
royal 14, 18
royalty 14, 20, 31
Rudra 25, 122

rūpacatuṣṭayam 27, 28

śabda 117
Śabdabrahman 44
ṣadguṇa-s 134, 136
sādhāraṇa 147
sadviveka 41
Sahakāri 88
Śaiva 41, 63, 64
Sajjanavaibhava 113
sakhī 85
Śakra 18, 30
Śakti (śakti) 5, 23, 24, 26, 28, 29, 32, 33, 36, 37, 39, 40, 44, 46, 47, 57, 60, 66, 73, 74, 75, 83, 84, 90, 91, 121, 134, 135, 136, 140, 141, 142, 143, 147
Śaktīśā 40
samānādhikaraṇa 118
sāmānya 126, 127
sāmarasyatā 41, 42, 63
saṃhṛti 24
Samitiñjaya 84
Saṃkalpasūryodaya 111, 113
Saṃkarṣaṇa 24, 28, 29, 30, 33, 34, 44, 46, 47, 98, 143
saṃpad 13
Saṃpatkumāra 64
saṃpradhāna 35
saṃṛddhi 13
saṃsāra 88, 100
saṃvid 35
Saṃvit Siddhi 55, 66
Śanaka 25
Sanatkumāra Saṃhitā 23
Śāṇḍilya Saṃhitā 23
śaṅka 16
Śaṅkara 34, 39, 79, 123
Sāṅkhya 19, 22, 25, 26, 27, 28, 43, 66, 74
śāntā 36, 37
Śāntiparvan 14, 18
śaraṇāgati 43, 70, 73, 115, 116, 155, 155, 156
Śaraṇāgatigadya 63, 67, 68, 69, 70, 72, 73, 75, 116, 125, 138, 139, 141, 156
śarīra-śarīri bhāva 118
Sārnāth inscription 19
sarvāṅgasundarī 47
Sarvārthasiddhi 112
sarvatyāga 43
śāstra 77, 124, 130
Śatadūṣaṇi 112
Śaṭakopa 119
Śatapatha Brāhmaṇa 13, 14, 15, 16, 18, 23
Satī 48
sattva 26, 33, 34, 69
sattva guṇa 24
Sāttvata 4, 6, 23, 125, 134, 153
Sāttvata Saṃhitā 130
Sāttvika 86, 115
satyatva 126
saulabhya 2, 71, 73, 119, 120, 121, 138, 146
saundaryam 14
sausīlya 119
Sautrāntika 112
Schönheit 12, 13
śeṣa (Śeṣa) 56, 73, 93, 97, 101, 103, 104, 105, 118, 121, 124, 128, 138, 140, 141, 146, 148, 156
Śeṣācala 64
śeṣatva 99, 109
Śeṣi (Śeṣin) 73, 74, 93, 97, 101, 103, 104, 105, 118, 119, 121, 128, 140, 141, 146, 148, 156
śeṣitva 92, 124, 125
Seśvaramīmāṃsā 112
sevā 86, 87
siddhānta 114, 115
Siddhitrayam 59, 61, 151
Siddhopāya 130
śiras 13
Śirimā 16
sisṛkṣā 28, 31, 32
Sītā 80, 83, 85, 91, 92, 97, 101, 103, 105, 106, 107, 108, 154
Śiva 25, 57, 58, 59, 62, 64, 88, 92, 123
six auspicious qualities 24, 41, 60, 61, 83, 136, 143, 147
six guṇa-s 26, 29, 60
Skandagupta 19
śloka 117, 118, 120, 121, 123, 125
Smṛtī 67
Smṛti 86, 97, 117
śobha-s 46
Soma 27, 124
sovereignty 13, 14, 23, 31, 67, 134
splendor 12, 48, 100
Śraddhā 16, 83
Śraddhā Sūktam 83
śreman 13
śreṣṭha 13
śreyas 13
Śrī Devī 69
Śrī Lakṣmīsahasranāma 82
Śrī Raṅga Aṣṭaka 77
Śrī Raṅgarājastava 77, 81

Śrī Sūkta 45, 83
Śrī Viṣṇusahasranāma 77, 78, 79
Śrī Viṣṇusahasranāma Bhāṣya 77, 78, 80, 82, 86, 91
Śrībhāṣya 51, 63, 65, 66, 67, 95, 111, 112, 114, 123, 125, 126, 127, 147, 151, 152
Śrīguṇaratnakośa 121, 125, 156
Śrīmān 59, 61, 122, 123
śrīmat 13, 67, 123, 128, 129, 130, 131
Śrīmate 67
Śrīmati 16
Śrīnivāsa 67, 123, 125, 126, 127, 147
Śrīnivāsatvam 126
Śrīpraśna Saṃhitā 22, 52
Śrīraṅgagadya 63
Śrīraṅgam 63, 64, 70, 71, 77, 78, 81, 82, 85, 95, 154, 156
Śrīraṅganātha 95
Śrīstava 9, 143
Śrīstuti 9, 113, 114, 121
Śrīsūkta 15, 16, 18, 19
Śrīvacanabhūṣaṇa 9, 96, 98, 125, 127
Śrīvallabhaḥ 67
Śrīvatśaṅka 77, 79, 86
Śrīvatśaṅkamiśra 154
Śrīvatsavakṣaḥ 126
Śrīviṣṇusahasranāma 143
Śriyaḥ kāntaḥ 67
Śriyaḥ Patiḥ 67
sṛṣṭi 24
Śrutaprakāśikācārya 70
Śrutaprakāśācārya 95
Śruti 80, 124, 126
sthāna 86
sthirā śakti 37
sthiti 24
stotra-s 79, 82, 112, 113, 114,
Stotraratna 9, 55, 56, 57, 58, 59, 61, 113, 125, 136
Sudarśana Bhaṭṭa 70
Sudarśanasūri 72
śuddha sattvam 140
suddha sṛṣṭi 134
Śūdra 64
Sugrīva 107, 108, 118
śukha 35
sūkṣmam 40
Sundarakāṇḍa 118
support 57, 58
supra-transcendent form 47
supremacy 58, 79, 83, 86, 88, 89, 90
Supreme Being 39
Supreme Puruṣa 56, 59, 61
Supreme Self 37, 93
supreme abode 80, 81, 86
suṣupsā 32
svabhāva 99, 135, 139, 146, 147
svādhyāya 22
svāmi 98, 118
svarūpa 31, 99, 122, 123, 128
svarūpa ekatva 147
svarūpaikya 118

Taittirīya Āraṇyaka 15
tamas 26, 33, 34, 35, 69
tāmasika 115
Tamil Veda 151
tamo guṇa 25
tanmātra-s 22, 25, 35
Tantra 44
Tantra Śāstra 6
Tantric 5, 6, 45, 73, 74
tapas 22
Tārikā 40, 45, 47, 48
Tātparyacandrikā 112
tattva-s 25, 47, 60
Tattvaṭīkā 112, 126
Tattvamuktākalāpa 112, 117
Tattvamātṛkā 113
Tattvaratnākara 77
Tattvaratnāvalī 113
tattvatraya 141
Tattvatrayam 96, 106
tejas 23, 26, 29, 32, 33, 35, 57, 60, 66, 121, 134, 141, 143
Teṅkaḷai 2, 95, 96, 133, 148
three guṇa-s 33, 69
tirodhāna 24
Tirukacci Naṃbi 152
Tirukkannamaṅgai Āṇḍān 101
Tirumaṅgai Āḷvār 78, 82
Tirumantra 96, 122, 124
Tirumoḷi 96
Tiruneḍum Taṇṭakam 78, 82
Tiruvaṇḍaḍi 123, 125
Tiruvāymoḷi 63, 78, 95, 96, 113, 114, 125, 142, 150, 151
triguṇa 26
Trivikrama 119

Ubhaya Vedānta 133, 151
ubhayavedāntin 96
udaya 38
Universal Father 84
Universal Mother 82, 83, 84, 88, 92, 93
unmeṣa 26, 32, 36
upadeśa 104
upalakṣaṇa 128, 129, 130

Upaniṣad 17, 27, 65, 79, 98, 138, 144, 151
upasti 87
Upeya 86, 87, 102, 129, 131, 146
Upādāna 88, 22
Upāsaka 87
upāsana 86, 87, 143
Upāya 43, 86, 87, 97, 101, 102, 103, 108, 124, 125, 128, 129, 131, 146
utsavamūrti 95
Uttara Nārāyaṇam 83
Uttaramīmāṃsā 112

Vāditrayakhaṇḍana 112
Vādukku Tiruvīthi Piḷḷai 95
Vaibhāṣika 112
Vaikhānasa Āgamas 113
Vaikuṇṭha 24, 81, 98, 100, 147
Vaikuṇṭhagadya 63, 70, 115
Vaiṣṇava Smṛti 83
Vājasaneya Saṃhitā 16, 17
Vāk 67
Vāmana 119
Vāmanāvatāra 123
Varadarāja 154
Varadarājapañcasat 113, 114
Varahapurāṇa 78
varṣiṣṭha 13
Varuṇa 135
Vāsava 18
Vāsudeva 15, 16, 19, 26, 28, 29, 33, 37, 44, 46, 47, 66, 83, 98, 117, 143, 149
vātsalya 72, 147
vaśiṣṭha 13
Vaṭakalai 2, 95, 113, 133, 148
Veda 65, 66, 79, 86
vedana 87
Vedas 22, 23, 27, 43, 44, 96, 97, 151
vedī 45
Vedic 11, 12, 13, 15, 16, 17, 18, 19, 20, 21, 27, 47, 83, 86, 88, 96, 133, 134, 135
Vedāṅgas 79
Vedānta 51, 53, 55, 60, 64, 71, 81, 96, 114, 124, 133, 136, 137
Vedānta Deśika 21, 133
Vedāntadīpa 63, 67
Vedāntasūtra-s 67
Vedāntasāra 63, 67
Vedāntic 51, 52, 53, 60, 63, 64, 79, 136, 137, 138, 141, 144
Vedāntist 96
Vedāntācārya 111
Vedārthasaṃgraha 63, 67, 68, 141, 151
Veṅkaṭanātha 2, 4, 5, 7, 8, 21, 39, 56, 95, 105, 111, 112, 113, 114, 115, 116, 117, 118, 119, 120, 121, 122, 123, 124, 125, 126, 127, 128, 129, 130, 131, 133, 134, 141, 146, 147, 148, 152, 155, 156, 157
Vibhava 22, 27, 28, 44, 58, 61, 62, 68, 90, 98
vibhava-s 24
Vibhīṣaṇa 80, 85, 107, 108
vibhūti 13, 62
Vidyā 34
vigrahas 129
vikalpa 35
vipāka 62
Viriñci 34
vīrya 23, 24, 26, 29, 32, 33, 57, 60, 66, 121, 134, 141, 143
viśeṣa 126, 127
viśeṣaṇa 128, 129, 130, 131, 147
viśeṣasūnya 125
viśeṣya 130
Viśiṣṭādvaita 7, 36, 60, 61, 63, 64, 112, 118, 126. 138, 142, 147, 149, 151
Viṣṇu 11, 14, 15, 16, 17, 18, 19, 20, 23, 24, 25, 26, 27, 28, 29, 30, 31, 37, 38, 39, 40, 41, 42, 44, 45, 46, 47, 48, 52, 56, 57, 58, 59, 60, 61, 62, 63, 64, 65, 66, 67, 68, 69, 70, 72, 73, 74, 78, 79, 80, 81, 82, 83, 84, 85, 86, 87, 89, 90, 91
Viṣṇu Purāṇa 79, 82, 83, 97
Viṣṇu Tattva 86
Viṣṇumitra 16
Viṣṇusmṛti 14, 17, 86
Viśvaksena 125
Viśvaksenasaṃhitā 124
viśvarūpa 137
Viśvāmitra 111
vyāvahārika 36, 40
vyoma 34
vyūha 22, 24, 27, 28, 29, 30, 33, 44, 46, 48, 90, 98, 134

Yādava Prakāśa 152
Yādavābhyudayam 112, 113
yādṛcchika sukṛta 100
yāja 116
Yāmuna 2, 4, 5, 6, 7, 8, 21, 23, 51, 52, 53, 55, 56, 57, 58, 59, 60, 61, 62, 63, 65, 66, 71, 72, 73, 74, 75, 76,

78, 79, 86, 112, 113, 114, 115, 125, 130, 133, 136, 137, 140, 141, 142, 143, 150, 151, 152, 153, 156
yaśas 13
Yoga 22, 23, 43, 51, 66, 116, 117
Yogarahasya 4, 51
Yogatantra 22
yogin 44
Yogācāra 112
Yudhiṣṭhira 14
yuga 88

www.ingramcontent.com/pod-product-compliance
Ingram Content Group UK Ltd.
Pitfield, Milton Keynes, MK11 3LW, UK
UKHW041417180426
11947UKWH00007B/179

9 780788 501999